How to Study
in College

How to Study in College

FIFTH EDITION

Walter Pauk

Director, Reading Research Center
Cornell University

Houghton Mifflin Company **Boston** **Toronto**

Dallas Geneva, Illinois Palo Alto
Princeton, New Jersey

Sponsoring editor: *Mary Jo Southern*
Senior project editor: *Susan Piland*
Senior production/design coordinator: *Renée Le Verrier*
Senior manufacturing coordinator: *Marie Barnes*
Marketing manager: *George Kane*

Printed in the U.S.A.

Library of Congress Catalog Card Number: 92-72391

ISBN: 0-395-64326-0

23456789-AH-96 95 94 93

Contents _____

12. Writing a Research Paper   259

To the Instructor _____

Time after time, students have told me that by learning a particular technique for, say, taking useful notes or reading and retaining a textbook assignment, they have achieved major breakthroughs. Moreover, these breakthroughs in a particular subject often jump-start the entire learning process and extend to all other subjects.

Students who are seeking help are not primarily interested in theory, and most of them have little patience with merely inspirational talk. They want practical instruction on how to succeed academically. They want something that they can readily understand and apply and that works. After a week of classes, they discover that the hit-or-miss tactics that got them through high school are grossly inadequate and inefficient at the competitive college level. So they turn to us for help.

Let's, then, teach these students proven techniques for studying and learning.

How to Study in College is brimming with exciting techniques, based on widely tested educational and learning theory, that have already helped myriad students. But the tail of theory is never allowed to wag the practical, feet-on-the-ground dog. While theory is always implicit, and is sometimes given in enough detail to explain the rationale behind a particular technique or reassure the skeptic, it is never presented without explicit applications and never used simply as exhortation. After all, the person who needs penicillin is hardly cured by learning the history of antibiotics!

Because it is so crucial that students learn for the long term, I am wholeheartedly against techniques that stress mere memorization. Such techniques fill the mind with "knowledge" that melts away after a test and leaves learning still to be done. The techniques presented in this book result in real learning. And real learning, like a real diamond, lasts.

Finally, no textbook—no matter how complete or current—is truly useful if it is boring, confusing, or excessively difficult to read. I have therefore tried to write in a conversational tone so that reading this book is like having a sincere, person-to-person chat.

THE FIFTH EDITION

- A new "concept map" at the beginning of each chapter provides a structured, at-a-glance overview of that chapter's contents.

- Each "Have You Missed Something?" chapter quiz now includes additional multiple-choice questions and new short-answer questions to reinforce students' understanding of key concepts.

- The new "Building Your Vocabulary Step by Step" section at the end of each chapter integrates vocabulary instruction throughout the book and lists words to learn from each chapter.

- *How to Study in College* has been streamlined throughout and carefully organized to show how its time-tested strategies and techniques apply to all aspects of learning.

- The "To the Student" introduction personalizes academic success by helping students establish their academic goals and directing students in using their schools' resources, their own learning styles, and this textbook to achieve these goals.

- Part I, "Preparing for Academic Challenges," lays the groundwork for effective learning with proven techniques for controlling stress, managing time, deepening concentration, and improving memory. Updated research findings support these techniques.

- Part II, "Devising a Note-Taking System," provides a system for taking notes from readings and lectures and then mastering those notes, plus ways of using both sides of the brain to increase understanding and recall. It also helps students develop their own study systems by customizing sound learning methods to accommodate personal learning styles.

- Part III, "Succeeding at Test-Taking and Writing," explains how to manage the anxiety that surrounds taking tests and writing papers, provides specific techniques for understanding and answering test questions, and sets up a methodology for doing research and writing. The expanded research section includes information on using libraries' computerized indexes and catalogs to select and investigate a topic.

- The Instructor's Resource Manual now includes six reproducible supplementary chapters that cover computers, math, science, effective speaking, foreign languages, and literature. It continues to provide additional multiple-choice questions (with answers) and short-answer questions for further study and discussion.

ACKNOWLEDGMENTS

Warm and sincere words of thanks go to those who are permanently linked to this book: the late Henry F. Thoma and Ian D. Elliot.

My sincere thanks also go to the contributors of material in previous editions: Professors Harrison A. Geiselmann, Kenneth A. Greisen, and Jane E. Hardy, all of Cornell University; Professor William G. Moulton of Princeton University; Professor James A. Wood of the University of Texas at El Paso; and Dr. Nancy V. Wood, now Director of Study Skills and Tutorial Services, the University of Texas at El Paso, but then a graduate teaching assistant in the Cornell Reading and Study Skills Program, for certain materials she originally prepared for that program.

I am also very pleased that for the current Instructor's Resource Manual a valued friend, John Rethorst of Cornell University, has combined his new chapter on computers with the chapter previously written by my esteemed colleague Professor H. Dean Sutphin of Cornell University. Professors Mike Radis and Ron Williams of The Pennsylvania State University prepared the in-depth questions for further study and discussion that appeared in the Instructor's Manual for the Fourth Edition, and Professor Carol Kanar of Valencia Community College assisted with the updating and revision of Chapter 1 of that edition. I thank them all for their valuable assistance.

Now for a very special acknowledgment: I am grateful to my friend Ross James Quirie Owens, whose experience as a writer, newspaper editor, director, and cinematographer prepared him to take full charge in revising, editing, and improving this book. His talents are particularly apparent in the mini-overviews and concept maps at the beginning of each chapter and in the quizzes at the end of each chapter as well as in all the quizzes and questions in the Instructor's Resource Manual.

I would also like to thank the reviewers of the text and manuscript for their many fine suggestions:

A. Cheryl Curtis   *University of Hartford*
Ceil Fillenworth   *St. Cloud State University*
Stephen D. Johnston   *Lane Community College*
Richard E. Lake   *St. Louis Community College at Florrisant Valley*
Lorita Manning   *Baylor University*
Kathryn E. Moore   *St. Louis Community College, Meramec*
C. David Moorhead   *Long Beach City College*
Thomas Musgrave   *Weber State University*
Jayne Nightingale   *Rhode Island College*
Jane Rhoads   *Wichita State University*
Sara Lee Sanderson   *Miami-Dade Community College*
Susan Steger-Farmer   *William Rainey Harper College*
Linda Wong   *Lane Community College*

Finally, I am eternally grateful to my many students, who have taught me much, so that I may pass on a little more to others.

W.P.

To the Student _____

I was recently startled by a full-page picture of a yawning baby in a CIGNA ad, which appeared in the *Wall Street Journal.* What struck me were these big, bold-faced words at the top of the page: "**ONLY 22,463 DAYS UNTIL RETIREMENT.**"[1]

My immediate reaction was "Oh, no! Life is not so short. We have more working days than this." I quickly punched 22,463 into my calculator and divided by 365. Sure enough, the figure confirmed the advertisement's point: "The average retirement age is now 61.5, not 65. And it's getting even lower." If you're already 18, you have only 15,163 days until retirement— and you're not through college yet!

But don't race breathlessly through your days. Rather, make the most of them by planning for college, for work, for fun, and for retirement. Plan so that you have control over your life. It is all up to you.

SHAPING YOUR FUTURE THROUGH GOALS

You can begin shaping your life now by setting definite, realistic goals for your college career and by mapping out plans to reach them. Your long-term academic goals may, for instance, be to choose a field of study or a specific career, to become proficient in a particular skill or set of skills, to gain more control over your time, or to learn how to work effectively despite stress. These are personal aspirations that you alone can determine. Of course, as you think about them and gather information to help you set them, you can consult with your academic advisor, other school or outside counselors, books, people who have achieved similar goals, and so forth. But *you* are the person who sets your goals, and *you* are the one who achieves them.

Just thinking about your goals is not enough, however. In the words of psychologist and philosopher William James, thinking alone "is an impression gone to waste. It is physiologically incomplete. It leaves no fruits behind." So complete the process by writing. Use the Shaping Your Future sheet (Figure 1) to begin putting your long-term academic goals down on paper.

---

[1]Reprinted by permission of CIGNA.

1 My Goal ——————— ——————— ——————— ——————— ——————— ——————— ———————	**2** Steps Leading to My Goal 1. ———————— 2. ———————— 3. ———————— 4. ———————— 5. ———————— 6. ———————— 7. ————————
3 Positive Factors 1. ———————— 2. ———————— 3. ———————— 4. ———————— 5. ———————— 6. ———————— 7. ————————	**4** Obstacles 1. ———————— 2. ———————— 3. ———————— 4. ———————— 5. ———————— 6. ———————— 7. ————————

FIGURE 1 Shaping Your Future

Step 1. On a clean sheet of paper, brainstorm about your goals. Jot down possible goals and words about them that come to mind, and do so quickly and freely. Use brainstorming as an opportunity to explore any aspects of any goals you choose. Do not stop writing to correct your spelling, polish a phrase, reorganize your notes, or analyze a thought. Just keep going until you've jotted down all that you can think of about your possible goals. Now look over your notes and group together similar items. Formulate each group into a goal by writing a summarizing sentence that states the main idea of each group. Select any one of these goals, and write it in block 1 of Figure 1.

Step 2.   On a separate sheet of paper, list in chronological order the steps you'll need to take to reach one of your goals. Transfer this list to block 2.

Step 3.   On another sheet, jot down those academic and personal strengths that will help you achieve this goal. List them in block 3.

Step 4.   Identify any academic weaknesses (such as difficulty with writing papers) or personal obstacles (such as financial, family, or health problems) that you will have to overcome to reach this goal, and list them in block 4. Repeat steps 2–4 for each goal you wrote in step 1.

With the completed Shaping Your Future sheets in hand, expand your resources. Talk with your academic advisor or with a counselor in your school's career center. Don't underestimate the value of discussing your goals and your plans for achieving them. Get as much feedback as you can. Then, if necessary, modify your goals and plans into realistic, attainable maps for your future.

You can also develop plans to achieve short-term goals such as completing textbook assignments. After writing out his academic goals, one college student enthusiastically said, "I now do almost everything in terms of goals, even my textbook assignments. I feel I'm in control of every day."

He then gave me a copy of a card that keeps him focused on his assignments (see Figure 2). "Using this card," he explained, "I waste no time. I comprehend better and remember more."

With this format as a guide, you can design your own Reading Assignment Card. Try it, refine it if necessary, and then reproduce the final version so you'll have a ready stack.

TAKING ACTION

Among the saddest words in life are "It might have been." If you take no action, your goals and plans will amount to nothing. For instance, let's say your short-term goal is to excel in your biology course. Anticipating that you may have trouble with some of the terms and concepts, you've decided to get help from a tutor. The biology department identifies the tutor for you, and now it's up to you to contact him or her. If you procrastinate

Date _____

Book _____

Starting page _____

Ending page _____

No. of pages _____

Time allotment _____

Time started _____

Time to finish _____

Time finished _____

Page reached _____

Goal achieved   yes — no

Reason (if no) _____

_____

No. min. worked _____

No. of pages read _____

Atmosphere: intrptns
              no intrptns

Work location _____

_____

FIGURE 2   Reading Assignment Card

here, all the thought, time and effort you put into your plan will have been wasted. Taking action simply means taking those steps necessary to complete your plan.

Let me pass on to you the technique that I use to push *myself* into immediate action. I whisper to myself, "Do it now. Life is not a rehearsal!"

If you muster up the self-discipline needed to take advantage of the resources that your college makes available, and if you make an effort to understand your learning style and develop your study skills, then you will have taken intelligent, decisive action in the pursuit of your goals.

Take Advantage of Your School's Resources

College Catalog.   General information about your college's requirements, policies, programs, and services appears in the college catalog. Make sure you have a copy, and use it often during the first weeks of classes to remind yourself of requirements and deadlines to be met. In the catalog you will find courses listed by department or by subject area and descriptions of course content. This information can help you plan your schedule of future courses. Whenever you have a problem, check the catalog for a listing that may help you.

Student Handbook.   The student handbook provides information on your school's procedures, regulations, and code of conduct. It may also describe the school's requirements for good academic standing and graduation. For details or for specific department requirements, consult your department office or your academic advisor. It's a good idea to read the student handbook to familiarize yourself with your school's codes and policies.

Admissions or Registrar's Office.   You can find answers to questions about grades, transcripts, and college requirements in the admissions or registrar's office. Admission to college and registration for courses begin with this office. This office stores all your records and at the end of each term issues your grade report.

Office of Financial Affairs.   For answers to questions about scholarships, loans, and grants, contact the financial affairs office. You will come here to pay fees and fines and to pick up your checks if you are in a work-study grant or program. If you want a part-time job on campus for which you must qualify on the basis of your financial status, you will fill out application forms in this office.

Career Development and Placement Office.   If you want help choosing a major or setting a career goal, contact the career development and placement office. People in this office can administer various interest, personality, and skills assessment tests to help you determine the kind of work for which you are best suited. They can help you find jobs on and off campus. Some career development centers sponsor on-campus recruitment, inviting businesses to interview prospective graduates and aiding them in submitting applications and résumés. After graduation, you can file a résumé in the placement office if you want your school's help in landing a job.

Academic Advising Office or Counseling Department.   Academic and guidance counselors can help you with everything from choosing the right course to solving personal problems that prevent you from meeting your academic goals. The academic office or counseling department may be part of the admissions office, or it may be a separate department. In many colleges students are assigned to an advisor or a counselor who follows their progress throughout their college careers.

Student Health Center.   If you become ill, you can go to a doctor at the health center. The health center may have a pharmacy and may provide a limited amount of hospital care. Some mental health services may be available through this center, through the office of a school psychologist or psychiatrist, or through a peer counseling group. The health center may also refer students to an agency outside the college.

Student Government Association.   Working with the dean of students, the student government association sponsors student activities such as intramural events, dances, special-interest organizations and clubs, and other social and academic events. (Joining a club or taking part in campus events is a good way to meet other students who share your interests.) In addition, your student government may publish a weekly bulletin that keeps you informed about campus life or a student handbook that summarizes college requirements and resources.

Student Publications.   The college newspaper or literary magazine offers contributors unique opportunities for self-expression and provides readers with information and entertainment. Serving on the editorial staff of one of these publications may also fulfill some journalism or English requirements.

Learning Lab or Skills Center.   You may turn to the learning lab or skills center for help in improving your study, reading, writing, math, or computer skills. Whether you are required to spend time in a lab because of your performance on a college skills assessment test or you choose to go on your own, take full advantage of the opportunity to gain the skills you need for increasingly demanding college courses.

Special Student Services.   Veterans, students with physical or learning disabilities, minority students, international students, and students who are economically disadvantaged may need the special assistance of a trained support group to meet their academic goals. If you think you qualify for these services, ask your counselor or advisor about them. Your college may also offer services such as off-campus residence listings.

Undergraduate Athletics Office. A listing of the college's athletic programs and events is available in the undergraduate athletics office. This is the office to visit if you are interested in participating in intramural or varsity sports or if you want to know how to get tickets for the next college sporting event.

Resident Assistant. For on-campus students, resident assistants (RAs) can be a great source of information about campus services. Although RAs are not professional counselors, they have recently been through many of the experiences you're undergoing and can probably direct you to the campus office best suited to your needs.

Discover Your Own Resources

"Know thyself" is wise advice for a student poised at the path that leads to an academic goal. Development of your skills begins with understanding your personal learning style and study skills. By identifying your preferences and strengths, you can zero in on the best study skills techniques for you.

The following list can help you identify your basic learning style. For each item, circle the letter that best matches your style. Keep your responses in mind as you read this book.

Learning Styles Self-Assessment

1. I study better   (a) by myself;   (b) in groups;   (c) in a combination of the two.
2. I remember best when   (a) I've *heard* something;   (b) I've *read* or *seen* something;   (c) I've *done* something active, like problem solving.
3. I think I'm   (a) better with facts, such as names or dates;   (b) better with concepts, ideas, or themes;   (c) about the same with both.
4. I learn better when I read   (a) slowly;   (b) quickly;   (c) either way.
5. I study more efficiently in   (a) one solid study period;   (b) small blocks of time.
6. I work   (a) well under pressure;   (b) poorly under pressure.

7. I work   (a) quickly, for short periods of time;   (b) at a steady, slower pace for longer periods of time.

8. I   (a) do learn best in a structured setting, such as a classroom or laboratory;   (b) do not learn best in a structured setting.

9. I think that the greatest strength of my learning style is _____ .

10. I think that the greatest weakness of my learning style is _____ .

Now that you've identified the characteristics of your style, take a couple of minutes to look at your study skills. The following list presents some statements students typically make about various aspects of studying. Circle the response in each sentence that best describes you and your study habits. Then use the page numbers that follow each item for additional self-study.

Study Skills Self-Assessment

1. Daily pressures do/don't make it difficult for me to relax and work efficiently.   (pp. 3–32)

2. I can/can't find enough time in the week for all that I need to accomplish. (pp. 35–56)

3. I have/don't have difficulty concentrating.   (pp. 59–73)

4. I do/don't have trouble remembering what I've learned.   (pp. 75–102)

5. I do/don't have a system for taking notes.   (pp. 107–121)

6. I recognize/don't recognize the kind of information that I should be jotting down in my notes.   (pp. 123–143)

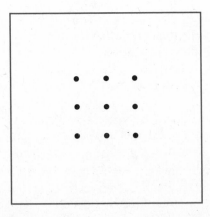

FIGURE 3   The Nine-Dot Problem
Connect these dots by drawing four straight lines without taking your pencil from the paper and without retracing any lines. The solution appears on page xxvi.

7. I do/do not find my notes useful after I've taken them.   (pp. 145–162)
8. Pictures, graphs, and diagrams help/don't help my understanding of what I've read or heard.   (pp. 165–185)
9. I usually do/don't become anxious about taking tests.   (pp. 189–208)
10. I could/could not use some improvement in my test-taking skills. (pp. 213–234)
11. I do/don't feel intimidated by essay questions.   (pp. 239–256)
12. I have/don't have difficulty writing research papers.   (pp. 259–285)
13. Learning new vocabulary is/isn't a problem for me. ("Building Your Vocabulary Step by Step" sections)

You'll improve your chances of success if you balance this knowledge of your learning style with a willingness to remain flexible. For example, you may be thinking, "It's true. I'm a sprinter who begins working with a burst of energy and then slacks off. That's the way I've always been. How can I possibly change?" Or you may believe that studying all night is an effective way of coping with a tight schedule and that you have no need for a more conventional strategy. These ways of thinking probably feel comfortable, but they may have created blind spots in your view of studying. To get a sense of how blind spots can limit you, try to solve the problem shown in Figure 3. Odds are that a blind spot will prevent you from solving it. Yet once you see the solution, you'll probably say, "How easy! Why didn't I think of that tactic myself?"

USING THIS BOOK

No matter what academic goals you've set for yourself, this book can help you achieve them. In theory, there is no limit to learning and no limit to how you can improve your natural abilities to understand the material you study. By reading and applying the techniques presented here, you will quickly begin to improve as a student, making your college experience a rich and rewarding one.

You will find many ideas, tips, techniques, and systems in this book, but do not try to use them all. Instead, try those you believe will help you the most. To discover the ideas that best suit you, follow this procedure. First, make sure that you comprehend the idea *and* that you also see the reason or principle behind it. Second, consider how the idea may fit in with the way you study and learn. Third, give the idea a test run to see if it works. In short, use this book as a collection of ideas from which you can select what you need for both immediate and future use.

How to Read Each Chapter

Use the first two pages of each chapter as an appetizer to whet your appetite for the courses to come. On the first page, read the short introduction to the chapter's main ideas and the list of key topics. Then to see how these ideas and topics are organized, turn the page and take a look at the concept map. This at-a-glance view of the chapter's main divisions and subdivisions shows you not only what is in the chapter but also how each section fits in with the whole.

With these overviews in mind, read the entire chapter thoughtfully—in one sitting if you can—and read the chapter summary carefully. Then go back and reread the parts of the chapter that particularly interest you. It is a good idea to make notes on any techniques or ideas you want to remember.

How to Use the "Have You Missed Something?" Questions

The end-of-chapter questions are designed to teach, not test; you'll find no trick questions and no traps to lead you to an incorrect answer. Take each

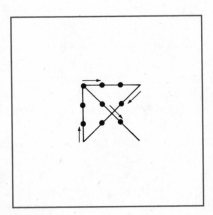

FIGURE 4   Answer to the Nine-Dot Problem
Begin at the top left corner and follow the arrows.

question at face value, and answer it to the best of your ability. Use any incorrect answers you give as opportunities to reread the pertinent portion of the chapter. By rereading and rethinking the question and answer, you will greatly strengthen your understanding of the entire concept.

A FINAL THOUGHT

To state in one sentence what I try to do in this book, let me rely on the words of Ralph Waldo Emerson: "The best service one person can render another person is to help him help himself."

How to Study
in College

Preparing for Academic Challenges

Managing Stress

**Rule No 1 is, don't sweat the small stuff.
Rule No. 2 is, it's all small stuff.**

ROBERT S. ELIOT, M.D.
Cardiologist

Stress, writes Dr. Hans Selye, a pioneer in the study of stress, is "the spice of life or the kiss of death—depending on how we cope with it."[1] Unfortunately, most of us cope with it badly. We worry too much, criticize too much, get angry too often, and become too tense. But if you can learn to deflect the stress that comes your way, you can thrive, as a student and as a human being. This chapter helps you manage stress by focusing on

• Developing a positive mental attitude

• Following a healthy physical routine

• Reducing stressors

---

[1] Hans Selye, "How to Master Stress," *Parents* 52 (November 1977): 25.

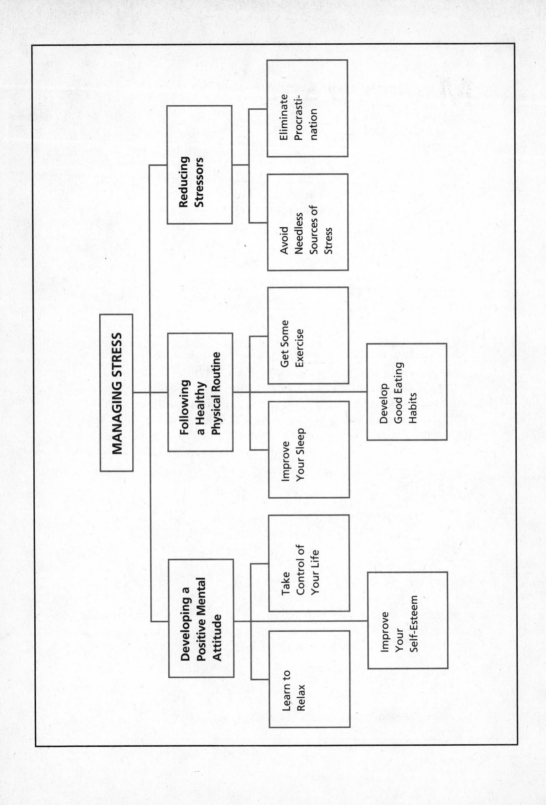

Mere mention of the word *stress* is enough to make most people anxious. It brings to mind images of frayed nerves, shortened tempers, and rising blood pressure. But being under stress isn't always a bad thing. In fact, stress can prompt us to respond effectively to a tough situation, to rise to the occasion when a paper comes due or a test is handed out. According to Marilyn Gist, a professor at the School of Business Administration of the University of Washington, "A certain amount of stress is healthy and beneficial; it stimulates some to perform, makes them excited and enthusiastic."[2]

"Stress," according to Hans Selye, "is the nonspecific response of the body to any demand made upon it."[3] In other words, it is the body's attempt to adjust to a demand, regardless of what the demand may be. You undergo stress when you run or walk at a brisk pace. Your body responds to the demand for more oxygen by increasing your breathing and causing your heart to beat faster. Yet most people view exercise, not as a source of stress, but as a means of stress relief. Likewise, watching a quiz show or doing a crossword can both be considered stressful. In each case, the brain responds with increased mental activity. Yet most people undertake these activities specifically for relaxation.

The problem is that we don't always respond to the sources of stress (known as *stressors*) in such a positive fashion. If instead of running for exercise, you're racing to catch a bus, or instead of solving a crossword puzzle, you're struggling with a math test that you didn't study for, your reaction is apt to be quite different. Rather than experiencing the exhilaration of exercising or the stimulation of solving a puzzle, you may wind up feeling exhausted or intimidated.

That's the two-sided potential of stress. Instead of compelling us to rise to the occasion, stress can sometimes plunge us down into a sea of anxiety, worry, hostility, or despair. The way we respond to stress, whether we use it as a boon or a burden, depends on two major factors: our overall approach to life and the number of stressors we face at any one time. These two factors can for the most part be controlled, which means you can basically decide whether stress will have a positive or negative effect on your life. To improve the chance that stress will affect you positively, you are wise to adopt a positive mental attitude, follow a healthy physical routine, and limit the number of stressors that confront you at any one time.

---

[2] Pam Miller Withers, "Good Stress/Bad Stress: How to Use One, Lose the Other," *Working Woman* (September 1989): 124.
[3] Hans Selye, *Stress Without Distress* (New York: J. B. Lippincott, 1974), p. 27.

DEVELOPING A POSITIVE MENTAL ATTITUDE

Although you can't turn away disaster simply by keeping a smile on your face, there are now abundant indications that your overall attitude can have a powerful influence on the outcome of potentially upsetting or stressful situations. The first evidence was offered around the turn of the century, when American philosopher and psychologist William James and Danish psychologist Carl Lange simultaneously developed a remarkable theory of emotion. You don't cry because you're sad, they suggested. You're sad because you cry. This revolutionary reversal of the apparent cause and effect of emotions briefly sent the scientific community into an uproar. As the twentieth century progressed, this controversial proposal, known as the James-Lange theory, was scoffed at by most members of the mainstream scientific community and was advocated instead by "inspirational" writers and speakers such as Dr. Norman Vincent Peale, who championed the virtues of "positive thinking." Now the James-Lange theory has been vindicated, and Peale's ideas, bolstered by recent scientific evidence, have garnered mainstream defenders.

As part of a study conducted in 1983 by Paul Ekman, Robert W. Levenson, and Wallace V. Friesen at the Department of Psychiatry of the University of California, San Francisco, subjects were given specific instructions for contracting various facial muscles to imitate six basic emotions: happiness, sadness, disgust, surprise, anger, and fear.[4] Instead of being told, for example, to "look scared," the subject was instructed to "raise your brows and pull them together, now raise your upper eyelids and stretch your lips horizontally, back toward your ears."[5] Expressions were held for ten seconds, while electronic instruments measured the subjects' physiological response.

The results were fascinating. Simply imitating an emotional expression was enough to trigger the physiological changes normally associated with that emotion. The most interesting contrast was between expressions for anger and for happiness. The average subject's heart rate and skin temperature increased more with anger than they did with happiness. Yet the subjects weren't truly angry or happy: they were just imitating the expressions associated with these two emotions.

We can conclude from this study that simply putting on a happy face may make you feel happier and that taking a dim or overly pessimistic view can lead to the discouraging outcome you expected. But managing

---

[4] Paul Ekman, Robert W. Levenson, and Wallace V. Friesen, "Autonomic Nervous System Activity Distinguishes Among Emotions," *Science* 221 (1983): 1208–1210.
[5] Ibid., p. 1208.

stress shouldn't simply be a fuzzy-headed smile-at-all-your-troubles strategy. Improving your attitude should be done systematically by learning to relax, by improving your self-esteem, and, above all, by taking control of your life.

Learn to Relax

The regular use of relaxation techniques, according to studies at the Mind/Body Medical Institute of Harvard Medical School, reduces stress and the prevalence of stress-related illness.[6] But many of us don't consider using such techniques because we misinterpret what the word *relaxation* means. Relaxation doesn't necessarily mean you're about to fall asleep. In fact, some World War II pilots used relaxation techniques, not to prepare themselves for sleep or to "take it easy," but to stay alert and avoid fatigue during bombing missions.[7]

Nor is relaxation a synonym for lethargy. "Relaxation," write psychologists Edward A. Charlesworth and Ronald G. Nathan in *Stress Management,* "simply means doing nothing with your muscles."[8] Relaxation therefore is relief from wasted effort or strain, an absence of tension. Indeed, explains author Emrika Padus, "tenseness wastes energy; tenseness causes anxiety.... The best performances come when the mind and body are floating, enjoying the activity just as we did when we were young children, completely absorbed in the experience and unaware of any consequences of the actions. This is true relaxation."[9]

There's nothing mystical about relaxation. Two simple techniques—breathing deeply and using progressive relaxation—can help you get the hang of this life-sustaining practice.

Breathe Deeply There's a strong connection between the way you breathe and the way you feel. When you're relaxed, your breaths are long and deep, originating from your abdomen. When you're anxious, your breathing is often short and shallow, originating from high in your chest.

This link between breathing and emotion operates in both directions. Just as the way you feel affects the way you breathe, changing your breathing alters your emotional response. A handful of experiments have

---

[6] Stephanie Wood, "Relax! You've Earned It," *McCall's* 118 (July 1991): 50.
[7] Edward A. Charlesworth and Ronald G. Nathan, *Stress Management* (New York: Atheneum, 1984), p. 41.
[8] Ibid., p. 42.
[9] Emrika Padus, *The Complete Guide to Your Emotions & Your Health* (Emmaus, Penn.: Rodale Press, 1986), p. 490.

Alcohol: The Wrong Way to Relax

Although some people believe that alcohol is not harmful and may even be helpful when taken in moderation, the potential dangers of drinking are daunting. Not only does alcohol actually undermine relaxation, it also has detrimental effects on other important aspects of managing stress.

* Alcohol triggers the stress hormone cortisol, which causes sodium retention and potassium loss. An excess of sodium can raise blood pressure, and a shortage of potassium makes the heart vulnerable to rhythm disturbances.
* Drinking can damage the heart's muscle fibers, impairing its ability to pump.
* As much as 11 percent of the incidence of hypertension in men can be attributed to consumption of three to four drinks per day.
* Alcohol consumption leads to higher levels of blood fats, including low-density lipoproteins, which are strongly associated with high cholesterol.
* Alcohol can cause gastrointestinal disorders. Peptic ulcers and pancreatitis are common in alcoholics, and even moderate drinkers become more susceptible to nausea and vomiting.
* Alcohol harms the body's ability to metabolize carbohydrates, resulting in impaired glucose tolerance and even hypoglycemia (excessively low blood sugar).
* A study done by U.S. and Italian researchers found that women develop alcohol-related ailments more quickly than men.
* According to conservative U.S. government estimates, beer, wine, and liquor account for approximately 100,000 deaths each year.

Sources: Robert S. Eliot and Dennis L. Breo, *Is It Worth Dying For? A Self-Assessment Program to Make Stress Work for You, Not Against You* (New York: Bantam, 1989); Michael F. Jacobson, "Alcohol Deaths: Sharing the Blame," *Nutrition Action Health Letter* 16, no. 3 (April 1989); G. Timothy Johnson and Stephen E. Goldfinger, eds., *The Harvard Medical School Health Letter Book* (Cambridge, MA: Harvard University Press, 1981); J. Raloff, "Women and Alcohol: A Gastric Disadvantage,"*Science News* 137 (January 20, 1990); *The Surgeon General's Report on Nutrition and Health* 1988 (Rocklin, CA: Prima Publishing and Communications, 1988).

established this connection. Dr. James Loehr found that when a relaxed group of subjects was asked to take short, rapid, and irregular breaths for two minutes—in other words, to pant—nearly everyone interviewed felt worried, threatened, and panicky.[10] Simply by imitating the response of an anxious person, the subjects had actually made themselves anxious.

Luckily, this principle can be used to encourage relaxation as well. By breathing slowly, steadily, and deeply and by beginning your breaths in your abdomen instead of up in your chest, you can encourage a feeling of relaxation. So just before an exam, an interview, or a dental appointment, when your palms are sweating, your body is tense, and your breath is short and shallow, try the count-of-three method to induce a more relaxed state. Count slowly and calmly through each step:

1. Inhale slowly through your nose while silently counting to three.
2. Hold your breath for the count of three.
3. Exhale slowly through your nose while silently counting to three.
4. With your breath expelled, count to three.
5. Repeat the cycle (steps 1 to 4) several times. (Once you have the rhythm, you need not continue counting; but maintain the same timing and the same pauses.)

Use Progressive Muscle Relaxation A big advantage of the count-of-three method is that it can be done inconspicuously almost anywhere, including in an exam room. But if you have some time, a quiet place, and a little privacy, you may want to try progressive muscle relaxation (PMR), a method for systematically tensing and relaxing the major muscles in your body.

PMR was developed more than seventy years ago by Edmund Jacobson, a doctor who saw the connection between tense muscles and a tense mind. PMR works by helping you become aware of the difference between how your muscles feel when they're tensed and how they feel when they're relaxed.

Start PMR by assuming a comfortable position, either sitting or lying down, and by closing your eyes. Make a tight fist in your right hand, and at the same time tense your right forearm. Hold this position for five seconds, feeling the tension in both your hand and arm; and then slowly release that tension, letting it flow out of you as you unclench your fist. Repeat the procedure with your left hand, noting the difference between how this hand feels tensed compared to your right hand and arm, which are now relaxed. Continue by separately tensing your shoulder muscles, your neck,

---

[10] James E. Loehr and Peter J. McLaughlin, with Ed Quillen, *Mentally Tough* (New York: M. Evans and Company, 1986), pp. 141–142.

and the muscles in your face. Then start with your feet and toes, moving up each leg; finish by tensing the muscles in your abdomen and chest. Once you've tensed and released every muscle group in your body, take a moment to savor the overall feeling of relaxation. Then open your eyes and end the exercise.

Improve Your Self-Esteem

Self-esteem is your personal assessment of your own value. Unfortunately, many of us are our own toughest critics. We overlook our positive attributes and forget our successes, emphasizing our shortcomings instead and providing ourselves with a silent but constant stream of discouraging dialogue. The stress that results from these inner discouragements is far worse than any criticism we might receive from a nagging parent, an insulting instructor, or an overly demanding boss.

A healthy level of self-esteem is crucial to keeping stress at bay. If your self-esteem needs improvement, rewrite the potentially destructive inner dialogue that haunts you throughout the day, and take some time out to dwell on your successes.

Rewrite Your Inner Dialogue   You can't rewrite your inner dialogue unless you've seen the script. Therefore, the first step in eliminating the destructive thoughts that undermine your self-esteem is to become aware of them.

Most of us talk silently to ourselves almost continually. Psychologists commonly refer to this inner conversation as *self-talk.* Although you may have learned to ignore the sound of your self-talk, the effect it has on your overall attitude can still be damaging. So when you enter a new situation or are faced with a difficult challenge, take a moment to express your apprehensions to yourself. Then listen to your self-talk. Whenever you have a negative thought, counteract it with a positive one. Remember that the thoughts you have are your own and they're under your control. You can open the door of your mind to whatever thoughts you want. Admit only the positive ones, and leave the negative thoughts out in the cold.

Build on Your Success   All of us have experienced success at one time or another. When you feel your self-esteem slipping, remember when you did a job you were proud of, when you overcame an obstacle in spite of the odds, or when everything seemed to go smoothly. It helps to congratulate yourself from time to time, to put yourself in an achieving frame of mind so that you can manifest success again.

Take Control of Your Life

One of the results of increased self-esteem is an increased sense of control, a quality that both medical doctors and psychologists are finding can have a measurable effect on your physical well-being and state of mind. According to the *Wellness Letter* from the University of California, Berkeley, "A sense of control may, in fact, be a critical factor in maintaining health."[11] When you're in control, you act; you set your own agenda instead of reacting to the wishes or whims of others or resigning yourself to what we often call "fate."

Appreciate the Significance of Control In the early 1960s, writer and magazine editor Norman Cousins was stricken with a painful and terminal illness. Determined not to let the illness control his life and sentence him to death, Cousins fought back. He watched movie comedies, one after another. The laughter the films elicited made the sleep that had eluded him come more easily and ultimately reversed the crippling illness.[12] In fact, the results were so impressive to the medical community that Cousins, who had no medical background, was awarded an honorary degree in medicine from the Yale University School of Medicine and was appointed adjunct professor in the School of Medicine at the University of California, Los Angeles.

Norman Cousins is not the only person who has demonstrated the importance of a sense of control. Author Richard Logan investigated the lives of people who were able to survive extreme stress—such as imprisonment in a concentration camp—and found that they all had at least one quality in common: a belief that their destiny was in their own hands. In other words, they had a sense of control.[13]

The importance of control was reinforced in a study that provided a physiological insight into the phenomenon. When your body is under stress, your adrenal glands release *cortisone,* a hormone that in small doses can fight allergies and disease but that in larger amounts can impair the body's ability to fight back. When the two groups of employees who made

---

[11]"Healthy Lives: A New View of Stress," *University of California, Berkeley, Wellness Letter* 6, no. 9 (June 1990): 4.

[12]*Managing Stress—From Morning to Night* (Alexandria, Va.: Time-Life Books, 1987), p. 21.

[13]Mihaly Csikszentmihalyi, *Flow: The Psychology of Optimal Experience* (New York: Harper & Row, 1990), p. 203.

up the study worked almost to the point of exhaustion, only one group experienced a significant increase in cortisone production. Those employees with high levels of cortisone had jobs that allowed them very little control. Those employees who experienced no increase in cortisone held positions with a high level of control.[14]

A lack of control can result in a sense of helplessness almost guaranteed to bring about the frayed nerves, tense muscles, and overall feeling of panic normally associated with short-term stress. If these conditions persist, they can have an adverse effect on your body's immune system, making you more susceptible to illness. Robbed of your sense of control, you not only react instead of acting you but also overreact. Turned outward, this overreaction may surface as anger. Turned inward, it can lead to fear, anxiety, and general depression.

In *The Joy of Stress*, Dr. Peter Hanson describes an experiment in which two groups of office workers were exposed to a series of loud and distracting background noises. One group had desks equipped with a button that could be pushed at any time to shut out the annoying sounds. The other group had no such button. Not surprisingly, workers with the button control were far more productive than those without. But what's remarkable is that no one in the button group actually pushed the button. Apparently the knowledge that they could shut out the noise if they wanted to was enough to enable them to work productively in spite of the distractions. Their sense of control resulted in a reduction in stress and an increase in productivity.[15]

Understand How Attitude Affects Control   Dr. Hanson's story of the control button underscores an important element of control: Taking control is primarily a matter of adjusting your attitude. As a student, you can achieve a sense of control by changing the way you view your courses, assignments, and exams.

Taking control of your classes and assignments means viewing them as choices instead of obligations. The stressed-out, overwhelmed student looks to the next lecture or reading assignment with dread, seeing it as a burden he or she would rather do without. The student who feels in control (and feels confident as a result) understands that he or she attends lectures and completes assignments as a matter of choice and that the benefits derived from both are not only practical but also enjoyable. According to psychologist Mihalyi Csikszentmihalyi, "Of all the virtues we can learn, no trait is more useful, more essential for survival and more likely to improve the quality of life than the ability to transform adversity into an enjoyable challenge."[16]

---

[14]Robert M. Bramson, *Coping with the Fast Track Blues* (New York: Doubleday, 1990), p. 217.
[15]Peter Hanson, *The Joy of Stress* (New York: McMeel & Parker, 1985), pp. 15–16.
[16]Csikszentmihalyi, *Flow*, p. 200.

Even students who feel they have their assignments under control can feel swamped by the prospect of an exam or a paper assignment. But by shifting their attitude, they can transform a dreaded paper or final into a challenge. Although the pressure is still on, students who take control prepare with confidence and relish the opportunity to demonstrate what they know.

Learn to Cope with Out-of-Control Circumstances   Clearly, a great many situations in life are out of your control. But even in unavoidable or unpredictable situations, you can still exercise some degree of influence. Psychologists have found that as your coping resources increase (both in number and in variety), so does your sense of control. Thus, a person with multiple coping strategies, instead of just one plan, is better able to adapt to the inevitable surprises that can accompany almost any undertaking.

For example, you have no control over whether an upcoming exam will be made up of essays or multiple-choice questions. If the instructor doesn't tell you which type it will be, you can increase your coping resources by preparing for both types of questions. Then regardless of what type the instructor chooses, you'll be ready. You'll have a feeling of control.

The same strategy can be applied to a number of mundane situations that often generate unwanted stress. An unexpected line at the bank or the grocery store can leave you feeling helpless and anxious. You can't make the line disappear or move more quickly, but you can put the situation back in your control by reading a book or reviewing a set of vocabulary cards while you wait. As you can see, even a small degree of control can be used to minimize a large amount of stress.

FOLLOWING A HEALTHY PHYSICAL ROUTINE

Stress isn't all in your head. It has a noticeable effect on your body and can often be avoided through changes in your physical routine. If you make a concerted effort to improve your sleep, develop good eating habits, and get some exercise, you'll make yourself more stress resistant and decrease your chances of being subjected to stress in the first place.

Improve Your Sleep

If your morning starts with the sound of an alarm clock, then you're probably not getting the sleep you need. According to Dr. Wilse Webb, a psy chologist at the University of Florida, Gainesville, "If that's how you wake up every day, you're shortening your natural sleep pattern."[17] And yet an alarm clock is a part of most people's lives. Does that mean *all* of us are cheating ourselves on sleep? Perhaps not all, but most Americans are getting less sleep than they actually need. In fact, according to a recent article in the *New York Times,* "sleep scientists insist that there is virtually an epidemic of sleepiness in the nation."[18]

The image of a nation filled with semiconscious citizens may seem comical, but in reality the effects of this widespread sleep deprivation are seldom humorous and are sometimes deadly. The U.S. Department of Transportation estimates that up to two hundred thousand traffic accidents each year are sleep related.[19] Furthermore, the worst nuclear power emergency in this country's history, at Three Mile Island, occurred at night, when workers were most susceptible to the effects of insufficient sleep.[20]

Although the consequences of sleep deprivation are not normally deadly, college students still suffer from them. Dr. Charles Czeisler, director of circadian and sleep disorders medicine at Brigham and Women's Hospital in Boston, has outlined some of the penalties that people pay for getting too little sleep: "Short term memory is impaired, the ability to make decisions is impaired, the ability to concentrate is impaired."[21] Clearly, a student who can't remember, can't make decisions, and has trouble concentrating will have a tough time surviving in an academic setting. Furthermore, the struggle to overcome the disabilities that sleep loss creates frequently leads to an even more pervasive problem: stress.

"Weariness corrodes civility and erases humor" read a recent article in *Time* magazine. "Without sufficient sleep, tempers flare faster and hotter at the slightest offense."[22] The day-to-day challenges and inconveniences of going to school and of living in the modern world are potentially stress inducing. Add in habitual sleep loss, and you turn a chronic problem into an acute one. Dr. Ernest Hartmann's study of "variable sleepers" (patients whose sleep and wake-up times are not consistent) revealed that people under stress tend to need more sleep than those who lead a life relatively free of anxiety and change. Yet stress often triggers insomnia, which leads

---

[17]Natalie Angier, "Cheating on Sleep: Modern Life Turns America into the Land of the Drowsy," *New York Times,* May 15, 1990, pp. C-1, C-8.
[18]Ibid., p. C-1.
[19]Anastasia Toufexis, "Drowsy America," *Time,* December 17, 1990, p. 80.
[20]Angier, "Cheating on Sleep," p. C-8.
[21]Ibid.
[22]Toufexis, "Drowsy America," p. 80.

to less sleep and the chance for even more stress.[23] The results can be a vicious circle of stress and sleeplessness.

Get the Right Amount of Sleep If an adequate amount of sleep is so important, then how much sleep should you be getting? Sleep experts have no easy answer to this basic question. The amount of sleep a person requires is based on a number of factors, including age, heredity, and day-to-day stress, and may vary widely. Sleep researchers generally agree that the average person needs between six and nine hours of sleep each night.[24] But college students aren't necessarily average people. A study done by Dr. Mary Carskadon, director of chronobiology at the E. P. Bradley Hospital in Providence, Rhode Island, found that teen-agers may require more than nine and a half hours of sleep each night to feel sufficiently rested.[25] And indeed, another study seems to add credence to Carskadon's findings. When healthy college students were allowed to lie down in a darkened room in the daytime, 20 percent of them feel asleep almost instantaneously, even though all of them were averaging seven to eight hours of sleep per night![26]

How can you be sure that you are getting the right amount of sleep? In general, your overall alertness should serve as a good indicator. If you are getting the right amount of sleep, you should be able to stay awake through twenty minutes of darkness at midday. Students in art history and film courses, where slides or movies are commonly shown, often complain that a darkened auditorium or classroom makes them sleepy. These situations don't *create* sleepiness. They simply reveal a problem of insufficient sleep and should serve as a warning to get more rest. Sleep behavior experts tell us that on the average, most people fall short of their needed length of sleep by sixty to ninety minutes each night.[27] Aggravating this daily deficit is the fact that sleep loss is cumulative; it adds up. If you feel tired on Monday morning, you're apt to feel even more so when Friday rolls around.[28]

Although sleep loss adds up, sleep does not. You can't stash away extra hours of sleep like money in the bank. You need to get sufficient sleep

---

[23]Lynne Lamberg, *The American Medical Association (Straight-talk, No-nonsense) Guide to Better Sleep*, Rev. (New York: Random House, 1984), p. 35.
[24]Milton K. Erman and Merrill M. Mitler, *How to Get a Good Night's Sleep* (Phillips Publishing, 1990), p. 5.
[25]Toufexis, "Drowsy America," p. 81.
[26]Angier, "Cheating on Sleep," p. C-1.
[27]Ibid.
[28]Ibid., p. C-8.

seven nights a week. Just as so-called weekend athletes engage in strenu-
ous exercise only on Saturday and Sunday and thereby jeopardize their
hearts and their overall health in their effort to "stay fit," people who
"sleep in" on weekends don't eliminate the effects of a week of sleep deprivation. In fact, they complicate the problem by disturbing their rhythm of
sleeping and waking.

Keep to a Schedule   Achieving full alertness isn't simply a matter of getting enough sleep. It's equally important to do your sleeping at the right
time of day.

The body has its own internal clock, a natural pattern of wakefulness
and sleep that roughly follows the rising and setting of the sun. These
cycles of waking and sleeping are known as _circadian rhythms_. Thanks to
your circadian rhythms, when morning arrives you instinctively become
more alert in anticipation of the day that lies ahead. With the advent of
evening, signals in your brain begin preparing you for needed sleep. You
go to sleep, and when you wake up the process is repeated.

The way to make the most of these circadian rhythms is to maintain a
regular sleep-wake schedule. Sleeping late on the weekends or going to
bed at widely varying times throws your circadian rhythms out of whack.
You find yourself feeling drowsy when you should be alert and wide
awake when you should be fast asleep.[29]

If you've ever traveled a great distance by air, you may have experienced a feeling known as _jet lag_, which was prompted because your body's
internal clock, "set" in the place where you started, didn't match the clocks
of the place where you landed. A person who flies from New York to San
Francisco, for example, may find herself feeling drowsy at 8 P.M. Pacific
time because her sleep-wake cycle was set out East, where the time is
already 11 P.M. And at 4 A.M., when the rest of the West is sleeping, she
may be feeling wide awake. But she will soon synchronize her internal
clock with Pacific time.

People who stay at home but go to sleep at widely varying times are
not so fortunate. They are often plagued by chronic drowsiness and insomnia, a sort of stay-at-home jet lag. If you go to bed at 11 P.M. one night and
at 2 A.M. the next, you may wake up the next day and feel as though
you've flown across the country. In these situations, even getting the right
amount of sleep won't be enough. Your rest will be reduced because you'll
be going against the beat of your body's natural rhythms.

Students who cheat themselves out of sleep feel they're adding extra
hours to their day. They are, of course, but in increasing the quantity of

---

[29]Richard M. Coleman, _Wide Awake at 3:00 A.M._ (New York: W. H. Freeman, 1986), p. 149.

their waking hours, they are reducing the quality. A well-rested student is usually more productive than one who is sleep deprived, even though the latter student may have more hours of study time available.

Recognize the Truth About Naps Students and others who have flexible schedules often see naps as the solution to sleep deprivation. Unfortunately, naps fall far short of their reputation and actually create a number of problems: They're impractical, they adversely affect learning, they harm both sound sleep and the sleep cycle, and they act as a convenient excuse for chronic procrastinators.

Admittedly, there is some scientific basis to the idea of a midafternoon nap. Most adults hit a low point of alertness at roughly 2 P.M. each day. Despite this daily dip in energy, technically known as a *circadian trough,* sleep researchers are quick to point out that a well-rested person will not need a nap at midday.[30]

If your goal is productive learning, napping may not be your best strategy. On waking suddenly from a nap (and few students have the time to do otherwise), you will experience *sleep inertia,* which results in poor performance for as long as a half-hour after waking.[31] A study of subjects who took naps of varying lengths reached the same conclusion in each case: If you follow your nap with a learning session, your memory will be impaired. Interestingly enough, the same study found that if subjects slept for at least six hours, their memories were not impaired when they awakened. These results seem to show that although napping harms your ability to remember, a traditional night's sleep does not.[32]

In addition, naps generally deprive you of two of sleep's more important components: dream, or rapid eye movement (REM), sleep, the period in which all our dreaming occurs, and deep sleep (also called *delta sleep*), which many sleep experts believe recharges our batteries and increases our overall alertness.[33] Therefore, if you take a nap, you may be adding to the quantity of your sleep but not to the quality of it because you will probably be lacking the dream and deep sleep that your body requires.

As you might expect, naps also interfere with your sleep-wake cycle. Unless you take a nap every day at the same time and for the same duration, you will probably wind up with stay-at-home jet lag and have difficulty falling asleep at night.

Finally, the temptation to misuse naps can be great. Many students give in to the urge to sleep, rationalizing that when they awake they will

---

[30] Robert K. Cooper, *The Performance Edge* (Boston: Houghton Mifflin, 1991), p. 225.
[31] Coleman, *Wide Awake at 3:00 A.M.,* p. 99.
[32] Dianne Hales, *The Complete Book of Sleep* (Menlo Park, Calif: Addison-Wesley, 1981), p. 56.
[33] Ibid., p. 18.

feel refreshed and perform more productively. Unfortunately, few students report this happy result. The harsh reality is that if you try to escape a mountain of work by taking a nap, you will wake up to face the same amount of work, and you'll have less time to do it in. It is far better to combat the desire to sleep, get the work done, and go to bed at your usual time with a clear conscience. You'll get the sleep you need, you'll minimize disruptions to your body's circadian rhythms, you'll feel healthier and more alert, and you'll be less susceptible to the potentially corrosive effects of stress.

Take Solid Steps for Better Sleeping   Optimum sleep promotes not only a more alert, energetic, zestful life but also, according to some studies, a longer life. If you're not concentrating, if you're dozing off in class and at your desk, or if you're feeling dragged out, take steps to put yourself on the right track.

Find out how much sleep you need.   If you have some free time at mid-morning, test your degree of alertness. Set a timer for fifteen to twenty minutes, darken your bedroom, and lie down on your bed. If the timer wakes you up, then you probably should be getting more sleep each night. If you're still awake when the timer goes off, you're well rested.

Wake up at the same time every morning.   If you consistently arise at the same time regardless of when you went to bed, you'll keep your circadian rhythms on tempo.[34] Furthermore, an unwavering wake-up time should help discourage you from staying up too late.

Schedule something active during your post-lunch slump.   Sitting in a dark room between 2:00 and 4:00 in the afternoon can be risky. If you're planning on taking a class where slides or movies are shown, try to avoid scheduling it during this time. If you don't have any class at this time, do something energetic, like running errands, sorting papers, practicing a musical instrument, or exercising to pull yourself through this daily dull period. If your energy seems to flag at other times, take frequent five-minute breaks, or slowly pace the floor while you read a book or recite a lesson.

Don't use caffeine after 4 P.M. or alcohol after 8 P.M.   The effects of caffeine can often result in insomnia and thus throw your sleep-wake schedule off.[35] Alcohol, although it has a reputation for making you drowsy, actually upsets your body's sleep pattern, first by reducing your REM sleep and

---

[34] Cooper, *The Performance Edge*, p. 222.
[35] Erman and Mitler, *How to Get a Good Night's Sleep.*

Caffeine: A Poor Substitute for Sleep

Caffeine is the most widely used drug in the United States. Many people drink a cup of coffee or a can of caffeinated soda to produce the feeling of alertness normally associated with sound sleep. Ironically, though, caffeine can actually lead to sleepiness.

* Although morning coffee can mean morning alertness, afternoon coffee may cause afternoon blahs.
* Regular use of caffeine reduces its ability to stimulate alertness.
* Large quantities of caffeine can induce behavioral depression, which results in sleepiness and decreased performance.
* Caffeine burns calories (energy) as it stimulates insulin production, leading to a sudden drop in blood sugar and a feeling of lethargy.
* Drinking only 250 mg. of caffeine can produce symptoms associated with clinical anxiety.

Sources: Richard M. Coleman, *Wide Awake at 3 a.m.* (New York: W.H. Freeman & Co., 1986); Susan Perry and Jim Dawson, *The Secret Our Body Clocks Reveal* (New York: Rawson Associates, 1988); Jere E. Yates, *Managing Stress* (New York: AMACOM, 1979).

then by triggering a "REM rebound," which can result in excessive dreaming and/or nightmares.[36]

Reserve your bed for sleeping. Eating, doing coursework, and even worrying in bed can scramble your body's contextual cues. If your bed becomes a multipurpose area, you may find it more difficult to fall asleep when the time comes.

Exercise! In addition to the benefits it provides to your heart, muscles, and self-esteem, exercise also enhances both the waking and sleeping phases of your circadian rhythms. Twenty minutes or more of vigorous aerobic exercise will boost your alertness in the daytime and improve the

---

[36]Coleman, *Wide Awake at 3:00 A.M.*, p. 124.

quality of your sleep at night. People who exercise regularly have been found to enjoy more deep sleep than people who don't.[37]

Develop Good Eating Habits

One aspect of a healthy physical routine involves developing good eating habits. That means taking time out for meals and eating the right foods.

Take Time Out for Meals   Stress can diminish or deplete certain vitamin and mineral supplies. An erratic meal schedule can help to aggravate this problem. According to nutritionist Jane Brody:

> Millions of Americans have fallen into a pattern of too-late-for-breakfast, grab-something-for-lunch, eat-a-big dinner, and nibble-nonstop-until-bedtime. They starve their bodies when they most need fuel and stuff them when they'll be doing nothing more strenuous than flipping the TV dial or pages of a book. When you think about it, the pattern makes no biological sense.[38]

The simplest way to put some sense back into your eating routine is by beginning each day with breakfast. Breakfast stokes your body's furnace so you have energy to burn for the rest of the day. Lunch and dinner simply throw a few coals on the fire; breakfast gets that fire burning.

Meals not only provide needed nutrients; they also supply you with a necessary break from the stresses of school or work. Here are some stress-relieving suggestions for mealtime:

Don't work as you eat.   Time will have been wasted, and you won't have gained the break you deserved when you sat down to eat. As a result, you'll probably feel more stressed than you were before you ate.

Eat quickly, but don't rush.   There's a difference. If you have a lot of work to do, you won't have time to while away the afternoon with a leisurely lunch. But if you keep one eye on your sandwich and the other on the clock as you eat, you'll increase your chances of getting indigestion and stress without significantly speeding up your meal.

Eat the Right Foods   Dieting advice varies widely, from the prudent to the downright absurd. Nevertheless, there are some basic principles most nutritionists agree on. A recent report from the U.S. Department of Health and Human Services confirmed what nutritionists have long suspected:

---

[37]Ibid., p. 146.
[38]Jane E. Brody, *Jane Brody's Good Food Book* (New York: Norton, 1985), p. 187.

Americans eat too much protein and fat and not enough carbohydrates. You can improve your diet by eating proteins sparingly but strategically, reducing your intake of fats and simple sugars, and increasing your intake of complex carbohydrates.

Eat Proteins Sparingly But Strategically. Although few nutritionists would dispute the necessity of protein as part of a healthy diet, the importance of protein has been blown out of proportion, while its shortcomings have been downplayed. Protein plays an integral role in your body's upkeep. It builds, maintains, and repairs muscle tissue. Protein also appears to have at least one psychological benefit: alertness. Among the amino acids that make up many proteins is *tyrosine*, which activates two hormones that nutritionist Dr. Judith Wurtman refers to as "alertness chemicals." When the brain produces these chemicals, there is "a tendency to think more quickly, react more rapidly to stimuli, and feel more attentive, motivated, and mentally energetic."[39]

Because protein isn't stored in the body (as sugar and fat are) you need to eat it every day. The National Research Council asserts that a diet that derives 8 percent of its total calories from protein should be adequate for 98 percent of the population. In a similar study, the Food and Nutrition Board came up with a figure of 6 percent. Yet the average American gets a whopping 17 percent of his or her calories from protein.

What happens to all that excess protein? It is stored as fat and sugar and used as an energy reserve. Unfortunately, the chemical process of turning protein into energy yields by-products that must be absorbed by the liver and kidneys and then excreted as waste. The task of absorbing those protein by-products puts a strain on the organs. And when the waste is excreted, minerals such as calcium, magnesium, and potassium are eliminated as well. All three of these minerals influence your ability to handle stress.

According to Dr. Michael Lesser in *Nutrition and Vitamin Therapy*, "Calcium shortage may result in a grouchy, irritable, tense disposition."[40] Even a moderate calcium deficiency can prompt symptoms that resemble an anxiety attack. Magnesium, considered a natural sedative by some researchers, was found to be deficient in subjects who exhibited aggressive, behavior. Finally, potassium has long been known to moderate the body's level of sodium, which can trigger hypertension if not kept in check.

Reduce Your Intake of Fats and Simple Sugars. The primary nutritional purpose of fat is to store energy. But, like protein, you need very little fat

---

[39] Judith J. Wurtman, *Managing Your Mind & Mood Through Food* (New York: Harper & Row, 1986), p. 19.
[40] Quoted in Padus, *The Complete Guide to Your Emotions & Your Health*, p. 11.

Fat: Where to Find It

A surprising number of common foods derive over 50 percent of their calories from fat. Unfortunately, most of these foods do little to meet the body's need for carbohydrates.

Food	Calories from Fat	Calories from Protein	Calories from Carbohydrates	Total Calories
Vegetable oil	100%	0%	0%	122
Butter (1 T)	100	0	0	108
Margarine (1 T)	100	0	0	108
Mayonnaise	98	1	1	101
Bacon/fried crisp (1 strip)	92	8	0	49
Cream cheese (1 oz.)	89	3	8	101
Bologna (1 slice)	86	14	0	88
Frankfurter (beef)	83	14	3	145
Peanut butter (1 T)	75	12.5	12.5	96
Cheddar cheese (1 oz.)	72	25	3	112
Egg, boiled (1 med.)	69	31	0	78
Ricotta cheese (1/2 cup)	67	7	26	216
Pork chop (3.5 oz.)	66	34	0	354
Tuna in oil (4 oz.)	66	34	0	285
Potato chips (3.5 oz.)	62	3	35	580
Hamburger (1 patty)	61	39	0	224
Roast chicken with skin intact (3.5 oz.)	56	44	0	243
Broiled tenderloin steak	54	46	0	149
Bass, striped, broiled (3.5 oz.)	51	35	14	229

Source: Adapted from *The Mount Sinai School of Medicine Complete Book of Nutrition*, Victor Herbert and Genell J. Subak-Sharpe, eds. (New York: St. Martin's Press, 1990), pp. 64–65.

to meet your body's requirement for it. Researchers from the National Institutes of Health recommend that we limit fat to roughly 25 percent of our daily calories. Because a gram of fat contains more than twice the calories that a gram of protein or carbohydrates does, meeting or even exceeding your daily requirement for fats is alarmingly easy. Eat a plate of macaroni and cheese, a dinner roll with butter, and a slice of pecan pie for dessert, and you've satisfied your body's fat requirement for the entire day!

Excess fat is even more dangerous than excess protein. Not only does consumption of too much fat lead to obesity, which places undue stress on the body's ability to function properly; it also results in a marked increase in blood cholesterol, which has been linked to a number of life-threatening cardiovascular diseases.

According to one nutritionist, simple carbohydrates such as white flour, refined sugar, and alcohol constitute more than 20 percent of the calories in a typical American diet. What nutritional benefit is derived from these caloric treats? None. With most of their fiber and nutrients removed in processing, these foods provide virtually empty calories—that is, short-lived energy with no long-term food value. In addition, they can take your blood sugar on a roller-coaster ride, leaving you up one minute and down the next. Finally, because simple carbohydrates often cause your blood sugar level to dip so dramatically, eating them can sometimes evolve into an addiction as you constantly seek to boost your energy level as quickly as you can.

Increase Your Intake of Complex Carbohydrates.   Complex carbohydrates, which we commonly call *starches,* are chains of sugars. Rice, whole grains, beans, and pasta are all examples of complex carbohydrates. Unlike simple carbohydrates, complex carbohydrates are valuable sources of nutrients and fiber. And because they occur in chains, complex carbohydrates take longer to digest, thus releasing their energy gradually instead of all at once.

Get Some Exercise

According to respected American cardiologist Dr. Paul Dudley White, "Vigorous…exercise is the best antidote for nervous and emotional stress that we possess."[41] In study after study, experts are corroborating that exercise decreases stress and anxiety. Many other researchers report that regular exercise raises self-esteem and well-being and decreases depression. A study of forty-eight students who had been suffering from test anxiety

---

[41] Robert K. Cooper, *Health and Fitness Excellence* (Boston: Houghton Mifflin, 1989), p. 100.

found that their anxiety was reduced after meditative relaxation and exercise.[42] In another study, both prisoners and prison guards took part in a carefully monitored exercise program. After a regimen of aerobic exercise, participants on both sides of the law found that they were able to sleep better, that their sense of well-being and self-esteem often improved, and that they experienced less tension and depression.[43]

The relationship between exercise and depression, one of the most damaging emotional outgrowths of prolonged stress, led psychologist William Morgan, recent president of the American Psychological Association's Division of Exercise and Sport Psychology, to suggest "that running should be viewed as a wonder drug, analogous to penicillin, morphine and the tricyclics [drugs used to treat depression]. It has a profound potential in preventing mental and physical disease and in rehabilitation after various diseases have occurred."[44] And the most effective exercise is that done regularly and aerobically.

Exercise Regularly   You don't have to be an Olympic athlete to reap the benefits of exercise. Exercising three or more times per week is usually enough to improve your overall conditioning, although many students who follow an exercise routine look forward to their time away from their desks and exercise between five and seven times per week. Aside from its well-documented benefits, one of the reasons that exercise is so effective in reducing stress is a simple one: Like eating, sleeping, or any other type of recreation, it provides a welcome break from your studying and recharges your mental and physical batteries.

Exercise Aerobically   Although all exercise can provide *relief* from stress, only aerobic exercise can actually *prevent* the harmful effects of negative stress. The word *aerobic* means "relating to oxygen." Aerobic exercise is any activity that causes a steady, prolonged increase in your breathing and heart rate. A quick sprint across a football field or a dash from home plate to first base is certainly exercise, but it isn't aerobic exercise. You are inhaling lots of oxygen and speeding up your heart, but you are doing so only for a few seconds, probably not at a steady rate, and definitely not for a prolonged period of time. If, however, you swim twenty-five laps or so, pedal your bike steadily for several miles, or take a brisk thirty-minute walk, in each case you are getting aerobic exercise.

---

[42]Kenneth H. Cooper, *The Aerobics Program for Total Well-Being* (New York: Bantam Books, 1982), p. 186.
[43]Ibid.
[44]Keith W. Johnsgård, "Peace of Mind," *Runner's World* 25, no. 4 (April 1990): 81.

Perhaps the greatest benefit of aerobic exercise is that it lowers your heart rate. Once your heart muscle has been strengthened through exercise, it acts more efficiently, beating fewer times to circulate the same amount of blood. And if anxiety should strike, the increase in the heart rate of an aerobically fit person is not as drastic as it is in someone who gets little or no aerobic exercise. Furthermore, if your heart rate remains comparatively low when subjected to stress, you are less likely to overreact emotionally. The result not only discourages overreaction to stress but also may save your life. A person in poor health who is subjected to unexpected stress can die from the sudden strain the excitement puts on his or her heart.[45]

Exercise provides a perfect example of good stress. It works as a stimulant to release the hormone *norepinephrine*, which promotes enhanced awareness, and *endorphins*, morphinelike hormones that provide the euphoric feeling commonly referred to as "runner's high." Exercise leaves you feeling simultaneously alert and relaxed, a nearly ideal state for efficient, prolonged, and stress-free study. According to Dr. Kenneth Cooper, if you exercise at the end of the day when stress levels are traditionally highest, "you can continue to work or play much later into the evening than might be possible otherwise."[46]

REDUCING STRESSORS

The number of stressors you encounter can be reduced by sidestepping unnecessary sources of stress and by avoiding procrastination.

Avoid Needless Sources of Stress

There are some stressful elements in life that must be faced head-on. But there are others that can be avoided; here are some suggestions for doing so:

Wake up a half-hour earlier. If you find yourself skipping breakfast or taking your last bite just as you race out the door, then you're starting your day on a stressful note. Although getting an adequate amount of sleep is crucial, waking up a half-hour earlier than usual won't significantly affect your sleeping habits but can do wonders to ease the pace of your morning preparations.

---

[45] Cooper, *The Aerobics Program for Total Well-Being*, p. 189.
[46] Ibid., p. 191.

Allow yourself plenty of travel time.   High-strung travelers are easily aggravated by slow drivers or long traffic lights. But slow drivers and long lights are facts of every driver's life. Factor them into your travel time.

Never wait empty-handed.   The stress that comes from standing in line or waiting in traffic stems from boredom and from irritation about wasting time. Both problems have the same easy solution: Have a book to read or some notes to review ready for the next time you're kept waiting, and you'll find that the time will fly by. Simply listening to the radio while waiting may be relaxing for some, but in general it won't provide the same sense of accomplishment.

Keep a note pad handy.   Needless stress and aggravation can accumulate if you spend your time trying not to forget what tasks you want to accomplish. Jot down reminders, and you'll free up your mind so that what you need to remember will no longer function as a stressor.

Eat dinner early.   If you eat at a college dining hall, it's usually wise to get there early. The trivial but real stress that comes from waiting in line, searching for a seat, or racing to get a second helping before the kitchen closes can be eliminated if you show up soon after the dining hall opens. Whether you eat your meals at home or at school, an early dinner gives you more time before bed to be productive.

Don't take your work to bed with you.   Your bed is for relaxation. Don't mix your mind's signals by turning your bed into an auxiliary workspace. If you establish a clear boundary between where you work and where you sleep, your work will become more productive, and your sleep will be more restful. And both will tend to improve your approach to life's stressors.

Eliminate Procrastination

"Nothing [is] so fatiguing as the eternal hanging on of an uncompleted task." These words by William James, distinguished American psychologist, strike at the hearts of us all. Every one of us has had many bouts with procrastination. The best ways to avoid future bouts is to learn why people procrastinate and what you can do to prevent procrastination.

Learn Why People Procrastinate   There's no single explanation for why people procrastinate. Nevertheless, many of the stressors already discussed in this chapter can trigger procrastination. Here's a list of the major sources:

Fear of failure.   Many students hesitate to even begin a task because they're afraid they won't be able to successfully complete it. Have some faith in yourself. Think back to past successes, and realize that if you've achieved success before, you can achieve it again. If you've failed in similar situations in the past, think of times when you've succeeded in other areas, and apply the confidence you gained then to the present.

Fear of success.   Some students put tasks off because they are afraid of succeeding. There are at least two reasons a person might be afraid of success. First, successful people are a minority. There is a kind of loneliness in success. Some students unconsciously procrastinate because they want to remain part of the group. They don't want to be resented by people who aren't as successful. Second, success brings on responsibility and choices. When a person succeeds, doors suddenly open. That should be good news, but some students view these opportunities as threats and burdens instead of challenges and choices.

Lack of time.   If you used all the time you've been spending worrying about the time you don't have, you'd be well on your way to completing the task you've been putting off. This is a problem of control. Realize that how you budget your time is up to you. If you feel in control, you'll find it easier to complete the jobs that need to be done.

Shortage of energy.   Claiming a lack of energy can hide the real reason for not doing something. If you truly don't have the energy, sleep, food, and exercise may be the root of your problem. Make sure you're getting enough regularly scheduled sleep, that you're eating a balanced diet, and that you're promoting good health and alertness through exercise. If you still feel tired, then some other cause is responsible. It may be a medical problem, in which case you should make a point to see a doctor. Or it may be a psychological problem masquerading as fatigue. In either case, find the cause and take care of it—right away!

Poor organization.   Perhaps you begin each day determined to get started on that task you've been putting off. But when nighttime comes, you find that despite your best intentions, you didn't get around to it. If that's your trouble, then the cause may be a lack of priorities and/or poor organization. If you organize what you plan to do each day into a schedule and list your activities in order of priority, then you should be able to accomplish those important tasks.

Devise Ways to Prevent Procrastination   Although the roots of procrastination are varied, the methods that follow for preventing procrastination should work regardless of the cause.

Make your plans a part of the public record.   When you have a job that has to be completed or a goal that you want to reach, resist keeping your objective as a foggy, easy-to-ignore idea in your head. Write down your plan. Once you've preserved it on paper, the job will be harder to ignore.

Or announce your intentions to close friends or family members. For example, "I plan to finish the bibliography for my research paper this weekend." Once you've made your intentions official, you're less likely to put them off. Procrastinators commonly fall into the habit of deceiving themselves, but they are less likely to deceive the people around them.

Step back and check your progress from time to time. One way that many people procrastinate is by getting entangled in the details of their work. If you plan on finishing an entire chapter assignment in a single evening but then find yourself spending most of your time reading, rereading, and fine-tuning your notes for a single section, you may not be looking for increased understanding. You may simply have found a way to procrastinate. If, however, you periodically step back and measure your progress, you'll realize that you've gotten bogged down, and you'll be able to pick up your pace so you can reach your goal in the allotted time.

Let your momentum work for you. If you've successfully completed a task you were anxious to finish, let your momentum carry over to an activity that you aren't as enthused about. This extra energy can help you get started on the dreaded task, and once you've begun (the hardest part), completion will become much easier.

Use the five-minute plan. William J. Knaus, author of *Do It Now: How to Stop Procrastinating,* recommends what he calls the "five-minute plan."[47] Tackle a long-neglected task by agreeing to work on it for only five minutes. When the five minutes are up, decide if you want to keep going. You usually will. The hardest part of almost any job is simply getting started. The five-minute plan takes the sting out of that painful first step.

Be specific. A task is almost always more intimidating when it looms large and undefined. For most students, the research paper is a classic example of this nebulous source of anxiety. Instead of constantly telling yourself, "I've got to start writing that research paper," zero in on a specific aspect of your paper, such as choosing the topic or compiling a working bibliography. Suddenly your goal becomes more concrete, more doable, and thus much easier to complete. Or as James R. Sherman, author of *Stop Procrastinating*, puts it, "A job well-defined is a job half done."[48]

Verbalize your excuses. You may think you've got perfectly good reasons for putting off what needs to be done. If you let your excuses see the light of day by writing them out or explaining them to a friend, you'll often find that your reasoning isn't nearly as logical as you'd thought.

---

[47] William J. Knaus, *Do It Now: How to Stop Procrastinating,* quoted in Padus, p. 393.
[48] James R. Sherman, *Stop Procrastinating* (Los Altos, Calif.: Crisp Publications, 1989), p. 38.

Visualize success or completion. Take a moment to imagine yourself accomplishing a task, passing a test, or achieving a goal. Through visualizing, you chart a course in your mind's eye. That course gives you a tangible game plan. The positive outcome you've imagined provides an incentive to follow that course until you reach the point of completion.

SUMMARY

What can you do to relax?

Try the relaxation techniques suggested in this chapter—deep breathing and progressive muscle relaxation—or others you're familiar with.

How can you improve your self-esteem?

Changing the script of your internal dialogue from words of discouragement to words of encouragement and building on your past successes should do a lot to boost your sense of your own value.

How do you take control of your life?

Taking control of your life involves shifting your attitude so that you are able to view threats as challenges and obligations as choices. It also means acknowledging and accepting those situations you are unable to control.

How can regular mealtimes discourage stress?

Regular mealtimes can alleviate some of the effects of stress by providing you with a consistent rest from your work and by replenishing some of the energy and nutrients that stress may have consumed.

How does your diet affect your response to stress?

Adequate nutrition can make you more resistant to stress, whereas poor nutrition can make you less stress resistant and can actually increase your susceptibility to stress.

How can exercise help reduce stress?

Regular exercise provides a needed rest from your work and improves the quality of your sleep and your general attitude.

What is the benefit of aerobic exercise?

Aerobic exercise builds up your heart muscle. (Most steady, sustained exercise, such as distance running, swimming, and brisk walking, is aerobic.) When you exercise aerobically, you increase your heart rate and your intake of oxygen. Your heart responds by getting stronger and working more efficiently.

How can you reduce the number of stressors you face?

You can minimize stressors by avoiding needless sources of stress and by eliminating the damaging habit of procrastination.

What can you do to avoid needless sources of stress?

You can deflect or avoid many potentially damaging sources of stress by getting into the habit of developing back-up plans and by learning to use time more efficiently. You can also identify the causes of procrastination and then find ways to prevent them.

HAVE YOU MISSED SOMETHING?

Matching. In each blank space in the left column, write the letter preceding the phrase in the right column that matches the left item best.

___b___ **1.** Jacobson

___f___ **2.** Panting

___e___ **3.** Aerobic

___c___ **4.** Proteins

___a___ **5.** Self-talk

___d___ **6.** Circadian trough

a. Has silent impact on self-esteem

b. Developed progressive muscle relaxation

c. Should be eaten sparingly but strategically

d. Dip in energy, usually in midafternoon

e. Means "relating to air"

f. Has been shown to cause feelings of panic

Multiple choice. Choose the word or phrase that completes the following sentence most accurately, and circle the letter that precedes it.

1. Relaxed breaths usually originate from the

    a. chest.
    b. waist.
    c. abdomen.
    d. neck.

2. Complex carbohydrates are chains of
   a. fats.
   b. starches.
   c. proteins.
   d. sugars.

3. One of the greatest benefits of aerobic exercise is that it
   a. takes only ten minutes to do.
   b. lowers your heart rate.
   c. burns only fats, not carbohydrates.
   d. builds up your arm muscles.

4. Common aerobic exercises include
   a. swimming.
   b. running.
   c. bicycling.
   d. all of the above.

5. Logan found that a group of survivors of extreme stress all
   a. believed in God.
   b. had a strong sense of control.
   c. avoided fats and sugars.
   d. had lowered heart rates.

6. Your learning may be impaired if you try to study right after
   a. exercise.
   b. a large meal.
   c. a brief nap.
   d. a final exam.

7. Taking control involves turning
   a. proteins into carbohydrates.
   b. threats into challenges.
   c. choices into obligations.
   d. food into calories.

True-false. Write *T* beside the *true* statements and *F* beside the *false* statements.

___ 1. Your body undergoes stress when you walk at a brisk pace.

___ 2. Experts don't all agree on how much sleep you require.

___ 3. Fear of success is one possible cause of procrastination.

_F_　**4.** It is difficult to meet your daily nutritional requirement for fat.

_F_　**5.** "Sleeping in" should eliminate the effects of sleep deprivation.

_T_　**6.** Your attitude can have a powerful effect on your sense of control.

Short answer.　Supply a brief answer for each of the following items. The number in parentheses refers to the page where the item is discussed in the text.

1. Explain the "two-sided potential of stress." (5)
2. What is the James-Lange theory? (6)
3. What makes an exercise aerobic? (24)

BUILDING YOUR VOCABULARY STEP BY STEP: HOW STRONG IS YOUR VOCABULARY?

Simply knowing a large number of words is not the same as understanding those words. Many of us routinely read and even use words that we can't define precisely.

　　The following quiz, which uses words from this chapter, is similar to the vocabulary section in the PSAT and SAT, standardized tests given to high school students who plan to attend college. After you have completed the test, check you answers with the key that follows.

Directions:　Each of the following items consists of a boldfaced word followed by five more words. Read the boldfaced word carefully. Then read each of the following words, and select the one that means the *opposite* of the boldfaced word. Circle the letter preceding the word you selected. (Answers appear on page 289.)

Example:

abundant	a. small	b. plenty	c. insufficient
	d. ample	e. large	

1. **aggravating**	a. loud	b. soothing	c. irritating
	d. monotonous	e. perplexing	
2. **bolstered**	a. improved	b. supported	c. hurt
	d. strengthened	e. weakened	
3. **deficit**	a. surplus	b. gap	c. windfall
	d. shortage	e. debt	

4. **corrodes**   a. oxidizes   b. eats away   c. improves
                   d. builds up   e. supports

5. **erratic**   a. weird   b. steady   c. restrained
                   d. unstable   e. sensual

6. **exhilaration** a. inhalation   b. depression   c. elation
                     d. relief   e. dismay

7. **controversial** a. disputable   b. heated   c. unquestionable
                      d. risqué   e. widely discussed

8. **habitual**   a. recurrent   b. rare   c. addictive
                   d. unusual   e. relentless

9. **impair**   a. enhance   b. hinder   c. invigorate
                   d. double   e. reduce

10. **integral**   a. calculated   b. essential   c. peripheral
                   d. unsung   e. damaging

11. **jeopardizing** a. stimulating   b. protecting   c. endangering
                      d. destroying   e. strengthening

12. **mundane**   a. extraordinary b. repetitive   c. commonplace
                   d. valuable   e. refined

13. **nebulous**   a. indistinct   b. precise   c. celestial
                   d. murky   e. solid

14. **obstacle**   a. wall   b. hindrance   c. antidote
                   d. boon   e. barrier

15. **scoffed**   a. praised   b. ridiculed   c. laughed
                   d. condemned   e. analyzed

16. **susceptible** a. strong   b. vulnerable   c. weak
                     d. resistant   e. irresistible

17. **undermine** a. subvert   b. cripple   c. buttress
                   d. build   e. dispose

18. **undue**   a. intolerant   b. inordinate   c. appropriate
                   d. reticent   e. prudent

Here are some additional words from the chapter that you may want to add to your vocabulary. The number after each word refers to the page where it was used.

aerobic (24)

analogous (24)

assuming (9)

contracting (6)

deprivation (14)

elicited (11)

erratic (20)

garnered (6)

inconspicuously (9)

inertia (17)

insight (11)

instantaneously (15)

instinctively (16)

intimidating (28)

lethargy (7)

optimum (18)

pessimistic (6)

phenomenon (11)

productivity (12)

prolonged (24)

regimen (24)

relish (13)

savor (10)

strategically (21)

tangible (29)

underscores (12)

Finding Time

2

I wish I could stand on a busy street corner, hat in hand, and beg people to throw me their wasted hours.

BERNARD BERENSON
Art historian

The people who worry about a lack of time are often the same ones who waste it. You can make the most of every minute by learning how to save time and by using schedules to help manage time. To help you find time, this chapter discusses

- Saving time
- Using time schedules

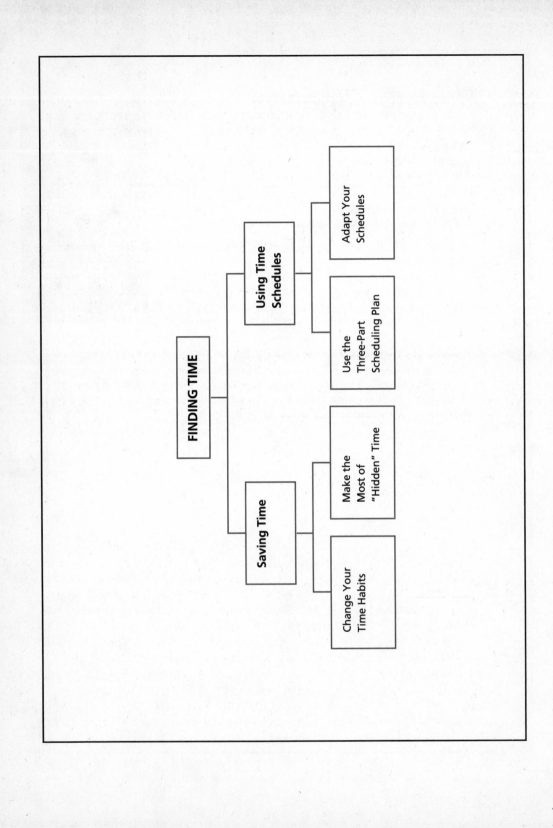

T ime is a precious and irreplaceable commodity. Few have noted that fact more convincingly and succinctly than Queen Elizabeth I of England (1533–1603). As she lay dying, she declared, "All my possessions for a moment of time."

How you use time can determine your success or failure in college. If you use time wisely, you'll prosper. If you use it poorly, you'll fail in the job you came to do. That's why the management of time is the number-one skill to master in college.

Yet students frequently squander time. A survey conducted at Fordham University in 1987 found that college freshmen spent roughly one-third of their waking hours during a typical weekday engaged in social activities or idle leisure. This "free time" amounted to nearly twice the time the students spent studying. And on the weekend the ratio of social and idle leisure time to study time for the same group was almost six to one!

Although the students in the survey seemed to waste time routinely, you needn't put yourself in the same position. You can gain extra time in two ways: (1) by doing a job in less time than usual and (2) by using small blocks of time that you usually waste. The first way requires you to study more efficiently, and this book provides a great many techniques to help you do just that. The second way requires you to save time by changing your habits and making the most of "hidden" time and to manage your time by using a three-part scheduling plan. This chapter offers a number of suggestions that can enable you to use time more productively.

SAVING TIME

All of us have claimed that we don't have enough time to accomplish what we need to do. But the fact is that everyone is allotted the same amount of time: twenty-four hours a day. It's our day-to-day habits, activities we no longer notice, that save time or waste it. You can put your time to better use by eliminating the bad habits that waste time, cultivating good habits that save time, and pinpointing areas of "hidden" time.

A good way to begin is by keeping a daily activities log. From the time you wake up to the time you go to sleep, note all your major activities, the time you started and finished each, and the time each activity consumed. With your day itemized on paper in this way, you can gain a clearer picture of where your time is being spent and where it's being wasted. The activities log in Figure 2.1 shows one student's daily routine and how he decided to put his time to better use.

Time		Time	Activity - Description
Start	End	Used	
7:45	8:15	:30	Dress
8:15	8:40	:25	Breakfast
8:40	9:00	:20	Nothing
9:00	10:00	1:00	Psychology - Lecture
10:00	10:40	:40	Coffee - Talking
10:40	11:00	:20	Nothing
11:00	12:00	1:00	Economics - Lecture
12:00	12:45	:45	Lunch
12:45	2:00	1:15	Reading - Magazine
2:00	4:00	2:00	Biology Lab
4:00	5:30	1:30	Recreation - Volleyball
5:30	6:00	:30	Nothing
6:00	7:00	1:00	Dinner
7:00	8:00	1:00	Nap
8:00	8:50	:50	Study - Statistics
8:50	9:20	:30	Break
9:20	10:00	:40	Study - Statistics
10:00	10:50	:50	Chat with Bob
10:50	11:30	:40	Study - Accounting
11:30	11:45	:15	Ready for bed
11:45	7:45	8:00	Sleep.

Paste 3 X 5 cards on mirror: laws of economics; psychological terms; statistical formulas. Study while brushing teeth, etc.

Look over textbook assignment and previous lecture notes to establish continuity for today's psychology lecture.

Break too long and too soon after breakfast. Work on psychology notes just taken; also look over economics assignment.

Rework the lecture notes on economics while still fresh in mind. Also, look over biology assignment to recall the objective of the coming lab.

Use this time to read a magazine or newspaper.

Not a good idea. Better finish work, then get a good night's sleep.

Break is too long.

Good as a reward if basic work is done.

Insufficient time allotted, but better than no time.

While brushing teeth, study the 3 X 5 cards. Replace cards that have been mastered with new ones.

FIGURE 2.1   Record of One Day's Activities and Suggestions for Making Better Use of Time

Change Your Time Habits

Once you have the concrete evidence of a daily activities log before you, you can see where to save time. The way to begin doing so is to eliminate common time-wasting habits and to develop time-saving habits.

Defy Parkinson's Law _Parkinson's Law_ says that work expands to fit the time allotted.[1] To avoid running out of time, work Parkinson's Law in reverse: For each task, set a deadline that will be difficult to meet, and then strive to meet that deadline.

Each time you achieve your goal, reward yourself with some small but pleasant activity. Take a break. Chat with a friend. Stroll around the room. Have a special snack, such as a bag of peanuts (keep it in your desk, to be opened only as a reward).

If you fail to meet a deadline, don't punish yourself. Just hold back your reward and set another goal. It is _positive_ reinforcement that is powerful in effecting a change in behavior.

Obey Your Alarm Clock How many times do you hit the snooze button on your alarm clock before you finally get out of bed? Even once is too many. Set your alarm for the time you want to get up, not for the time you want to _start_ getting up. If you can't obey your alarm, you'll have a hard time sticking to your time schedule. After all, it doesn't even buzz.

Take "Time Out" Reward yourself with regular short breaks as you work. Learning in several small sessions, rather than in one continuous stretch, actually increases comprehension. In one study, students who practiced French vocabulary in three discrete sessions did 35 percent better on an exam than those who tried to learn the words in one sitting.[2] So take a breather for ten minutes every hour, or spend five minutes resting every half-hour. Whichever method you choose, keep your breaks consistent. This way, you'll study with more energy and look forward to your regular rests. And when you return to your desk, you'll find that you feel more refreshed.

Jot Down Thoughts on a Notepad Keep a memo pad or a plain sheet of paper by your side, and write down any obligations or stray ideas that occur to you as you're studying. By putting them on paper, you'll free your brain to focus entirely on the task before you. You will work more efficiently, and as a result you'll save time.

If the thoughts you've written down don't relate to your studies, you can deal with them when your work is done or even while you're taking a break. If your jottings do relate to your work, you can use them to get the

---

[1] C. Northcote Parkinson, _Parkinson's Law and Other Studies in Administration_ (Boston: Houghton Mifflin, 1957).
[2] Kristine C. Bloom et al., "Effects of Massed and Distributed Practice on the Learning and Retention of Second-Language Vocabulary," _Journal of Educational Research_ 74, no. 4 (March–April 1981): 245–248.

jump on the subject they pertain to. Often the hardest part of shifting from one activity to another is just getting started. Your jottings may provide an impetus to overcome the inertia that seems to characterize the outset of a new activity. If so, they may save you some valuable time. Here is an example, from the notepad of one student who, while working on a calculus assignment, came up with a topic for an upcoming paper. As soon as she finished her calculus, she was able to begin doing preliminary research on the topic without delay.

—Call Mr. Soames about make-up test.

—Check Campbell book for discussion of brain laterality.

—What about "Earthquake Prediction" as possible paper topic?

—Look up definitions for leftover vocab. cards.

—Tennis at 6 tonight, not 7!

Make the Most of "Hidden" Time

Another way you can gain time is by tapping into "hidden time" that goes unused because you don't recognize it as available.

Carry Pocket Work   Many situations may leave you with a few moments of unexpected free time—a long line at the bank or supermarket, a delayed bus or train, a wait at the doctor's office, a lunch date who arrives late. If you make a point to bring along a book, a photocopied article, or 3 x 5 cards carrying key concepts or formulas, you'll be able to take advantage of potentially frustrating experiences.

Use Your Mind When It's Free   Some activities may still afford the opportunity for studying if you're prepared. For example, if you're shaving, combing your hair, or washing dishes, there's no reason you can't be studying at the same time. Attach small metal or plastic clips near mirrors and on walls at eye level. Place a note card in each clip. Or do a problem or two in math or master some new vocabulary words as you eat a sandwich at work.

Put Information on Audio Cassettes   Another way of using hidden time is by listening to information you've recorded on audio cassettes. Recorded information enables you to keep studying in situations where you're moving about or your eyes are otherwise occupied, such as when you're getting dressed or driving. In addition, recorded information can provide a refreshing change from written material.

Employ Spare-Time Thinking You can make the most of the moments immediately before or after class by recalling the main points from the last lecture as you're heading to class or by quickly recalling the points of a lecture just completed as you're leaving class.

Use Your Subconscious At one time or another, you have awakened during the night with a bright idea or a solution to a problem that you had been thinking about before bedtime. Your subconscious works while your conscious mind is resting in sleep. If you want to capture the ideas or solutions produced by your subconscious, write them down as soon as you wake up; otherwise, they'll be lost. Many creative people know this and keep a pad and pencil near their beds. For example, Nobel Prize winner Albert Szent-Györgyi said, "I go to sleep thinking about my problems all the time, and my brain must continue to think about them when I sleep because I wake up, sometimes in the middle of the night, with answers to questions that have been eluding me all day."[3]

USING TIME SCHEDULES

A time schedule is a game plan, a written strategy that spells out exactly what you hope to accomplish—for a day, a week, or even the entire term—and how you plan to do it. Committing yourself to planning out and keeping to a schedule can seem a bit frightening at first, but following such a schedule soon becomes a source of strength and a boon to your life. There are several benefits to a schedule.

A schedule provides greater control. A thoughtfully constructed time schedule can increase your sense of control in four ways. First, because your schedule is written down, your plans seem more manageable. You can start working without delay. Second, you know you'll study all of your subjects—even those you dislike—because you've allotted time for them in your schedule. There's less of a temptation to skip disliked subjects when study time has already been allotted for them in your schedule. Third, a schedule discourages you from being lazy. You've got a plan right in front of you, and that plan says, "Let's get down to business!" Fourth, you can schedule review sessions right from the start and avoid last-minute cramming for tests.

---

[3] Originally published in *Some Watch While Some Must Sleep,* by William C. Dement, as a volume in The Portable Stanford series published by the Stanford Alumni Association. Copyright © 1972. Reprinted by permission of the Stanford Alumni Association.

A schedule encourages relaxation.   At the same time, because your plan is written down instead of floating around in your head, your mind is freed for other things. There's no time wasted worrying about what to do next. It's all there on paper. There's no guilt either. Both work and play are written into your schedule. This means that when you take a break, you know you deserve it.

Despite these benefits, many students are reluctant to start using a time schedule. They feel not only that a schedule will do them very little good but also that keeping track of time will turn them into nervous wrecks. Neither worry is warranted.

A schedule saves time.   Yes, it takes time to devise a schedule, but that time is rewarded. You will be able to shift smoothly from one activity to the next, without the pauses and panics involved in wondering what to do next.

A schedule provides freedom.   Scheduling frees you from time's control. The people you see dashing from class to library to gym, or eating lunch on the run, are slaves to time. The students who schedule time, who decide how it will be used, are the masters of time.

A schedule increases flexibility.   Disorganized people often waste so much time that there's no room for flexibility. People who do scheduling free their time for a variety of activities and are therefore more flexible.

Use the Three-Part Scheduling Plan

If you're attending classes full time, your best strategy for scheduling is to use a three-part plan. The three schedules—a *master schedule,* a *weekly schedule,* and a *daily schedule*—work in concert to help you manage each day as well as the term as a whole. If you are balancing your studies with the extra responsibilities that come with working at a job, participating in a time-consuming extracurricular activity, or raising a family, the basic principles that underlie the plan are still valuable, but you may want to tailor them to your particular needs.

The three-part scheduling plan provides a system for handling the assignments and activities that make up your daily life. The master schedule serves as a basic structure for organizing your activities. The weekly schedule adds specific details to the master schedule, and the daily schedule puts the weekly schedule in a portable form. Although each schedule performs a different function, all three follow the same scheduling guidelines:

1. *Plan your time in blocks.*   A father once tied a bundle of small, thin sticks together with a strand of twine, handed the bundle to his youngest son, and said, "Son, break these sticks in half." The boy used his hands and knees but could not break the bundle. Sadly, he handed it back to his father. Without a word, the father untied the twine and, using only his fingers, snapped each stick one by one.

When the sum total of your obligations and academic assignments seems overwhelming, it helps immensely to split them up into small, manageable units. By dividing each day into blocks, time schedules provide you with a method for breaking up your responsibilities and dealing with them one by one. Assigning a block of time to each activity ensures that you will work at peak efficiency.

When you're faced with an assignment, particularly a long-term one, remind yourself right from the start that you do not intend to accomplish everything in one sitting. The "divide and conquer" tactic applies to academic assignments just as it does to military campaigns.

2. *Study during prime time.* For most of us prime time is daytime. In fact, research has shown that each hour used for study during the day is equal to one and a half hours at night. Even so, you may find that you have dead hours during the day when you are less productive than you'd like to be. Schedule less-demanding tasks for these hours.

3. *Study before recitation classes and after lecture classes.* A study session before a recitation or discussion class (a foreign language course or a psychology seminar, for example) helps warm you up. When you walk into class, the material is fresh in your mind. For lecture classes, use the time immediately after class to fill in any gaps in your notes and to review the information you've just learned.

4. *Schedule your time effectively.* Account for all your time, but do so without being overly detailed. The time you'd take to make a meticulous schedule can be better used in studying a subject directly, and the chances of your following such a plan are slim.

5. *Include nonacademic activities.* Always set aside time for food, sleep, and recreation as well as the other activities of your life. Cheating yourself out of a meal, a good night's sleep, a swim, a family get-together, or a meeting with friends won't save you time in the long run. In fact, this may cost you time because all these activities are necessary for your overall mental and physical wellness. Make your plan for living, not just for studying.

Lay a Foundation with a Master Schedule A master schedule provides a schedule of fixed activities around which your varying activities are arranged. Unless changes occur in your basic program, you need to draw up a master schedule only once per term.

A master schedule grid lists the days of the week at the top and the hours of the day down the left side. The boxes within the grid are filled in

	Mon.	Tues.	Wed.	Thurs.	Fri.	Sat.	Sun.
7-8	← —————— Dress and Breakfast —————— →						
8-9	History		History		History	Dress + Breakfast	
9-10		Phy. Ed		Phy Ed.		Phy Ed.	Dress + Breakfast
10-11		Chem.		Chem.		Chem.	
11-12	French		French		French		
12-1	← —————— Lunch ——————————————————— →						
1-2	Math	Film making	Math	Film making	Math		
2-3				↑			
3-4				Chem. lab.			
4-5	English		English	↓	English		
5-6							
6-7	← —————— Dinner ——————————————————— →						
7-8							
8-9							
9-10							
10-11							
11-12	← —————— Sleep ——————————— →						

FIGURE 2.2   A Master Schedule

with all your required activities: sleep, meals, job, regular meetings, community time, sports, and, of course, classes. The empty boxes that remain represent your free time. Figure 2.2 provides an example of a typical master schedule.

Such a master schedule, on a 5 x 8 card taped over your desk or carried in your notebook, unclutters your mind. More important, it enables you to visualize the blank boxes as actual blocks of time into which you may fit necessary activities.

Account for Changing Details with a Weekly Schedule The weekly schedule takes over where the master schedule leaves off. To construct it, photocopy your master schedule and then fill in the empty blocks with the activities you have planned for the upcoming week. If you have a math test on Friday, for example, you will need to schedule a little extra study time for math. Next week you may be assigned a research paper. If so, you'll probably want to leave space in your schedule for library research. The weekly schedule helps you adapt your time to your changing priorities. Keep it posted by your desk or pasted on the inside cover of your notebook.

A sample weekly schedule is shown in Figure 2.3. The lists that follow show how the guidelines for scheduling were used to set it up.

Monday Through Friday/Saturday

7–8 A.M.   Avoid the frantic dash and the gobbled (or skipped) breakfast by getting up on time.

12–1 P.M.   Take a full, leisurely hour for lunch.

5–6   Relax before dinner—your reward for a day of conscientious work.

7–9   Keep up with current notes and assignments through systematic studying.

9–10   To forestall cramming at quiz and examination times, give some time every day to a review of previous assignments and ground covered to date.

10   A cease-study time of 10 P.M. provides an incentive for working hard during the day and early evening.

10–12   Devote some time every day to reading books that truly interest you. Recreational reading and conversation help you unwind for a good night's sleep.

Tuesday/Thursday/Saturday

8–9 A.M.   Because chemistry (10–11) is your hard subject, build your morning study program around it. An hour's study before class will make the class period more meaningful.

11–12 P.M. Another hour's study immediately after chemistry class will help you remember the work covered in class and move more readily to the next assignment.

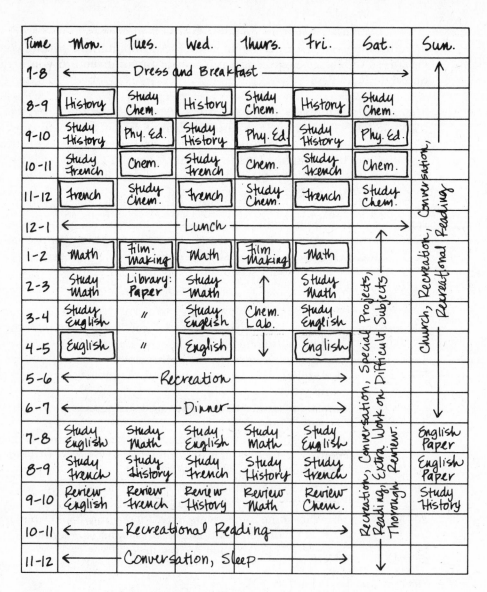

FIGURE 2.3   A Detailed Weekly Schedule Based on a Master Schedule

Special

Tuesday   2–5 P.M., library: paper
Sunday   7–9 P.M., English paper

For some assignments you will need to schedule blocks of time to do research or to develop and follow up ideas.

Saturday   From noon on, Saturday is left unscheduled—for recreation, for special projects to which you must devote a concentrated period of time, for extra work on difficult subjects, for thorough review.

Sunday   This is your day until evening. Study history before you go to bed because it is the first class you'll have on Monday morning.

Provide a Portable Game Plan with a Daily Schedule   A daily schedule is a brief, yet specific list of the day's tasks and the time blocks you plan to

FOR MONDAY

8 - 9	Psychology - Review Chapter V and lecture notes
9 - 10	Psychology lecture
10 - 11	Economics lecture
11 - 12	Economics - fix up notes, begin Chapter VII
1 - 2	Campus store - Pick up paper and binder, pen, lead, calculator
2 - 5	Engineering - work on assignment
5 - 6	Exercise - Tennis court with Joan.
7 - 10	Accounting and Math

Review: Just before class is a good time to review the high points of chapters previously studied. Also review the previous lecture for continuity.

Fix up notes: The very best time to fix up lecture notes, and review them simultaneously, is immediately after the lecture.

After lunch: This is a good time to give yourself a semi-break from academic work and do some necessary errands.

2-5 block: This is a valuable block of time during which you should be able to read the assignment and work out the assigned problems without losing continuity.

Exercise: After an entire day with the books, some exercise and a shower will help to put an edge on your appetite, as well as making a definite break between study during the day and study during the evening.

After dinner: Both subjects need unbroken time for efficient production. Use the block of three hours to do a balanced amount of work for each, depending on the assignments.

Breaks: Breaks are not listed. You judge for yourself when a break is best for you. Also, the break should be taken when you arrive at a good stopping point.

FIGURE 2.4 A Daily Schedule

accomplish them in. You should be able to fit all this information on a 3 x 5 index card that you can carry around with you all day. Make up your daily schedule each night before you go to bed. Once you have put your worries and concerns on paper, your mind will be free for sleep. You will also have thought through your day and will be better prepared when the morning comes. Figure 2.4 shows one student's daily schedule and explains why it is effective.

Adapt Your Schedules

If you have a job, a family, or some other commitment that requires a great deal of your attention, the predictable time blocks that characterize traditional time schedules may not be as useful for you. You may need a system that helps you use scattered bits of time instead. And if you are faced with a long-term assignment, your schedules and scheduling strategies may require some adjustment as well.

Develop When Necessary, a Task-Based Master Schedule   A task-based master schedule enables you to keep track of one or more assignments or goals over an extended period of time. Figure 2.5 provides an example of a task-based master schedule. Across the top of the schedule, instead of the days of the week, list the major goals you hope to accomplish or the assignments you plan to complete. Deadlines for subgoals may be written down the left-hand side where the hours of the day would normally be written in a standard master schedule.

Now divide up each goal or long-term assignment into manageable subgoals. List these in a column beneath the task they refer to. For example, if you've been assigned a research paper, you may arrive at the following subgoals: Do preliminary research, choose topic, plan outline, conduct research, complete first draft, and revise first draft. As you reach each milestone on the way to completing your assignment, cross it off your schedule. As you do, you provide yourself with visual evidence and positive feedback of the progress you've made.

Make Your Weekly Schedule Assignment Oriented   If the span of your goal or assignment is a week or less, you can use an assignment-oriented weekly schedule as a supplement to your master schedule. Figure 2.6 shows such a schedule. The format is simple. Draw a horizontal line to divide an 8 1/2 x 11 sheet of paper in half. In the top half, list your subjects, assignments, estimated study times, and due dates. Then, with the due dates and estimated times as control factors, check your master schedule for your avail-

	Psychology Research Paper April 21	Train for Amateur Triathlon may 1	Self-Paced Computer Course
Feb. 7	~~Select Three Topic Ideas~~	~~Up Minimum to 60 Laps~~	~~Complete Ch. 1-3~~
Feb. 10	Do Preliminary Research	Try Ride Up Satyr Hill	
Feb. 14	Make final Topic Choice	Run 30 miles per week	Complete Ch. 4-6
Feb. 18	Complete Bibliography		
March 15	Finish First Draft		Mid-term exam
March 18	Begin Rewriting		
April 21	Paper Due		Final

FIGURE 2.5   A Task-Based Master Schedule

Subject	Assignment	Estimated Time	Date Due	Time Due
Electronics	Chap. V - 32 pp. - Read	2 hr.	Mon. 13th	8:00
English	Paper to Write	18 hr.	Mon. 20th	9:00
Math	Problems on pp. 110-111	3 hr.	Tues. 14th	10:00
Industrial Safety	Make shop layouts	8 hr.	Fri. 17th	11:00
Graphics	Drawing of TV components	6 hr.	Fri. 17th	1:00
Electronics	Chap. VI - 40 pp. - Read	2½ hr.	Weds. 22nd	8:00

Day	Assignment	Morning	Afternoon	Evening
Sun.	Electronics - Read Chap. V English - Find a Topic			7:30 - 9:30 9:30 - 10:30
Mon.	English - Gather Notes Math - Problems		2:00 - 6:00	7:00 - 10:00
Tues.	English - Gather Notes Industrial Safety	8:00 - 10:00	3:00 - 6:00	7:00 - 10:00
Wed.	English - First Draft Graphics		2:00 - 6:00	7:00 - 10:00
Thurs.	Industrial Safety English - Paper Graphics	8:00 - 10:00	3:00 - 6:00	7:00 - 10:00
Fri.	English - Final Copy Electronics		2:00 - 6:00	7:00 - 9:30
Sat.				

FIGURE 2.6   A Weekly Schedule Based on Assignments

able time. Choose enough hours to do the job, and write them on the appropriate line on the bottom half of the sheet. Stick to your schedule. As long as you give study hours top priority, your remaining hours will be truly free.

Turn Your Daily Schedule into a List of Things to Do   If your available time is unpredictable, your daily study schedule should simply be a list of things to do arranged in order of priority on a 3 x 5 card. In this case, assigning specific times is likely to lead only to frustration.

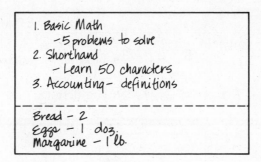

1. Basic Math
   - 5 problems to solve
2. Shorthand
   - Learn 50 characters
3. Accounting - definitions

Bread - 2
Eggs - 1 doz.
Margarine - 1 lb.

FIGURE 2.7   A Things-to-Do List

Figure 2.7 shows a typical daily list. To be successful, you need a sense of urgency about referring to your list and studying whenever an opportunity presents itself. Then cross off the tasks as you complete them.

Use the *Pareto Principle* to help you draw up your list. Named after Vilfredo Pareto (1848–1923), an Italian economist and sociologist, the Pareto Principle states that the truly important items in any given group constitute only a small number of the total items in the group. This principle is also known as the *80/20 rule.*

For example, in almost any sales force, 80 percent of the business is brought in by 20 percent of the salespeople. In any committee, 80 percent of the ideas come from 20 percent of the members. In a classroom, 80 percent of the teacher's time is taken up by 20 percent of the students.

In any list of things to do, 80 percent of the importance resides in 20 percent of the list. In a list of ten items, 80 percent of the list's value lies in two items, which constitute 20 percent of the list. Because of Pareto's Principle, in your lists of things to do always put the most important items first. Then, if you accomplish only the first few items, you will have accomplished the most important tasks on the list.

Keep the Pareto Principle in mind whenever you make up a list or a schedule or must decide which subject to study first. Apply the principle by listing first things first.[4]

---

[4]Reprinted with the permission of Charles Scribner's Sons, an imprint of Macmillan Publishing Company, from GETTING THINGS DONE, Revised and Updated Edition by Edwin C. Bliss. Copyright © 1991, 1976, Edwin C. Bliss.

SUMMARY

How can you gain time?

You can gain time by changing your time habits and by finding hidden time throughout your day.

What time habits can you change?

If you defy Parkinson's Law and obey your alarm clock, you can break time-wasting habits and add time to your day. You can save time by taking regular breaks when you study and by jotting down distracting thoughts on a notepad.

How can you take advantage of hidden time?

You can carry pocket work to do for unexpected free time, use your mind when it's free, listen to audio cassette versions of your notes, think in your spare time, and draw on your subconscious.

What is the value of using a time schedule?

A time schedule enables you to plot out and manage your time. Using a time schedule can increase your control over your life, leave you feeling more relaxed, and add to your freedom and flexibility.

How do you choose the right type of schedule?

If you're attending classes full time, you can use a three-part scheduling plan with separate master, weekly, and daily schedules. If you have additional demanding commitments, you may want to use schedules that emphasize the tasks you want to accomplish.

What general guidelines should you follow in making up a master, weekly, or daily schedule?

All three schedules should be made up of separate time blocks that enable you to tackle your tasks in manageable units. Schedule most of your important activities for daylight hours. For recitation classes, study before the class; for lecture classes, study after class. Schedule your time effectively—list all of your tasks, but not in daunting and unrealistic detail. Finally, schedule nonacademic activities (meals, sleep, recreation) as well as those that relate to your schoolwork. Your schedule should serve as a plan for living, not just for studying.

What are the purpose and content of a master schedule?	A master schedule provides you with a basic framework for a term's activities. Written on a grid, this schedule includes those obligations that stay the same week in and week out. The blocks that are left blank signify the time you have available for scheduling weekly and daily activities.
What is a weekly schedule?	A weekly schedule picks up where the master schedule leaves off, filling in the blanks with your daily activities as they vary from week to week.
What is a daily schedule?	A daily schedule is a portable game plan, showing your day's schedule on a 3 x 5 card.
How can you adapt schedules to your life outside school?	If you have a job, a family, or other time-consuming demands, or if you are faced with a long-term assignment, set up your schedules to emphasize the tasks you need to accomplish instead of the time when you will do them. Devise a special master schedule that focuses on long-term goals. Make your weekly schedule more assignment oriented, and turn your daily schedule into a list of things to do.
What is a task-based master schedule?	A task-based master schedule is a list of the major goals you hope to accomplish and the deadlines you set on the way to reaching those goals.
What is an assignment-oriented weekly schedule?	An assignment-oriented weekly schedule budgets your week's school-related activities. It begins with a list of your upcoming assignments and a time estimate for eac and then shows a time block for each.
What is a list of things to do?	A daily list of things to do is an outline in order of priority of what you plan to accomplish.

HAVE YOU MISSED SOMETHING?

Matching.   In each blank space in the left column, write the letter preceding the phrase in the right column that matches the left item best.

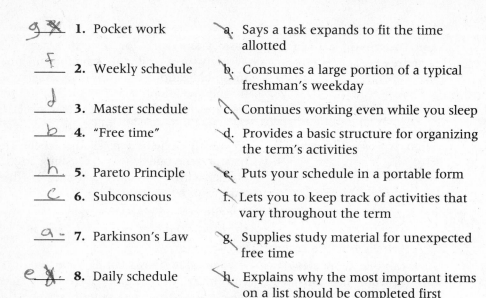

_g_ ~~x~~ **1.** Pocket work   a. Says a task expands to fit the time allotted

_f_ **2.** Weekly schedule   b. Consumes a large portion of a typical freshman's weekday

_d_ **3.** Master schedule   c. Continues working even while you sleep

_b_ **4.** "Free time"   d. Provides a basic structure for organizing the term's activities

_h_ **5.** Pareto Principle   e. Puts your schedule in a portable form

_c_ **6.** Subconscious   f. Lets you to keep track of activities that vary throughout the term

_a_ - **7.** Parkinson's Law   g. Supplies study material for unexpected free time

_e_ ~~x~~ **8.** Daily schedule   h. Explains why the most important items on a list should be completed first

Multiple choice.   Choose the word or phrase that completes the following sentence most accurately, and circle the letter that precedes it.

1. The three-part scheduling plan is particularly helpful for

   a. working mothers.
   b. full-time students.
   c. student athletes.
   d. none of the above.

2. A time schedule functions as a

   a. game plan.
   b. computer.
   c. punishment.
   d. reward.

3. All your time should be accounted for, but without too much

   a. hesitation.
   b. recreation.
   c. detail.
   d. interest.

4. Energy is increased and efficiency is improved when you

   a. work or study continuously.
   b. take brief but regular breaks while studying.
   c. do most of your studying at night.
   d. use only one schedule instead of three.

5. The master schedule provides

    a. an alternative to a weekly schedule.
    b. an excuse for increased recreation.
    c. <u>a framework of fixed activities.</u>
    d. a solution to the problem of hidden time.

6. The best approach to a long-term assignment is

    a. increase and multiply.
    b. <u>divide and conquer.</u>
    c. meals and recreation.
    d. rules and regulations.

7. An assignment-oriented weekly schedule is appropriate

    a. as a supplement to your master schedule.
    b. when you face an unusual or long-term assignment.
    c. if you don't have big blocks of uninterrupted time.
    d. <u>for all of the above.</u>

8. Unlike a daily schedule, a list of things to do

    a. works efficiently.
    b. is only 80 percent useful.
    c. <u>has no time blocks.</u>
    d. is written on an index card.

True-false. Write *T* beside the *true* statements and *F* beside the *false* statements.

  F   **1.** Taking regular breaks wastes valuable time.

  T   **2.** Free time can often occur unexpectedly.

  T   **3.** The master, weekly, and daily schedules all follow the same basic guidelines.

  F   **4.** Time schedules can make you feel like a slave to time.

  T   **5.** Scheduling saves time that might otherwise be wasted.

  T   **6.** Most of us work more efficiently in the daytime.

Short answer. Supply a brief answer for each of the following items. The number in parentheses refers to the page where the item is discussed in the text.

1. What is the purpose of keeping a daily activities log? (37–38)
2. How does a time schedule increase your sense of control? (41)
3. In what ways does a schedule promote relaxation? (42)

4. What is the advantage of scheduling your time in blocks? (42–43)

5. Discuss how to prepare a task-oriented master schedule. (48–49)

BUILDING YOUR VOCABULARY STEP BY STEP: DEVELOPING A MORE PRECISE VOCABULARY

A strong vocabulary is based on precision. Because the fundamental building blocks of learning and knowledge are words—words with precise meanings—if you get the meanings wrong, you have learned false information. As Mark Twain once expressed the matter, "The difference between the right word and the almost right word is the difference between lightning and the lightning bug."

The size of your vocabulary is also important—the larger it is, the better it can be. But precision comes first. You take a number of steps to build a more precise vocabulary.

Pay close attention to context. Definitions in isolation, like words by themselves, can be confusing and even misleading. If you view only part of the picture, your perspective can sometimes be comical. For example, one student who had learned that the word *provoke* means "to stir up" supposedly wrote, "The cook *provoked* the pot of soup."

If you understand the context of the word *provoke,* you can appreciate the student's mistake. People frequently make similar mistakes with other words that may not be as comical but are just as incorrect. By learning the context of a new word, you decrease the chance of misunderstanding it.

Look up the synonyms and see how they differ. Most dictionary entries include synonyms along with definitions. One excellent way of honing your understanding of a new word is by looking up not only the new word but also the synonyms. For example, some dictionaries list *imply* and *infer* as synonyms. Although the two words are closely related, their meanings are still quite distinct and in fact mutually exclusive. Whereas *imply* basically means "to drop a hint," *infer* means "to take a hint." Learning the definitions of both words instead of just one makes it easier to know which one to choose. As semanticist S. I. Hayakawa notes:

> Nothing is so important to clear and accurate expression as the ability to distinguish between words of similar, but not identical, meaning.... To choose wrongly is to leave the hearer or reader with a fuzzy or mistaken impression. To choose well is to give both illumination and delight. The study of synonyms will help the reader come closer to saying what he really wants to say.[5]

---

[5]S. I. Hayakawa, *Modern Guide to Synonyms and Related Words* (New York: Funk & Wagnalls, 1968), p. vii.

Consult the dictionary. Even when a word is used repeatedly in the same way, there's no guarantee that the word has been used correctly.

Take the word *fulsome,* for example. Do you know what it means? Would you stop reading to consult a dictionary if you came across this sentence: "The mayor's speech gave *fulsome praise* to the head of the finance committee."?

Although the word may sound like a compliment, its actual meaning is radically different. According to *The American Heritage Dictionary,* Second College Edition, fulsome means "offensively flattering or insincere" or "offensive to the taste or sensibilities." In truth, fulsome praise is nothing to be proud of.

Failure to consult a dictionary can sometimes lead not only to imprecise definitions but also to completely incorrect use of words. The safest, simplest way of verifying the meaning of a word is to consult a dictionary.

Be aware of changing meanings. Our language is constantly in flux. In some instances, those changes are drastic; in others, they're steady but imperceptible.

When the king of England first saw the recently completed St. Paul's Cathedral, he described the structure as both "awful" and "artificial." Yet he wasn't upset. In fact, he was delighted with what he saw. In his day, *awful* lacked its modern-day meaning of "terrible" or "bad" and was used exclusively to describe something awe inspiring; *artificial,* instead of meaning "phony" or "fake," referred to a creation of superior artistry.

Many of the most recent examples of words that have changed their meanings come from computer technology. Although verbs such as *interface, access,* and *network* were once used exclusively by technicians, they are now gaining wider use as general-purpose verbs. Only the most recent dictionaries include the latest definitions of these words.

Following are some of the words from the chapter you've just read. Use them to find out just how precise your vocabulary is. Beside each word is the page number on which the word appears, so you can go back and read it in context. (And, of course, you'll find each of these words in the dictionary.) Try comparing each word to its synonyms to sharpen the precision of your vocabulary. For example, what's the difference between *constitute* and *contain* or *stall* and *forestall?* Many of the words in the list have synonyms that you already know.

allotted (33)	forestall (45)	signify (53)
constitute (51)	meticulous (43)	succinctly (37)
dashing (42)	overwhelming (43)	supplement (48)
daunting (52)	posted (45)	urgency (51)
discrete (39)	refreshing (40)	warranted (42)
extracurricular (42)		

Learning to Concentrate

The key to music, the key to life, is concentration.

BOBBY HACKETT
Cornetist and bandleader

Everyone—from astronauts to athletes, from merchants to musicians—appreciates the value of concentration. Yet few of us know how to attain and then sustain it. Although concentration does not appear at the snap of the fingers, there are ways you can improve the conditions for concentration. To aid you in learning the art of concentration, this chapter deals with

- Understanding what concentration means
- Eliminating distractions
- Adopting strategies that encourage concentration

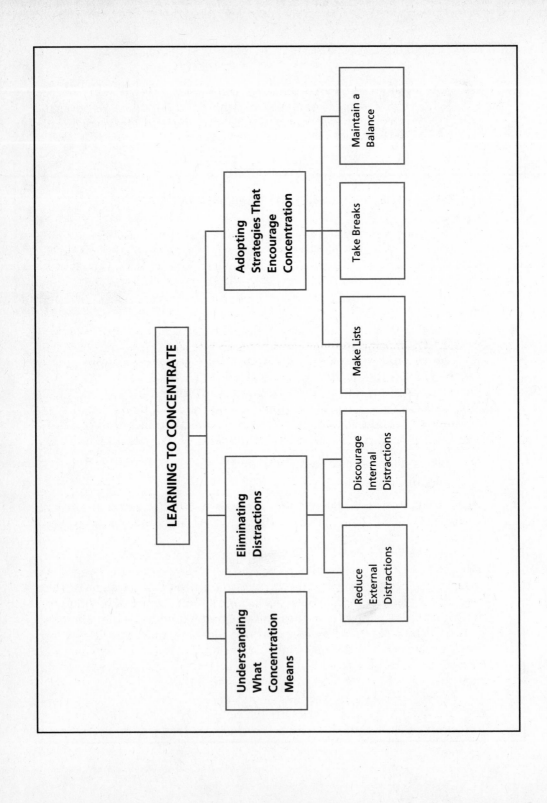

Concentration is focused thinking. During our waking hours we are, with varying degrees of intensity, thinking all the time. We never run out of things to think and worry about. Thoughts and ideas bang, rattle, and knock on the door of our consciousness trying to gain entry.

UNDERSTANDING WHAT CONCENTRATION MEANS

Watch a good bowler as she takes her position and directs all her thoughts on knocking down the pins at the end of the alley. Watch a quarterback as he focuses entirely on getting a pass to an open receiver, even while line-backers rush in on him from several directions. That's concentration!

Imagine becoming so absorbed in your textbook that you find yourself "talking" to the author: "That's not proof enough," or "Other writers explain it differently," or "I never thought about the problem that way before." Or imagine studying your notes so intently that when you finally look up, you see that it's been two hours since you last checked the clock. That's concentration!

Just as light waves can be focused into a single powerful beam—a laser—concentration can focus the power of your thoughts, enabling you to think with greater precision and penetrate difficult ideas. But powerful as it can be, concentration has an elusive quality. In fact, concentration comes only when you don't think about it. For example, if you were thinking deeply about a subject and suddenly realized that you were concentrating, at that moment you would have broken your concentration. Such prolonged, undivided attention can be difficult to achieve. After all, in normal circumstances there are dozens of things competing for your attention.

Figure 3.1 provides a vivid illustration of the natural tendency to divide attention. As you gaze at this picture, you'll probably discover that your visual focus is shifting every few seconds so that you first see a goblet, then two profiles, and then the goblet again. Once you're aware of both images, it is difficult for your eyes to focus on one and ignore the other. Similarly, it is hard for your mind to focus on one idea at a time. People who *can* focus exclusively on the task before them have a much better chance of completing that task more quickly and accurately than those who divide their attention even when they don't mean to do so.

Because you can't strive for concentration directly, you must instead try to improve the conditions that promote concentration. That involves eliminating distractions and adopting strategies to enhance concentration.

FIGURE 3.1   A Goblet or Two Profiles?

ELIMINATING DISTRACTIONS

Trouble in concentrating may come from external distractions, such as sights or sounds that compete for your attention, or from internal distractions, such as worries or daydreams. Once recognized, these obstacles to concentration can be overcome.

Reduce External Distractions

Anything that stimulates your senses and in the process disrupts your concentration can be considered an external distraction. Study halls and living quarters are overflowing with such distractions, everything from banging doors to baking bread. To work in a way that is compatible with concentration, you need the proper environment as well as the right equipment.

Select the Right Environment   Your study environment should be used exclusively for study. In addition, it should be quiet and well lighted. You can take your work to a place that is already designed for study, or you can create your own study environment.

Find a Workshop.   You'd be hard pressed to find an environment more suitable for high-quality concentration than a library. It offers a minimum of nonacademic distractions, a quiet atmosphere (usually as a matter of policy), and sufficient lighting. Get in the habit right away, on the first day of class, of studying at the library. Even the walk to the library can be used productively as a review session or a refreshing break.

Whether you choose to work in the library or somewhere else, make sure your study area is reserved only for studying. Psychologists emphasize that a conditioning effect is created between the desk and you: If you nap or daydream a lot while sitting at the desk, then the desk can act as a cue for napping or daydreaming. By the same token, if you read or work in bed, you make it difficult to work energetically and to fall asleep easily. To avoid this negative conditioning, use your desk only for studying. When you feel the urge to nap or daydream, leave your desk and nap or daydream elsewhere.

Your study area should be your workshop, a place where you feel secure and comfortable. You can ensure that you have the proper environment for study and concentration if you minimize visual distractions, avoid or eliminate distracting noises, refrain from playing music, control the impulse to register distractions by using the spider technique, and provide the area with plenty of light.

Minimize Visual Distractions. A sheet of notes or a page from a textbook can seem dull compared with a glimpse of a softball game being played on a nearby diamond or a view of gently falling snow. To improve your chances of concentration, avoid competition for your eyes' attention. Study by a window so you can take advantage of the natural light, but keep your head turned away from the potentially distracting view.

Of course, not all visual distractions lie on the other side of a window pane. If your study area contains photographs you're liable to look at, gadgets you're likely to fiddle with, or books you'll be tempted to pick up and read, remove them until you have completed your work.

Eliminate Noise. If you need a quiet spot for efficient study, do your utmost to find one. Noise can be one of the most serious obstacles to effective study. Nothing is more wasteful than going over the same paragraph again and again because there is too much noise for you to absorb what you are reading. If the library is the right place for you, then make an effort to study there whenever you can. If you study at home, achieving quiet can sometimes be as simple as closing a door or inserting ear plugs.

Turn Off the Music. When you are studying, music is noise. Some students report that they studied successfully throughout high school with music in the background. But success in passing high school courses is no proof that background music will not interfere with college-level studies. If you passed your high school courses with music in the background, take a moment to ponder this: How much better could you have done in a music-free environment that allowed you to concentrate all your energy on your schoolwork?

By exerting extra energy when music is playing, you may be able to keep your mind on your studies 75 percent of the time. But your mind and body will be bombarded by sound waves 100 percent of the time. Such bombardment is physically tiring. Shutting out the music saps you of energy that could be put to better use. Concentration is already difficult to achieve. Why make your job even harder?

Try the Spider Technique.   A vibrating tuning fork held close to a spider's web sets up vibrations in the web. After the spider makes a few hurried investigations and finds no fly in the web, it learns to ignore the vibrations. The next time you are studying in the library and the door opens, don't look up. Controlling your impulse to look up will disturb your concentration the first few times. But very soon, like the spider, you'll learn to ignore these external disturbances.

Turn On the Lights.   Good lighting makes for good studying. By contrast, poor lighting makes for eyestrain, general tension, headaches, and sleepiness—irritations that interfere with concentration. If you study under good light but your eyes still bother you, have them examined by an ophthalmologist or optometrist. Clear and comfortable vision is essential to good studying.

Use the Right Equipment

Because proper lighting is an important component of your study environment, the right light should head the list of the equipment you need to promote concentration and reduce external distractions.

Find the Right Light.   Whether it comes from conventional light bulbs, fluorescent tubes, or the new compact fluorescent bulbs, the best light for study is bright, even, and steady (remember B, E, and ST).

Bright.   The emission of light is measured in lumens. For studying, you need at least 2,500 lumens. Two standard 100-watt bulbs (1,750 lumens each) will meet that requirement. So will a double-tube fluorescent lamp; it provides the same amount of light as two 100-watt incandescent bulbs and can last up to one hundred times longer!

Even.   Shadows in your work area or "hot spots" caused by glare will tire out your eyes and make concentration difficult. Get rid of glare by shielding your lamp with a shade and by using a light-colored, nonglossy blotter on your desk. Eliminate shadows by using two lamps, fluorescent light, or diffuse light.

STeady.   A constant flicker will undermine concentration. If you use fluorescent light, try a double- or triple-tube lamp. These multitubed fix-tures eliminate the natural strobe of fluorescent light. If you are using conventional (incandescent) light, make sure the bulb is screwed in properly.

Find a Comfortable Seat.   Don't be misled into believing that you need a hard, uncomfortable chair to stay alert and maintain your concentration. Whether you stay awake or fall asleep does not depend on your chair.

Use a Bookstand.   A bookstand promotes alertness and encourages concentration by tilting your text at an optimum angle and permitting you to sit back with your arms folded to contemplate the meaning of what you are reading.

Keep Other Equipment Nearby.   Other basic equipment that can help keep you studying without interruption includes an up-to-date dictionary, a calculator, a clock, a calendar, paper, notebooks, paper clips, tape, rubber bands, pencils, pens, erasers, and note cards. If you make it a habit to keep your desk well stocked, you won't derail your concentration with unplanned emergency trips to obtain necessities.

Discourage Internal Distractions

Internal distractions are distractions that *you* create: daydreams, personal problems, anxiety, indecision, forgetfulness, and unrealistic goals. These distractions are as disruptive as the sights, sounds, and smells that make up the external variety, even though in this case the only one who is aware of them is you. Because internal distractions come from within, you have the power to eliminate or at least control them.

Use a Concentration Scoresheet   Keep a sheet of paper handy by your book. Then whenever you catch your mind wandering, keep score by putting a checkmark on the sheet. The mere act of doing this reminds you to get back to work. Students report that when they first tried this system, they accumulated as many as twenty checkmarks per textbook page, but after one or two weeks, they were down to one or two checkmarks per page.

The concentration scoresheet encourages self-observation. Taking note of your breaks in concentration—when they happen, how often they occur, and what triggers them—will make you realize just how intrusive the lapses are and will enable you to gradually eliminate them.

Put Stray Thoughts on a Worry Pad   Although pleasant plans and diverting daydreams are major sources of internal distraction, nagging worries and obligations can also take your mind off your work. The concentration scoresheet will alert you to these breaks in your attention, but it won't address the problems that prompted the distraction. To prevent the same worries from interfering with your concentration again and again, you must address them. A worry pad provides an excellent short-term solution to the problem.

When an intrusive thought disrupts your concentration, write it down on your worry pad with the idea that you will attend to it just as soon as you get the chance. Then with your conscience clear and your bothersome thought recorded on paper, you can get back to the business of concentration. After you have finished studying, read over your list and give these concerns your full attention. If you cannot alleviate them yourself, get the help of friends or counselors.

ADOPTING STRATEGIES THAT ENCOURAGE CONCENTRATION

Although the best way of encouraging concentration is usually to discourage distractions, you can take other actions to improve your concentration. Get into the habit of making lists, taking regular breaks, and maintaining a balance between the challenge of a particular assignment and the level of your skill.

Make Lists

As we have seen, keeping random thoughts and information in your head instead of writing them down is a primary impediment to concentration. Use lists to remind yourself of day-to-day obligations, and catalog all the study equipment you're likely to need.

Use a Reminder List   To avoid worrying about the possibility of missing personal appointments and forgetting those things you've set out to do, write them down on your daily schedule (see Figure 2.5, page 49). As a result, you will be able to shift smoothly from one activity to the next without breaking your concentration.

Keep an Inventory List   There's nothing more annoying and more disruptive to your concentration than to be working steadily when you suddenly discover you are missing something simple, such as a ruler, a sharp pencil, or a pocket calculator. By the time you've searched for what you need, found it, and then gotten back to work, you will almost surely have broken your concentration. Before you sit down to study, check a list of your most-used supplies to make sure you have everything you need: sharp pencils, fresh paper and cards, necessary books. Then stay in your chair until you have studied a half-hour or so.

Take Breaks

If you allow physical energy to build up unabated, your mind will race. If you keep repressing concerns that compete for your attention, those concerns will eventually triumph and scuttle your concentration. And if you persist in denying such a basic instinct as hunger, all you'll be able to think of is food.

If, however, you take a few minutes to defuse these distractions, stand up and stretch, address a problem you've been avoiding, or grab a healthy snack to tide you over, you can return to your work ready to concentrate.

Maintain a Balance

Psychologist Mihaly Csikszentmihalyi believes that the most intense and rewarding kind of concentration (which he calls "flow") comes when you develop a balance between the challenge of the work you are doing and the level of skills you possess.[1] If the challenge of an assignment overwhelms your skill level, then anxiety—not concentration—is likely to result. Conversely, if your skills are high but the assignment isn't challenging, then you're apt to become bored and easily distracted. Finally, if both your skill level and the challenge of an assignment are low, then you'll probably become apathetic and have no desire to concentrate.

Here are some strategies for boosting your skills and raising you interest level.

Find a Tutor   If you find yourself struggling with a subject, don't procrastinate. Before you reach the point of anxiety—or worse, apathy—get a tutor. Either go to the campus learning skills center or tutoring office, or find a classmate who has time to help you. In most cases, it won't take long before a tutor will pinpoint your problem, help you work it out, and send you off to tackle the rest of the term on your own.

Join a Study Group   Get together regularly with a small group of students to discuss specific assignments and the course as a whole. During the give-

---

[1]Richard Flaste, "The Power of Concentration," *New York Times Magazine,* (October 8, 1989), p. 26.

and-take of the discussions, you are bound to learn a great deal, and the subject may come alive, or the enthusiasm of some of the members may rub off on you. As you grow more familiar with the subject, your interest level will rise. The only prerequisite for a group meeting is that all members do their homework. Only then can each member become an active contributor.

Pick Out an Alternate Textbook   If you're struggling with a course, the textbook, not the subject, may be at the root of your problem. A little investigating at a library or bookstore may turn up books in which other authors discuss the same topics in ways you may find more accessible. After you have consulted some alternative books, read the material in your assigned textbook. The two texts may discuss the same topic, but your class will probably be focusing on aspects and approaches specific to the assigned text.

Use Programmed Materials and Workbooks   If your skills don't seem to match the requirements of a course, you may need some extra practice. Programmed materials furnish questions and problems closely followed by their answers, thereby enabling you to teach yourself every incremental step of each lesson. Workbooks provide exercises that apply the ideas explained in your textbooks. Either of these study aids can help minimize the anxiety that arises from feeling uncertain about putting newly learned ideas to use. They can also stimulate your interest by helping you take what you've learned a step further.

Set Realistic Study Goals   In some cases when the challenge of your work outstrips your skills, the problem lies with you and is easily remedied. For instance, don't expect to acquire a term's worth of skills in a few marathon study sessions. If up to now you have done little or no studying, change your habits gradually. Start by studying for only two hours on that first evening; then work up to longer sessions in which you'll be able to achieve increasingly large goals.

SUMMARY

What is concentration?	Concentration is thinking that is focused. It occurs when nearly all your thinking energy is devoted to a single subject instead of to a variety of scattered ideas.
How do distractions affect concentration?	Distractions compete for your mind's attention. External distractions, such as loud

noises or interesting scenery, or internal distractions, such as nagging worries or vivid daydreams, divert your attention and destroy your concentration.

What is the proper environment for concentration?

The proper environment is a place you use only for studying and use consistently. The area should be relatively free of visual distractions and noise, including music. The area should be brightly and evenly lit to discourage fatigue and prevent eyestrain.

What equipment aids concentration?

Good lights head the list of equipment that encourages concentration. A comfortable chair is important as well. A bookstand can free your hands and keep your textbook in a position that encourages active, focused thinking. Well-stocked and accessible supplies help you keep your mind on your work.

What is a concentration scoresheet?

A concentration scoresheet is a tally of the times when your concentration is broken. To keep score, put a checkmark on a sheet of paper each time you realize you are no longer concentrating. The checkmarks will motivate you to keep your mind on your work.

What is a worry pad, and how do you use it?

A worry pad acts as a holding tank for stray thoughts that divert your attention from your studying. Putting these thoughts on paper takes them off your mind until you have the time to focus on them.

What strategies encourage concentration?

Strategies that help promote concentration and reduce the chance that distractions will arise in the first place include making lists, taking breaks, and maintaining a balance between your skills and the level of the material you're learning.

How do lists promote concentration?

Simply putting things on paper sends your mind a strong message: You're serious about getting work done and about maintaining concentration. If you have a written list of things to do, instead of a vague plan you keep in your head, you'll be able to move smoothly and confidently from one task to the next. In addition, if you make up a complete inventory of the study supplies you need and then run through a checklist of those supplies before you begin studying, you'll avoid the annoying problem of breaking your concentration to search for a missing supply.

What is the value of taking a break?

Taking a break can help defuse the distractions—hunger, fatigue, boredom—that commonly accumulate during study sessions.

What is meant by "maintaining a balance"?

This phrase means matching your personal skills to the level of challenge of a particular task. Otherwise, if the challenge overwhelms your skills, you may become anxious. If your skills exceed the challenge, you may become bored. And when both challenge and skills are low, you will probably feel apathetic.

What techniques allow you to maintain a balance and concentrate?

If you find yourself off balance, you have several strategies from which to choose. Find a tutor to help raise your level of skills. Study in a small group to boost the challenge of a course. Search out alternative texts that challenge you if your assigned text seems boring or that set your mind at ease if the text seems intimidating. Use programmed materials and workbooks to test your skills if you're feeling unsure of yourself or to provide an extra challenge when the course seems too easy. Finally, set realistic study goals, which will help keep the challenge within the range of your skill level.

HAVE YOU MISSED SOMETHING?

Matching. In each blank space in the left column, write the letter preceding the phrase in the right column that matches the left item best.

_g-f_ **1.** "Flow"

✳ _h_ **2.** Boredom

_a._ **3.** Spider technique

_f_ **4.** Reminder list

_b._ **5.** Self-observation

_d._ **6.** Checkmark

_e._ **7.** Worry pad

_c_ **8.** Programmed materials

a. Technique for tuning out external distractions

b. Encouraged by the concentration scoresheet

c. Used to promote interest and raise skill levels

d. Can serve as a signal for broken concentration

e. Stopgap measure for dealing with internal distractions

f. Enables you to shift smoothly from one task to the next

g. Term that describes an especially rewarding kind of concentration

h. Results when skills exceed the challenge of the task

Multiple choice. Choose the word or phrase that completes the following sentence most accurately, and circle the letter that precedes it.

1. Trouble in concentrating is due primarily to
   a. internal and external distractions.
   b. boredom.
   c. anxiety.
   d. poor eyesight.

2. To promote concentration, your work area should be
   a. quiet.
   b. well lighted.
   c. used only for studying.
   d. all of the above.

3. When you're studying, music should be considered
   a. a help.
   b. a reward.
   c. noise.
   d. an internal distraction.

4. Internal distractions are
   a. disruptions that you create.

    b.   caused by such problems as headaches and indigestion.
    c.   a by-product of concentration.
    d.   encouraged by a comfortable study area.

5. Although concentration is powerful, it is often
    a.   unnecessary.
    b.   elusive.
    c.   underestimated.
    d.   time consuming.

6. When the challenge is high but your skill level is low, you will probably experience
    a.   concentration.
    b.   boredom.
    c.   anxiety.
    d.   apathy.

True-false. Write *T* beside the *true* statements and *F* beside the *false* statements.

_T_   **1.** You can't realize you're concentrating while you're concentrating.

_F_   **2.** Music provides a suitable background for studying.

_T_   **3.** In normal circumstances, there are dozens of things competing for your attention.

_F_   **4.** Most internal distractions are beyond your control.

_F_   **5.** The best way of achieving concentration is by striving for it directly.

_F_   **6.** Your study environment will be more effective if you use it for recreation as well.

_T_   **7.** Concentration involves achieving a balance between challenges and skills.

Short answer. Supply a brief answer for each of the following items. The number in parentheses refers to the page where the item is discussed in the text.

1. What are the two general ways in which concentration can be promoted? (61)

2. How will a tutor help minimize your anxiety and apathy? (61)

3. Explain the conditioning effect that occurs when you use your desk only for studying. (63)

4. What are some ways you can eliminate noise? (63)

5. Discuss how you can use lists to encourage concentration. (66–67)

BUILDING YOUR VOCABULARY STEP BY STEP: LEARNING HOW *NOT* TO BUILD YOUR VOCABULARY

Some people repeatedly try to increase their vocabulary as compulsively as others try to lose weight. Boosting your vocabulary by reading "good books," letting your vocabulary increase "naturally," or following the lists in so-called word-power books may all seem like reasonable techniques. The problem is that the most common word-building methods, like many of the popular diet plans, simply don't work.

Reading good books.   There's nothing wrong with reading good books; but don't read them to increase the size of your vocabulary. A book is only as good as its ideas and themes. All the big words in the world cannot improve a book that has nothing to say. Conversely, a great book can coax profound ideas from simple words. And even if a book is good and makes use of a large vocabulary, simply reading new words is not enough. You have to learn them.

Relying on "natural growth."   The theory behind natural growth is that your vocabulary will grow automatically like the hair on your head. But your vocabulary is more like a muscle than a strand of hair. To build your vocabulary and keep it strong, you have to exercise the words you already know by using them regularly and increase the size of your vocabulary by constantly replenishing it with new words. Simply sitting back and waiting for your vocabulary to get larger without work will result instead in its shrinking.

Reading word-building books.   So-called word-power books entice students who want to increase their vocabularies and are willing to put in the work. Unfortunately, most of the effort put into learning the long lists of words that these experts have compiled, is lost because these word-power books have a fundamental flaw: They are based on the notion that new words should come from the word lists of experts. In fact, new words must be built on words you already know. There's no guarantee that the words you find in word-power books will have any connection with your existing vocabulary. Without this link, it's unlikely that you will be able to thoroughly learn and retain even a fraction of words from such a list.

Unlike the words in word-power books, those that follow are taken from the chapter you've just read (page numbers indicate where). Instead of relying on natural growth to automatically make them a part of your vocabulary, pick up a good book—the dictionary—and actively add these words to those you know.

absorbed (61)	elusive (61)	prerequisite (68)
apathetic (67)	exerting (64)	programmed (68)
bombarded (64)	incandescent (64)	prompted (65)
compatible (62)	indecision (65)	repressing (67)
conditioning (63)	intensity (61)	scuttle (67)
contemplate (65)	intently (61)	suitable (62)
conventional (64)	intrusive (66)	unabated (67)
cue (63)	ophthalmologist (58)	utmost (63)
derail (65)	ponder (63)	vivid (61)

Combating Forgetting

Memory is the art of attention.

SAMUEL JOHNSON
Author

Forgetting is like an ocean wave steadily washing away what you've learned. You can't stop forgetting any more than you can stop a wave. But you *can* reinforce what you've learned and strengthen your memories in the face of the incoming tide. To aid you in doing so, this chapter focuses on

- Understanding how we forget
- Making an effort to remember
- Controlling the number and form of your memories
- Strengthening memories
- Allowing time for memories to consolidate

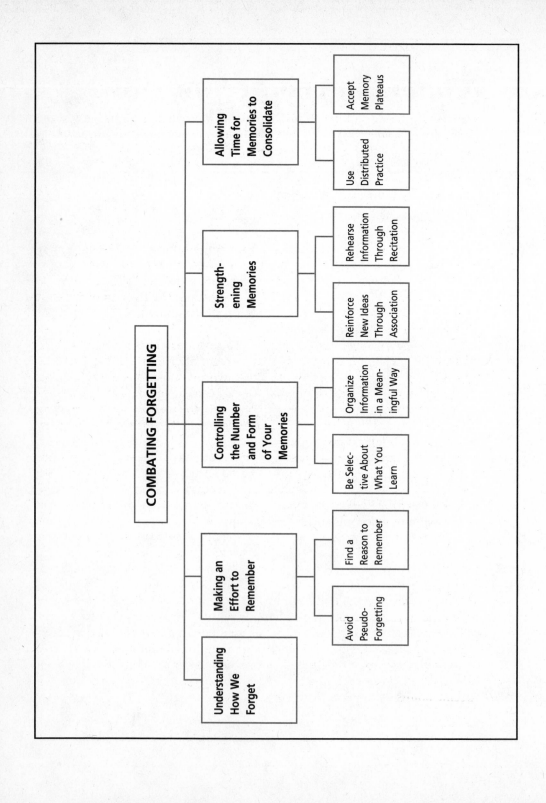

COMBATING FORGETTING

- Understanding How We Forget
- Making an Effort to Remember
  - Avoid Pseudo-Forgetting
  - Find a Reason to Remember
- Controlling the Number and Form of Your Memories
  - Be Selective About What You Learn
  - Organize Information in a Meaningful Way
- Strengthening Memories
  - Reinforce New Ideas Through Association
  - Rehearse Information Through Recitation
- Allowing Time for Memories to Consolidate
  - Use Distributed Practice
  - Accept Memory Plateaus

Most of us become annoyed when we realize we've forgotten something crucial or when something "we should have known" has managed to slip our minds. But just how big a problem is forgetting? In the hierarchy of academic woes, forgetting holds sole possession of the summit. It is the biggest single problem you will encounter in school.

UNDERSTANDING HOW WE FORGET

Memory is under constant assault from forgetfulness. Forgetting works both massively and rapidly to undo the work that learning has done. Unfortunately, forgetting's acts of sabotage are extremely successful. After you learn something new, you will forget most of it by the end of the day. Numerous studies and experiments have shown how quickly we forget what we read and what we hear.

In one experiment, people who read a textbook chapter forgot 46 percent of their reading after one day, 79 percent after fourteen days, and 81 percent after twenty-eight days. In other words, subjects could remember only slightly more than half of what they'd read the previous day; after less than a month, the information they were able to retain from their reading had dwindled down to 19 percent. Therefore, eighty percent of what they had originally read was now lost.

Not surprisingly, remembering what you have heard is even more difficult than recalling what you have read. After all, as you read you are able to slow down, pause, reflect, and, if necessary, reread. Listeners have no such luxuries; they usually have just one chance to catch the words and ideas being spoken.

For instance, in an experiment researchers secretly recorded a seminar held by the Cambridge Psychological Society.[1] Two weeks later, the society members who had attended the seminar were asked to write down all they could recall of it. The results were shocking. More than 90 percent of the points from the lecture had been forgotten or confused with the passage of time. The average proportion of specific points each member correctly recalled was 8.4 percent! Much of what members recalled was at odds with what had actually been said. Events were mentioned that never took place; casual remarks were embellished; points were reported that had only been hinted at. This learned group of psychologists forgot 91.6 percent of the specific points made in the seminar.

---

[1] See Ian M. L. Hunter, *Memory: Facts and Fallacies* (Baltimore: Penguin, 1957), p. 83.

How does this devastating forgetting occur? Although the experts are divided on the answer, they have formulated a number of interesting and plausible theories to explain forgetting.

Use it or lose it: Fading theory.   According to fading theory, the trace or mark a memory etches in your brain is like a path you make when you walk across a meadow. If you don't continue to walk over the path, grass will grow up and obliterate your trail. In the same way, a fact that's learned but never used will become fainter until it is obliterated completely by forgetfulness.

I know it's here somewhere: Retrieval theory.   Unlike proponents of fading theory, some psychologists believe that once a fact or idea is thoroughly learned, it remains a memory for life. According to this retrieval theory, a forgotten fact hasn't faded; it has been misfiled in the vast storehouse of your mind. Whether the information has disappeared completely or has simply been lost, the net result is the same: Information you once learned and remembered has now been forgotten.

Fighting for a spot: Interference theory.   According to interference theory, limited space puts old and new memories at odds. Memories become like a bunch of competitive basketball players fighting for a spot beneath the basket. Old memories and facts elbow out new information (forward interference), thereby causing us to forget what we've recently learned. Meanwhile, new facts and ideas battle for a coveted position by forcing out facts that we've known for a while (backward interference). The result is a constant battle, with old and new memories both jockeying for position. Some win and some lose.

Caught in a crossfire: Interactive interference theory.   Imagine you have learned three facts at three different times. For example:

Oldest: *Photosynthesis* is the process whereby plants employ sunlight to turn chemicals into food.

Middle: A *photomicrograph* is a picture taken through a microscope.

Newest: *Phototropism* is the movement of a plant in response to light.

According to interactive interference theory, you'll lose the middle fact rapidly because it will be bombarded by the oldest learning and the newest learning. To complicate things, the middle fact, fighting for survival, will do its best to bombard the newest and the oldest learning (fighting both frontal and rear attacks). In the course of this fighting, the middle fact, while going down in defeat, will inflict some damage (forgetting) to both the oldest and the newest learning.

Tuning out what you don't like: Reactive interference theory. According to reactive interference theory, your general attitude toward the facts you learn plays a crucial role in whether you will recall them. Facts related to a subject you don't like or find boring can be difficult to understand and even harder to remember. The implications of this theory are clear: Attitude has a noticeable effect on what you are able to learn and remember.

MAKING AN EFFORT TO REMEMBER

To remember something, you have to make a conscious effort to learn it. If you don't learn new information in the first place, it isn't really yours to forget. And even if you do learn new information, it won't last very long unless you're convinced that it's worth hanging onto. The effort you initially make determines whether you'll remember for a lifetime what you've heard or read or forget it in a matter of seconds.

Avoid Pseudo-Forgetting

Whenever you cannot remember a name, a telephone number, a fact, an idea, or even a joke, it's quite natural to say, "I forgot." Yet forgetting may not have anything to do with your problem. You may never have learned the information in the first place. As the poet Oliver Wendell Holmes apparently put it, "A man must *get* a thing before he can *forget* it."

If you are introduced to someone but don't hear that person's name, it's only natural that the name will slip your mind. You didn't forget it. You pseudo-forgot it. The word pseudo means "false" or "phony." Thousands of instances we blame on forgetting are actually a result of this "phony forgetting."

If an idea or a fact is to be retained in your memory, it must be impressed on your mind clearly and crisply at least once. A record of that idea or fact must be laid down in your brain before you can truly recall or forget what you've learned.

Find a Reason to Remember

If you can find a reason for holding onto information you've learned, you have a much better chance of remembering it. In a carefully designed study, H. H. Remmers and M. N. Thisted showed how intention can influence the life span of a memory. Two groups of students were given identical material and asked to master it. The only difference was that the first group was told it had to remember the material for only a single day, whereas the second group was instructed to master the material for recall after two weeks.[2] The difference in intention had a noticeable effect. Although the two groups studied the same material in a similar fashion, after two weeks the students who had intended to remember over the long term retained more than the students who had intended to hang on to what they had learned for only a day.

Psychologists agree that to learn something thoroughly, you have to be properly motivated. Indeed, a strong motivation can have a surprising effect on your memory. A basketball coach at Cornell University recalled that although as a student at DePauw University he had first found physics uninteresting, his attitude changed when he encountered material dealing with angles, trajectory, and force. He used this information to better understand how basketballs carom off the backboard. Because of his new found interest, he was able to raise his grade from a C to an A by the end of the semester. What was his reason for remembering? Information from physics, a subject he had once dreaded, could be applied to basketball, a sport he loved.

Of all the sources of motivation, interest is the strongest. If you could study every one of your subjects with motivated interest, you would not have to worry about your final grades. When you are naturally interested in a subject, you have no problem. If, however, you are not naturally interested, try to combat boredom by artificially creating interest (see Chapter 2). Once you begin to learn something about a new subject, the chances are great that you will find it genuinely interesting. Use the power of interest to work *for* you, not against you.

Whether genuine interest or simple academic survival serves as your motivation, when you hear or read information you want to hold onto, there are ways to strengthen your intention to remember, so that what you've learned will be recalled:

Pay attention.   If you're distracted while you're trying to learn, it's unlikely you'll remember anything. Therefore, make a point to minimize distractions as you read your assignments or listen to lectures.

Get information right the first time.   False ideas and misunderstood facts can hang on as tenaciously as information you learn correctly. Therefore, it pays to be attentive when you learn something new. For example, many

---

[2]H. H. Remmers and M. N. Thisted, "The Effect of Temporal Set on Learning," *Journal of Applied Psychology* 16 (June 1932) 257–268.

people incorrectly pronounce the word *nuclear* (NEW-clee-er) as "NEW-cue-ler." One look at the word shows you that this pronunciation is incorrect. But if you learn a word incorrectly, you'll have difficulty replacing the old memory with the correct pronunciation. If you learn something correctly in the first place, you'll have no bad habits to break.

Make sure you understand. Ideas that aren't clear to you when you read or hear them won't miraculously jell and become clearer in your memory. You cannot fashion a lucid, correct memory from a fuzzy, poorly understood concept. Therefore, don't hesitate to ask the instructor to explain any point that you are not clear on. And don't be reluctant to read and reread a passage in your textbook until you're sure you fully grasp its meaning.

Interestingly, the same motivation that enables you to remember can also help you forget. Recall that reactive interference theory suggests we have a tendency to "tune out" information that bores or bothers us. But motivated forgetting can be used positively to clear your mind of information you no longer need to retain.

This conscious intention to forget is well demonstrated by servers in restaurants. They exhibit a remarkably good memory for what their customers have ordered up to the moment the bill is paid. Then experienced servers jettison the entire transaction from their minds and give their full attention to the next customer. Just as they intend to remember, so they intend to forget.

Dr. Hans Selye, a pioneer in stress management, explains how he used motivated forgetting to help minimize the anxiety caused by an overburdened memory:

> I make a conscious effort to forget immediately all that is unimportant
> and to jot down data of possible value (even at the price of having to
> prepare complex files). Thus, I manage to keep my memory free for facts
> which are truly essential to me. I think this technique can help anyone
> to accomplish the greatest simplicity compatible with the degree of
> complexity of his intellectual life.[3]

This idea of intending to forget explains why Albert Einstein, unquestionably one of the great minds of the twentieth century, was nonetheless unable to provide his home telephone number from memory. Although the famous physicist's forgetfulness may have seemed like absent-mindedness to some, it was usually deliberate. Einstein used his exceptional brain as the incubator for ideas and theories that fundamentally changed the way we view the world. He saw no point in clogging his mind with simple

---

[3] Hans Selye, *The Stress of Life* (New York: McGraw-Hill, 1956), p. 269.

numbers that could easily be stored in an address book, and so he purposely forgot them.

CONTROLLING THE NUMBER AND FORM OF YOUR MEMORIES

The forgetting that many of us practice instinctively seems to imply that there is a limit to how much we can remember at once. In 1956, psychologist G. A. Miller produced scientific support for this notion. In his article "The Magical Number Seven, Plus or Minus Two," Miller points out that most people are able to hold only seven items in short-term memory at one time. The size of each item, however, can be virtually unlimited as long as the information in it is meaningfully organized. For example, you couldn't expect to remember the following thirty-one items:

aabceeeeeeeilmmmnnnnoorrrssttuvy

But if you organized these items in a meaningful way—as words—you could reduce the number of items to seven and increase your odds of remembering them:

You	can	learn	to	remember	seven	items.
1	2	3	4	5	6	7

As Miller explains, "Our language is tremendously useful for repackaging material into a few chunks rich in information."[4]

The lesson to be learned from Miller's research is this: Improve your chances of remembering by being selective about what you learn and by making sure that what you do choose to remember is meaningfully organized.

Be Selective About What You Learn

Long before Miller's "magical number seven," Herman Ebbinghaus (1850–1909), a German psychologist, had spent more than twenty years investigating forgetting and the limits of memory. In his most famous experiment, Ebbinghaus counted the number of trials required to learn a series of six nonsense syllables (such as *bik, luf, tur, pem, nif,* and *wox*). He then counted the number of trials required to learn a series of twelve such syllables.

---

[4]G. A. Miller, "The Magical Number Seven, Plus or Minus Two: Some Limits on Our Capacity for Processing Information," *Psychological Review* 63 (March 1956): 81–97.

Ebbinghaus's tabulations yielded surprising results: The number of trials required to memorize the twelve syllables was fifteen times greater than the number required to learn the six syllables.[5] So, for example, if it took four minutes to memorize six syllables, it would take an hour to memorize twelve.

Although Ebbinghaus dealt only with nonsense syllables, his careful research teaches us a valuable lesson that can be applied to both textbook and lecture material: To improve your chances of remembering what you've learned, you must condense and summarize. In practical terms this means picking out the main ideas from your lecture and textbook notes and leaving the supporting materials and examples aside. Once you have selected the important points from what you've read, you should be able to memorize them in a manageable amount of time.

Of course, reducing pages and pages of notes down to just a handful of main ideas is often easier said than done. If you need a painless method of extracting the highlights from your notes, consider the *Silver Dollar System.*

The Silver Dollar System

Read through your notes and make an *S* in the margin next to any idea that seems important. Depending on the number of pages of notes you read, you'll probably wind up with several dozen *S*'s.

Now read only the notes you have flagged with an *S*. As you go through these flagged notes for a second time, select the ideas that seem particularly important, and draw a vertical line through the *S*'s that are next to them. Your symbol will look like this: *$*.

Make a third and final pass through your notes, reading only those ideas that have been marked *$*. Out of these notes, mark the truly outstanding ideas—there will be only a handful of them—with another vertical line so your markings look like dollar signs: *$*.

The Silver Dollar System shows you at a glance which ideas are crucial to remember and which are not. The *$* sign alerts you to the truly important ideas, the "Silver Dollar" ideas that should receive most of your attention. Next come the *$* ideas; they are worthy, but shouldn't clutter up your memory if you have a lot to remember in a limited amount of time. Finally, the *S* ideas can be ignored. Although you flagged these as potentially important ideas, since then you've twice marked ideas that were even more important.

---

[5]R. D. Williams and G. W. Knox, "A Survey of Dynamic Principles Governing Memory," *Journal of General Psychology* 30 (April 1944): 167-179.

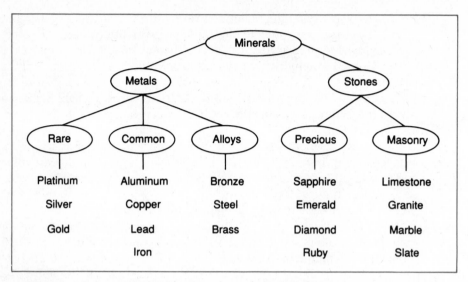

FIGURE 4.1   The Category and Cluster System of Organizing Items

In normal circumstances, deciding what's important can be a time-con-suming and even frightening experience. It requires real courage to select just a few ideas from pages and pages of notes and ignore the rest. With this system, you can select the Silver Dollar ideas gradually and relatively easily.

Organize Information in a Meaningful Way

The papers on your desk are easier to keep track of if you organize them into groups and put them into several file folders. A textbook is easier to understand because the information in it has been divided into chapters. A single item is easier to find in a supermarket because the products have been grouped together and arranged in different aisles. If you had to look for a jar of peanut butter in a supermarket where the items were randomly placed, you might give up the search.

The same idea applies to memories as well. If the material you try to remember isn't well organized, you'll have trouble remembering it. But if you organize information in a meaningful way, you'll have a much easier time recalling it.

When you have a large list of items to remember, try to cluster similar items around a natural heading or category. Once clustered and categorized, the items will resist the decaying power of forgetting. Just as the stem holds together the individual grapes, so categories and clusters hold together individual facts and ideas.

This hanging together is especially useful during an exam: Remembering one item from a cluster is usually the key to remembering all the items. For example, it would take a long time to memorize by rote the following words, which you might encounter in a geology course:

slate	diamond	sapphire
bronze	lead	aluminum
iron	marble	silver
emerald	steel	brass
gold	limestone	ruby
granite	platinum	copper

But when these words are organized into categories and are clustered as shown in Figure 4.1, memorization is relatively easy and remembering is strong.[6]

STRENGTHENING MEMORIES

The stronger a memory is, the longer it lasts. If you reinforce new ideas by connecting them to ones already in your memory, and if you conscientiously rehearse what you've learned, that result should be strong enough to stand up to forgetting.

Reinforce New Ideas Through Association

That famous saying "No man is an island" applies to memories as well. An idea that stands alone is not likely to be recalled because the ideas you remember are woven into a network that connects a single memory with hundreds and often thousands of other memories. The more connections there are in the network and the stronger those connections are, the better the chance for recall is.

Sometimes these connections are made automatically. Most people easily recall, for example, where they were and what they were doing

---

[6]This example is from Jerome Kagan and Ernest Havemann, *Psychology: An Introduction,* 4th ed. (New York: Harcourt Brace Jovanovich, 1980), p. 153. Reprinted by permission of the publisher.

when President Kennedy was assassinated in 1963 or when the space shuttle *Challenger* exploded in 1986. In these cases, you instantly connect the memory of the event with the memory of where you were.

But in normal circumstances, relying on your memory to automatically make these connections is risky. If you want to improve your chances of remembering something, you must make a real effort to link what you've learned to your memory network. You can strengthen the staying power of information when you add it to your memory by consciously making either logical or artificial connections.

Make Logical Connections   Consider how you can recall the written directions to a friend's house by keeping in mind a map you once saw of the location or strengthen your memory of the bones of the body by recalling a diagram of a human skeleton. These are examples of logical connections you make to improve your recall. The best ways of strengthening your memory network through logical connections are by building on your basic background or by using images to support what you're trying to remember.

Build on Your Basic Background.   The principle behind basic background is simple but powerful. Your understanding and memory of what you hear, read, see, feel, or taste depend entirely on what you know, on what you already have in your background. Some of this information has been with you for years, whereas other parts of it may be just seconds old. When listening to a speaker, you understand his or her points as long as you can interpret them in light of something you've already learned. When you make connections this way, you increase the power of your memory.

Here are some concrete steps to help you build a solid background:

Give basic courses the attention they deserve.   Many students make the mistake of thinking that the basic courses they take in their freshman year are a waste of time. Yet these introductory courses create the background essential for all the courses that follow. Indeed, each student's professional life begins with freshman courses.

Make a conscious attempt to link what you learn to what you already know. When you learn something new, ask yourself questions such as "How does this relate to what I already know?" and "How does this *change* what I already know?"

Ask an instructor to explain what you don't understand.   At times an entire class can hinge on a single point. Miss that and you miss the purpose of the class. Don't feel hesitant or shy about asking an instructor to go back over a point you can't quite get a fix on. After all, the instructor is there to help you learn.

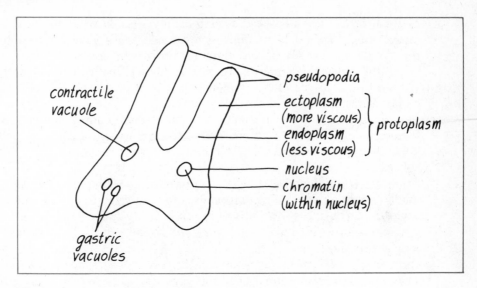

FIGURE 4.2 Structure of the Amoeba

Strengthen Memories with Pictures. Another way of reinforcing what you've learned is by creating a picture of it. Whether you draw the new information on paper or simply visualize it in your mind, you add an extra dimension to your memory. After all, only one-half of your brain thinks in words; the other half thinks in pictures. When you convert words into pictures, you are using both sides of your brain instead of just one.

A student who attended a lecture on amoebas included a sketch of this one-celled organism in her notes (see Figure 4.2). The combination of words and picture gave her a clearer understanding of the subject than she would have gained from relying exclusively on written information. When a question about amoebas appeared on a test, the student handled it easily by recalling the picture she had drawn.

Even when material doesn't lend itself to drawing, you can still devise a mental image. According to Dr. Joseph E. Shorr of the Institute of Psycho-Imagination Therapy in Beverly Hills, California, "The human memory would be worthless without the capacity to make mental pictures." Almost any memory can be turned into a mental image. If you need to remember, for example, that Abraham Lincoln was born in 1809, you can picture a log cabin with "1809" inscribed over the doorway. The image you recall doesn't have to be especially detailed; it only has to be strong enough to jog your memory. (Chapter 8 provides a detailed discussion of how to tap into your natural ability to think visually.)

Make Artificial Connections   Strong connections don't always have to be logical ones. They can be completely artificial. After all, what natural link is there between the word *face* and a group of musical notes? Yet many beginning music students rely on this word to help them recall the notes written in the spaces of the treble clef (F, A, C, E). These connections are by no means limited to music.

Suppose you have just been introduced to a man named Mr. Perkins. To remember his name, you immediately associate it with a coffeepot *perking.* You even visualize the perking pot and smell the aroma of freshly brewed coffee.

What you have done is tie *new* information (Mr. Perkins) to *old* information (perking coffeepot) that is already well established in your memory. When you meet Mr. Perkins at some future time, you will recall the perking coffee pot, which will prepare you to say, "Hello, Mr. Perkins. Nice to see you again."

The majority of memory tricks (known as *mnemonic devices*) rely on such artificial connections.

Use Classic Mnemonic Devices.   Nearly everyone employs at least one or two mnemonic devices to recall specific hard-to-remember facts and information. Probably the most widely used mnemonic device is the old jingle by which many of us keep track of the irregularities in the calendar:

> Thirty days hath September,
> April, June, and November.
> All the rest have thirty-one,
> Except February alone.

Rivaling this days-in-the-month mnemonic is one for spelling:

> *i* before *e* except after *c*
> or when sounding like *a*
> as in *neighbor* and *weigh*

Many people have their own personal mnemonics, such as "Surround the *r* with *a* for the word *separate.*"

As we've already learned, the cardinal rule for dealing with masses of information is to make sure that information is organized in a meaningful way. A mnemonic device is an organizational system pure and simple. It is an ordinary means to an important end. Gerald R. Miller conducted a study to evaluate the effectiveness of mnemonic devices as aids to study.[7]

---

[7] Gerald R. Miller, *An Evaluation of the Effectiveness of Mnemonic Devices as Aids to Study,* Cooperative Research Project no. 5-8438 (El Paso: University of Texas, 1967).

He found that students who used mnemonics raised their test scores by as much as 77 percent!

Miller recognizes that the use of too many mnemonics can overload the memory. Nevertheless, he argues that learning a large number of mnemonics well creates no greater hazard for a student than learning a large amount of material in the traditional way. Here's a sampling of some classic mnemonics that you may have encountered:

Spelling.   The greatest number of mnemonic devices are aids to spelling. Here's how to remember the correct way to spell two words that confuse many students:

A principal is a pal.

A principle is a rule.

If you use classic mnemonic devices to help you recall information, make certain you memorize the sentence, word, or jingle thoroughly. The slightest error can throw you off completely. For example, some algebra students use the FOIL method to remember the order for multiplying a binomial: First, Outer, Inner, Last. But if you recall the wrong word instead, say FILE, you wind up hopelessly confused.

Biology.   The first letters of the words in the following sentence stand for the major categories and subdivisions of the animal world—kingdom, phylum, class, order, family, genus, species, variety:

Kings Play Cards On Fairly Good Soft Velvet.

Geography.   Remembering the names of the Great Lakes is easy if you keep HOMES in mind, but recalling the lakes in a particular order is not so easy. Here's a mnemonic device that organizes them from west to east (Superior, Michigan, Huron, Erie, Ontario):

Super Machine Heaved Earth Out.

History.   The royal houses of England (Norman, Plantagenet, Lancaster, York, Tudor, Stuart, Hanover, Windsor) are difficult to remember without the help of a mnemonic device:

No Plan Like Yours To Study History Wisely

Medicine.   Even doctors and pharmacists use memory systems to help keep certain chemicals straight. To distinguish between cyanates, which are harmless, and cyanides, which are extremely poisonous, they use this device:

-ate, I ate; *-ide,* I died.

Medical students are expected to remember massive amounts of information. Often, a mnemonic comes to the rescue. Some med students use the word SKILL to help them recall the body's excretory organs:

<u>S</u>kin <u>K</u>idneys <u>I</u>ntestines <u>L</u>iver <u>L</u>ungs

Devise Your Own Mnemonics.   Associating new information logically is generally better than doing so artificially, and truly knowing something is always better than using a system to remember it. But if you're required to learn facts that you can't connect with your memory network and that have no classic mnemonic, you may want to invent your own mnemonic device to help you remember.

Keyword mnemonic.[8]   Connecting a man named Perkins with a perking coffee pot provides a good example of a *keyword mnemonic* in action. The procedure for devising a keyword mnemonic has two steps, a verbal step and a visual step.

1. *The verbal step.*   Find a familiar word or a phrase that sounds like the word you are trying to remember. This is your keyword. For the name *Perkins* the keyword is *perking.*

2. *The visual step.*   Connect your keyword with what you want to remember. For example, form a mental image of Mr. Perkins' face on a perking coffeepot. Then when you see him again, you'll recall that image which will remind you of his name.

The keyword system isn't limited to helping you remember the names of people you meet. It also comes in handy for remembering vocabulary words from a foreign language. For example, if you want to recall the French word for butter, *beurre,* connect it with a keyword like *burr,* or *brrr,* and then link the two with a visual image, a pat of butter covered with burrs or a stick of butter wearing a parka and shivering (brrr!).

Create-a-word mnemonic.   The letters of a "created" word can be used to help you remember important information in the same way the classic mnemonics FACE and FOIL are used. Here's an example: The task is to devise a mnemonic that will enable you to recall five guidelines for preventing heart attack and stroke.

1. After <u>age</u> 40, get a medical checkup every year.
2. Do not <u>smoke</u>.
3. Keep your <u>weight</u> down.
4. <u>Exercise</u> moderately and wisely.

---

[8]The keyword mnemonics section is based on a discussion in K. L. Higbee, *Your Memory: How It Works and How to Improve It,* 2/e (New York: Prentice Hall, 1988).

5. Get sufficient <u>rest</u>.

To devise a *create-a-word mnemonic,* proceed as follows:

1. Underline the key word in each item (as has been done in the previous list).

2. Write down the first letter of each key word. (Here we have A, S, W, E, and R.)

3. Create a word or several words from the first letters of the key words. Change the order of the letters as necessary to do so. (Here we can make SWEAR, which will help us recall the five key words: <u>S</u>moke, <u>W</u>eight, <u>E</u>xercise, <u>A</u>ge 40, <u>R</u>est.)

4. If possible, make a link between your key word and the idea for which it acts as a mnemonic. ("If you want to reduce your risk of heart attack or stroke, you must *swear* to do the following.")

Your mnemonic may be a real word or a word you just made up. If you use a made-up word, be sure you will be able to remember it.

Create-a-sentence mnemonic.   This is a variation on the create-a-word mnemonic. In fact, most of the steps are the same. A *create-a-sentence mnemonic* is devised as follows:

1. Underline the key word in each main point in your notes.
2. Write down the first letter of each key word.
3. Construct an easy-to-remember sentence using words whose first letters are the same as the first letters of the key words.
4. Devise a sentence that relates to the information you're trying to remember.

As an example, here are eight main points taken from a long article about what to do if you are in a building that is on fire. The key words have been underlined.

1. Feel the <u>door</u> with your hand. If it is hot, the room or hall on the other side is on fire.

2. If the door is cool, check the <u>air</u> coming under the door. If it is cool, then there's probably no fire on the other side.

3. Even so, don't take chances. Open the door just a <u>crack</u> while kneeling with your face turned away. Listen and smell for fire and smoke.

4. When you leave, <u>shut</u> all doors and windows.

5. If your room is smoke filled, <u>crawl</u> with your nose about one foot from the floor.

6. Never use an elevator; use a <u>stairway</u>.

7. If you are trapped, use <u>wet</u> cloths to protect your face, hands, and breathing passages.

8. <u>Hang</u> something out of a window to attract attention.

The first letters of the key words are D, A, C, S, C, S, W, and H. An easy-to-remember sentence using words beginning with the first letters of the key words is

<u>D</u>ry <u>A</u>ir <u>C</u>reates <u>S</u>parks, <u>C</u>ausing <u>S</u>moke <u>W</u>ithin <u>H</u>ouses.

The letters need not appear in the same order as the key words. But in this case, the sequence of steps was considered important, so the original order was retained.

In general, creating a simple sentence is easier than taking the first letters from your key words and turning them into a word or two, especially if the order of the points has to be maintained. Of course, if the initial letters are mainly consonants, both methods can be difficult. To circumvent the problem of having too many consonants, choose some key words (or synonyms of the key words) that begin with a vowel.

Employ Commercial Memory Methods.   Most commercial memory courses rely on *the peg.* This system for memorizing items in sequence employs a master list of words that act as hooks or pegs on which to hang the information you want to remember. A peg word often rhymes with the number it stands for. For example, one is bun, two is shoe, three is tree, and four is door. To remember a group of items, you associate them with the peg words, often by employing bizarre images.

For example, if you want to remember a shopping list consisting of butter, sugar, and sausage, you might visualize a pound of butter melting atop a gigantic bun, a shoe filled with loose sugar, and a sausage as tall as a tree. Then when you arrive at the supermarket, you run through the peg words in sequence (bun, shoe, tree) and recall the words with which each is associated.

The peg may work for buying groceries but not for doing schoolwork because the system assumes you'll be able to memorize the original list. When you are unable to do this, the entire system falls apart. In addition, the peg works with only one list at a time, it may cause interference, and it does little to reinforce information in your long-term memory. Commercial memory courses do have some value, and peg words can help out in a pinch, but in general the cost of the courses outweighs their usefulness, and the techniques are better for survival than success.

Rehearse Information Through Recitation

No single activity is more important in strengthening your memory than recitation. That's because recitation forces you to think seriously about what you've read or heard. This deep thinking (experts call it *deep cognitive processing*) is the key to making memories last.

To reap the benefits of recitation, you need to know how to recite. But it also helps to understand how reciting strengthens your memory and why reciting is more effective than rereading.

Learn How to Recite Most students have only a vague idea of what reciting involves. Others more familiar with reciting incorrectly assume that there is only one method of doing so. Although there is a traditional method of reciting, if you follow some basic guidelines, you can recite in several ways. In fact, the best method of reciting is not the best known.

Do Traditional Reciting. Traditional reciting involves restating information out loud, in your own words, and from memory. For example, if you read a paragraph from a textbook, look away, and then explain the meaning of what you have just read, then you are reciting.

Unfortunately, not all students are keen on this kind of reciting. Some feel that the process is strange or unnatural, like talking to themselves. Others are reluctant to recite in a quiet place where people are studying. Still others are embarrassed to be heard reciting no matter what. As a result, many students don't recite. But there are other ways to recite that avoid such embarrassments. The trick is to stick to the basics of reciting.

Understand the Process of Reciting. All reciting follows three basic steps: You *read,* you *convert* what you've read, and then you *test* yourself on what you've learned. A simple way to recall these steps is to think of the consonants in the word *recite*. The *R* stands for read, the *C* for convert, and the *T* for test.

1. *How to read.* Read one paragraph at a time if you're reciting from your textbook or one note at a time if you're reciting from your note sheets. In each case, extract the main idea as you do so. If you're reciting from your notes, your job is a breeze: The main idea is the note you wrote down. If you're reading from your textbook, remember that each paragraph typically contains just one main idea, which all the other sentences support.

2. *How to convert what you've read.* Once you've read the paragraph or note and extracted the main idea, convert this main idea into a key word or two that hint at the idea or a question that uses the idea as its answer.

3. *How to test yourself.* Use the converted form to show your knowledge of the original paragraph or note. Use the key words or the question you've devised to demonstrate out loud or on paper your knowledge of the main idea.

Recite by Writing Out Questions and Answers.   The best way to recite is by converting what you've read into questions, reading those questions, and then writing down answers. Converting ideas into questions is usually more effective than coming up with a key word or two. In addition, writing down answers on paper provides better practice than simply stating those answers out loud.

The difference between using key words and asking questions is basically the difference between recognizing and recalling. Recognizing a correct answer is always easier than recalling one without any clues. Key words "cheat" by enabling you to recognize part of the answer, whereas questions emphasize recall. With no clues to go on, if you can answer your question, you have probably recalled the right answer and not simply recognized it. And because most of the answers you'll be asked to give in tests and quizzes will be written, not spoken, this kind of reciting provides excellent practice for test taking.

When done properly, reading out loud can be an excellent way of reciting. But some students who are reluctant to recite out loud either skip the reciting step altogether or mumble instead of speaking clearly. Reciting under your breath makes it too easy to convince yourself that you know the correct answer when you don't. But when you do your reciting by writing, you have solid proof that you can answer your questions.

Understand Why Recitation Works   Whether you recite by speaking or by writing, the effect on your memory is basically the same. Recitation strengthens the original memory trace by prompting you to think actively about the new material. The physical activity of thinking, pronouncing, and hearing your own words involves your body as well as your mind in the process of learning. The more physical senses you use in learning, the stronger the memory in your brain will be. In addition, recitation provides a number of psychological benefits that improve your ability to learn and remember.

Recitation Gets You Involved.   Reading is not the same as comprehending. It's possible, for example, to read a book aloud to a child without paying attention to the story. Likewise, if you're having a tough time concentrating, you can read every word on a page and still not recall what you've read. To truly comprehend what you've read, you need to know both what the words *say* and what they *mean*. When you recite, you make yourself stop and wonder, "What did this just say?" You're transformed from a detached observer into a participant.

Recitation Provides Feedback.   Reciting not only gets you involved in your reading, it also demonstrates how involved you are. Rereading can give you a false and dangerous sense of confidence. It takes a lot of time and leaves you with the feeling that you've been hard at work, yet it provides no concrete indication of what you're learning. When test time comes, you may blame your mental blanks on test anxiety or on unfair questions when the real culprit is ineffective studying.

Unlike rereading, reciting lets you know right away where your weaknesses lie. You find out at the end of every paragraph whether you understand what you've just read. This gives you a chance to clarify and solidify information on the spot, long before you're tested on it.

Recitation Supplies Motivation. Because it gets you involved and checks your progress regularly, recitation provides motivation for studying. And motivated interest promotes stronger memory.

If you struggled to extract the information from a paragraph you just read, you may be motivated to get the point of the next paragraph more easily. If you had no trouble finding the meaning in that paragraph, then the momentum of your reading may serve as a motivation.

Recognize the Difference Between Reciting and Rereading

Students who don't recite usually reread their notes or chapter assignments until they feel they "know it." They do this in the hope that repetition will lead to comprehension. Unfortunately, any real learning that takes place through rereading usually occurs by accident. This all-too-common study method really does little to strengthen memory.

Recitation, however, works in several ways at once to help improve the chances that you'll remember what you've learned. Recitation gets you involved. It provides immediate feedback so you can test yourself and check your progress. It motivates you to keep on reading.

ALLOWING TIME FOR MEMORIES TO CONSOLIDATE

The fact that recitation helps new information to jell hints at another aspect of memory: New ideas don't instantly become a part of your memory. Your memory needs time to consolidate what you've learned.

A dramatic illustration of the memory's need to consolidate comes in a story of a mountain climber who fell and hit his head. Although the man was not permanently injured, he couldn't remember falling. In fact, he couldn't recall anything that had happened to him in the fifteen minutes *before* the accident. Why not? According to the principle of consolidation, the climber's memories before the accident had not had a chance to consolidate. As a result, when the climber hit his head, those unfinished memories were lost.[9]

This principle helps explain why in most cases the most effective way to study is in short blocks of time instead of in one long stretch. An understanding of consolidation will help you live through those frustrating times when you don't seem to retain what you're studying.

Use Distributed Practice

In *distributed practice*, you engage in relatively short study periods broken up by rest intervals. In *massed practice*, you study continuously until the task is completed. A number of studies have demonstrated that several short "learning sprints" are more productive than one grueling, long-distance study session.

In an extensive experiment, Irving Lorge found that with the introduction of distributed practice, students immediately improved their performance.[10] When distributed practice was discontinued, their performance suffered. Students had an immediate reaction to the initiation and to the withdrawal of distributed practice.

Bertram Epstein used two experimental groups to find out whether distributed practice had an effect on retention.[11] One group studied in bite-sized stretches with rest periods in between (distributed practice), while the other worked in one long session with no rests (massed practice). Both groups were tested immediately after studying as well as two weeks and then ten weeks later. Epstein concluded that distributed practice was superior to massed practice for both immediate and long-term retention.

The memory's need to consolidate information seems to play a key role in explaining why distributed practice is superior to massed practice. But there are other advantages as well that support these bite-sized study sessions:

Periodic "breathers" discourage fatigue. They refresh you both physically and emotionally.

---

[9]R. S. Woodworth and H. Schlosberg, *Experimental Psychology*, rev. ed. (New York: Holt, Rinehart, and Winston, 1954), p. 773.
[10]Irving Lorge, *Influence of Regularly Interpolated Time Intervals upon Subsequent Learning*, Contributions to Education no. 438 (New York: Bureau of Publications, Teachers College, Columbia University, 1930).
[11]Bertram Epstein, *Immediate and Retention Effects of Interpolated Rest Periods on Learning Performance*, Contributions to Education no. 949 (New York: Bureau of Publications, Teachers College, Columbia University, 1949).

Motivation is stronger when you work within short blocks of time. The end of each session marks a minivictory that provides momentum and a sense of accomplishment.

Distributed practice wards off boredom. Uninteresting subjects are easier to take in small doses.

In spite of all the advantages of distributed practice, there are a few cases where massed practice is superior. For instance, when you are writing the first draft of a paper, massed practice is often essential. You have organized your notes in stacks, discrete bits of information are waiting in your mind like jigsaw puzzle pieces to be fitted together, and the organizational pattern of your paper, though dimly perceived, is beginning to take shape. To stop working at this point would be disastrous. The entire effort would collapse. So in such a circumstance, it is far more efficient to overextend yourself—to complete that stage of the process—than to take a break or otherwise apply the principle of distributed practice.

Accept Memory Plateaus

No two people learn at exactly the same rate, yet the learning patterns of most people are quite similar. We all experience lulls in our learning. Progress is usually slow and steady at first, but then for a period of time there might be no perceptible progress even though we are making a genuine effort. This "no-progress" period is called a *plateau*. After days, weeks, or even a month of effort, suddenly a surprising spurt in learning occurs and continues until another plateau is reached.

When you reach a plateau, do not lose heart. Plateaus are a normal part of learning. You may not see any progress, but learning is occurring nevertheless. Once everything is in place, you'll be rewarded for your effort.

SUMMARY

How powerful is forget-fulness?

Forgetting works quickly and thoroughly to rob you in less than a day of much of the new information you've read or heard. As time goes on, the forgetting continues.

What causes forgetting to occur?

Experts propose several theories about why we forget. Fading theory says that rarely used information fades away. Retrieval theory argues that forgotten information is misplaced. Interference theory contends that old and new memories interfere with each other. Interactive interference theory suggests that middle memories are squeezed out by older and newer memories. Reactive interference theory maintains that you tune out and consequently forget information you don't want to know.

What is pseudo-forgetting?

Pseudo-forgetting is false forgetting. It occurs when you fail to learn something in the first place.

Does having a reason to remember affect your memory?

Yes. A study showed that simply intending to remember can significantly increase the life span of a memory. There are numerous examples of people who are motivated to remember and then do so. Of these motivations, the most effective one is interest.

How can you strengthen your intention to remember?

Start by paying close attention. If you're distracted, you aren't as likely to remember. When you learn something new, be sure that you understand it and that you learn it correctly. If you confuse or fail to understand the original information, you aren't going to miraculously correct it in your memory.

How do the number and form of your memories affect your ability to retain information?

Limiting what you try to learn and organizing it in a meaningful way will improve your ability to retain this information. The Silver Dollar System can aid you in memorizing information. Organizing such information into meaningful categories further improves recall.

Why is it crucial to connect what you learn with what you already know?

Linking new, individual memories to a memory network improves recall. Sometimes you make these connections automatically, but consciously establishing connections (either logical or artificial) between new information and a memory network ensures greater remembering.

What is the principle of basic background?

The principle of basic background says that what you are able to learn and remember is based on what you already know.

How do pictures strengthen your memory?	By connecting new information to something you've drawn or visualized, you add a new dimension to that memory by getting the visual side of your brain involved.
How do you make artificial connections?	You make artificial connections by using memory tricks, or mnemonic devices, to link new information with old information.
How do you recite?	The most common method of reciting involves repeating information out loud, from memory, and in your own words. There are, however, other ways to recite. All can be effective if you follow the basic process of reciting.
What is the basic process of reciting?	The basic process comprises three steps: (1) read, (2) convert what you've read, and (3) test yourself on what you've learned.
What is the best method for reciting, and why?	The best way of reciting is by transforming what you've read into questions, reading them, and then answering them. This is the best method because when you convert a main idea into a question, you force yourself to remember what you've just read. Reciting by writing causes no embarrassment, creates no disturbance, and provides you with written evidence of whether you've understood what you've read. And because most tests are written, reciting by writing provides excellent practice in taking tests.
How does reciting strengthen your memory?	Reciting holds information in your short-term memory long enough for the material to jell and then move on to long-term memory.
How does distributed practice aid consolidation?	Distributed practice aids consolidation because memory needs time to coalesce what you've learned and the breaks in this practice provide that time.
What are some advantages of distributed practice?	In addition to allowing time for consolidation, distributed practice provides breathers that discourage fatigue and burnout, increases motivation by creating a sense of accomplishment, and wards off boredom

by dividing dull or intimidating subjects into more manageable pieces.

Are there times when it's better to study continuously?

Continuous studying, or massed practice, is appropriate for doing prolonged creative work, such as writing a paper or preparing an oral report. In these situations it's usually best to keep working while you have ideas and information in your mind so they have time to interact and jell.

What are memory plateaus?

Memory plateaus are periods when you appear to be making no progress even though you are making an effort. During these lulls, your mind is consolidating what you've learned thus far.

HAVE YOU MISSED SOMETHING?

Matching. In each blank space in the left column, write the letter preceding the phrase in the right column that matches the left item best.

__C__ 1. Pseudo-forgetting

a. Primary cause of reactive interference

__b.__ 2. Basic courses

b. Suggests that memories fight each other for space

__g.__ 3. Memory network

c. Failure to recall what you never really learned

__e__ 4. Plateaus

d. Method for selecting key ideas from your notes

__a.__ 5. Negative attitude

e. No-progress periods that occur during learning

__b.__ 6. Interactive interference

f. Study sessions divided by regular breaks

__d.__ 7. Silver Dollar System

g. Connects and strengthens related memories

__f.__ 8. Distributed practice

h. Lay the foundation for basic background

Multiple choice. Choose the word or phrase that completes the following sentence most accurately, and circle the letter that precedes it.

1. Memory acquires an extra dimension when information is

    a. written on note cards.
    b. drawn or visualized.
    c. reread or recited.
    d. condensed or reduced.

2. The most valuable facts from your notes are known as

    a. Silver Dollar ideas.
    b. mnemonic devices.
    c. memory traces.
    d. none of the above.

3. According to fading theory, old memories are like a(n)

    a. basketball court.
    b. filing cabinet.
    c. underused path.
    d. oil slick.

4. In general, mnemonic devices supply

    a. visual cues.
    b. an organizational system.
    c. consolidation time.
    d. interference insurance.

5. No single activity is more important to strengthening memory than

    a. recitation.
    b. rereading.
    c. revising.
    d. none of the above.

True-false. Write *T* beside the *true* statements and *F* beside the *false* statements.

T   **1.** In creative work, massed practice is often preferred over distributed practice.

T   **2.** In general, it's easier to recall what you've read than it is to remember what you've heard.

T   **3.** Rereading does very little to strengthen your memory.

F   **4.** Gerald Miller found that mnemonics had no effect on learning.

F   **5.** New information is automatically transferred to long-term memory.

Short answer.   Supply a brief answer for each of the following items. The number in parentheses refers to the page where the item is discussed in the text.

1. What does retrieval theory suggest about memory? (78)
2. What is the nature of G. A. Miller's notion of memory? (82)
3. Explain the three steps used in all types of reciting. (93)
4. Explain why in recitation questions are preferable to key words. (94)
5. List some of the advantages of distributed practice. (96–97)

BUILDING YOUR VOCABULARY STEP BY STEP: USING THE DICTIONARY

Consider this sentence: "Restless and irresponsible, Alex was considered the prodigal son." What does the word *prodigal* mean? If you think it means "wandering," you're mistaken. It can be risky to rely solely on context to determine the meaning of a word you don't know. Your safest bet is to avoid all the guesswork and go straight to the dictionary.

Many scholars and businesspeople rely on a pocket dictionary as a handy source of definitions. Eddie Rickenbacker (1890–1973), auto racer, ace fighter pilot in World War I, and businessman, who left school when he was only twelve years old, carried a small dictionary with him wherever he went.

Follow the example of thousands of successful people. Get yourself a pocket dictionary such as *New Webster's Best Pocket Dictionary* or *Webster's New World Vest Pocket Dictionary*, and always carry it with you. Instead of reading the print on cereal boxes, looking at advertising placards on buses and subways, or staring into space, you can take out your dictionary and read it. Its definitions are terse, consisting mainly of synonyms, but its value lies in its ability to spark a lifelong interest in words as well as increase your vocabulary. Of course, a pocket dictionary is no substitute for a large, desk-size dictionary; but as a portable learning tool, the pocket dictionary is worth at least its weight in gold.

For your study periods, buy and use the best abridged dictionary that you can afford, but be aware that no word is ever fully defined even by a good abridged dictionary. Words have multiple shades of meaning that add richness to your language. These various shades will become apparent to you as you keep reading, listening, and using words in many contexts. Good abridged desk dictionaries include the following:

The American Heritage Dictionary (Houghton Mifflin Company)

The American College Dictionary (Random House)

Webster's New Collegiate Dictionary (G&C Merriam Company)

Webster's New World Dictionary of the American Language (World Publishing Company)

For intensive word study, however, there is no substitute for an unabridged dictionary. Locate the unabridged dictionaries in your library—usually they are in the reference room—and use them to supplement your own abridged desk dictionary. An unabridged dictionary provides more definitions, more about the derivations of words, and more on usage. Good one-volume unabridged dictionaries include *Webster's New International Dictionary of the English Language,* and the *New Standard Dictionary of the English Language.*

Dictionaries can provide you with valuable information, including the pronunciation, derivation, and definitions of the following words from the chapter you just completed. Page numbers indicate the locations of these words in the chapter.

bizarre (92)	hinge (86)	proponents (78)
caroming (80)	interactive (78)	reap (93)
cognitive (93)	jettison (81)	reinforcing (87)
coveted (78)	jog (87)	retention (96)
devastating (78)	lucid (81)	rote (85)
embellished (77)	obliterate (78)	sole (77)
etches (78)	overburdened (81)	tenaciously (80)
excretory (90)	plausible (78)	woes (77)
hierarchy (77)		

Devising a Note-Taking System

Creating a Note-Taking Framework

Learn, compare, collect the facts!

IVAN PETROVICH PAVLOV

Physiologist

Strong buildings start with firm foundations. And what holds true for buildings applies to note taking as well. Note taking, which enhances your ability to comprehend and remember what you've read or heard, has to be established on solid ground to be effective. The time-tested Cornell system provides just such a base. To help you understand the architecture of note taking, this chapter focuses on

- Learning the value of taking notes
- Using the Cornell system
- Recording information efficiently

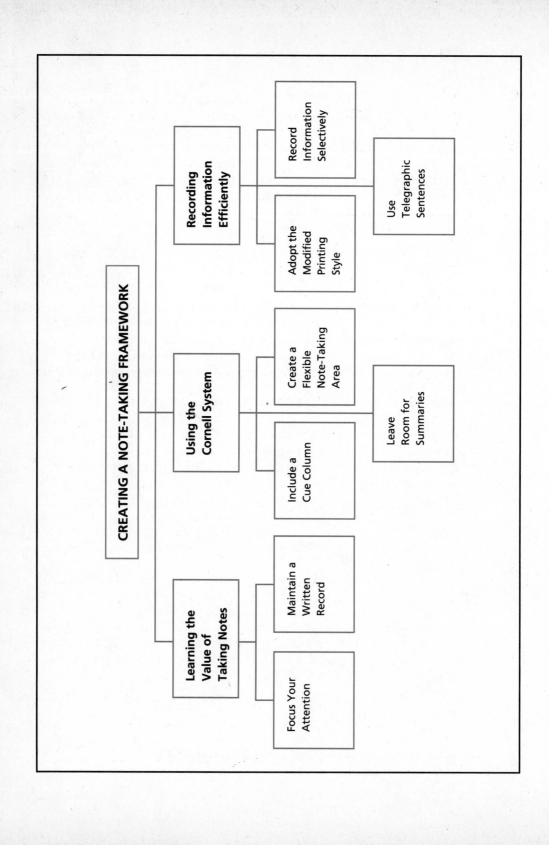

Learning begins with information gathering. The lectures you hear in class and the chapters, articles, and books you're asked to read for assignments provide the raw material for knowledge. Because you spend so much of your academic life accumulating information, it's unwise to do so haphazardly. The best way to gather information is by taking notes, and the best way to take systematic notes is by learning the value of taking notes, by building a solid note-taking framework, and by recording information as efficiently as possible.

LEARNING THE VALUE OF TAKING NOTES

Note taking works on two levels to bolster your memory. First, it focuses your attention on what you're reading or hearing, which in turn helps strengthen the original memory trace of the material. Second, it provides you with a written record of what you've learned. This enables you to keep the information fresh in your mind just by conducting a handful of brief review sessions.

Focus Your Attention

Information improperly learned can be easily forgotten. If you're sitting through a lengthy lecture or reading a long textbook assignment, the risk is high that you will tune out or skip over some important information. With your hands free, your mind is free to wander as well. In short, there's no real incentive for paying attention. By providing instant feedback as well as a conditioning effect, note taking supplies the incentive you need to keep your mind on your work.

The instant feedback you get is the notes you write down. You know right away whether you're paying attention and understanding what you're hearing or reading. The evidence is right there on paper.

An additional advantage of taking notes is a conditioning effect called the *Pencil Technique.* The act of gripping the pencil and of jotting down notes encourages attention, which leads to stronger memories and improved concentration.

Maintain a Written Record

Although taking notes keeps your mind on your work, the primary goal of note taking is to provide you with a written record of what you've read or heard. Your short-term memory isn't equipped to retain all the ideas in a typical chapter or lecture. As a result, forgetting can be instantaneous and complete. In fact, recent experiments have shown that unrehearsed information is sometimes forgotten in as little as twenty seconds.[1] Hermann Ebbinghaus, a German psychologist who investigated remembering and forgetting, found that almost half of what is learned is forgotten within an hour.[2] Recently, psychologists carrying out experiments similar to Ebbinghaus's affirmed his findings.

The following true story further confirms the rapidity and massiveness of forgetting. Three professors eating lunch in the faculty lounge had this conversation:

Clyde: Did you hear last night's lecture?
Walter: No, I was busy.
Clyde: Well, you missed one of the best lectures in recent years.
Leon: I agree. The four points that he developed were gems.
Clyde: I've never heard anyone make his points so clearly.
Walter: I don't want you to repeat the lecture, but what were those four points?
Leon: (Long silence) Clyde? (Passage of two or three minutes; seemed like an hour.)…Well, I'd better get back to the office.
Clyde: Me, too!
Walter: Me, too!

Both Leon and Clyde were brilliant men, yet neither of them was able to recall even a fragment of any point made in the previous night's lecture. Each had forgotten the four points because neither had transferred the points from short-term memory to long-term memory by silently reciting them. Instead, they both had recited that the speaker was clear, forceful, and wise and that he had made four points—and they remembered only what they had recited. As you can surmise from the anecdote, the only sure way to overcome forgetting is by taking notes and then studying and reciting them.

USING THE CORNELL SYSTEM

The notes you jot down can become a handwritten textbook. In fact, in many instances your notes are more practical, meaningful, and up-to-date than a textbook. If you keep them neat, complete, and well organized, they will serve you splendidly.

---

[1] Douglas A. Bernstein, Edward J. Roy, Thomas K. Srull, and Christopher D. Wickens, *Psychology* (Boston: Hougton Mifflin, 1988), p. 293.
[2] Hermann Ebbinghaus, *Memory* (New York: Dover, 1964), p. 76.

The best way I know of to ensure that the notes you take are useful is by adopting the Cornell Note-taking system, which I developed at Cornell University more than forty years ago. Since then, the Cornell system has been adopted by countless colleges and universities not only in the United States but also in other countries, including China. Although the system is far-reaching, its secret is simple: Wide margins on the left-hand side and at the bottom of each page provide the keystone.

Although many office and school supply stores now sell Cornell-style note paper, you can easily use a pen and a ruler to adapt standard loose-leaf paper to the task. First draw a vertical line down the left side of each page two-and-a-half inches from the edge of the paper; end the line two inches from the bottom of the sheet. This creates the *cue column*. Next draw a horizontal line two inches up from the bottom of the page. This is the border for your *summary area*. The large space to the right of the cue column and above the summary area is where your notes should be taken. Figure. 5.1 shows a Cornell note sheet.

Include a Cue Column

The cue column is a two-and-one-half-inch margin on the left-hand side of each page of your note sheets. It helps to ensure that you will actually put the notes to good use instead of simply stashing them away in a notebook until test time.

As you're taking notes, whether from a textbook assignment or a classroom lecture, keep the cue column empty. But when you review and recite what you've jotted down, draw questions from the ideas in your notes, and write them in the cue column. Writing questions helps clarify meanings, reveal relationships, establish continuity, and strengthen memory.

Leave Room for Summaries

The two-inch space at the bottom of each note sheet is the summary area in which you sum up each page of your notes in a sentence or two. The virtues of the summary area are twofold. Not only does it provide a convenient in-a-nutshell version of a page full of notes; it also helps you step back and look at the implications of what you've written down. There's always a danger that in paying close attention to the specific facts and details that make up your notes, you lose sight of their overall meaning. By encouraging you to look at "the big picture," the summary area provides perspectives and helps avoid this potential note-taking pitfall.

Create a Flexible Note-Taking Area

The information that goes in the largest space on the page varies from class to class and from student to student. Different courses come with different

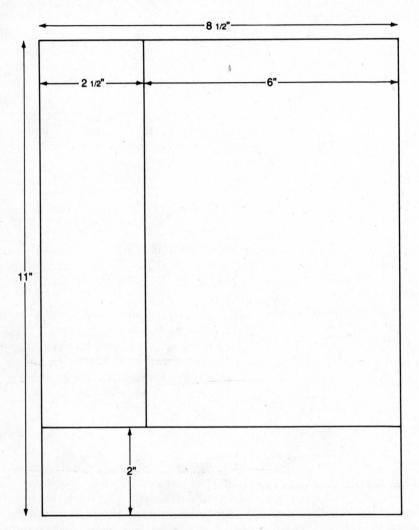

FIGURE 5.1   The Cornell Note Sheet
To use the Cornell System, the student writes notes in the wide (6") column. To study from the notes, the student writes questions in the narrow column and a summary in the space at the bottom of the note sheet.

Psych. 105 – Prof. Martin – Sept. 14 (Mon.)

MEMORY

Memory tricky – Can recall instantly many trivial things of childhood; yet, forget things recently worked hard to learn & retain.

Memory Trace

How do psychologists account for remembering?	— Fact that we retain information means that some change was made in the brain.
What's a "memory trace"?	— Change called "memory trace." — "Trace" probably a molecular arrangement similar to molecular changes in a magnetic recording tape.

Three memory systems: sensory, short-term, long-term.

How do psychologists account for remembering?

What's a "memory trace"?

What are the three memory systems?

How long does sensory memory retain information?

How is information transferred to STM?

What are the retention times of STM?

What's the capacity of the STM?

How to hold information in STM?

What are the retention times of LTM?

What are the six ways to transfer information from STM to LTM?

Memory Trace
— Fact that we retain information means that some change was made in the brain.
— Change called "memory trace."
— "Trace" probably a molecular arrangement similar to molecular changes in a magnetic recording tape.

Three memory systems: sensory, short-term, long-term.
— <u>Sensory</u> (lasts one second)
Ex. Words or numbers sent to brain by sight (visual image) start to disintegrate within a few tenths of a second & gone in one full second, unless quickly transferred to S-T memory by verbal repetition.
— Short-term memory [STM] (lasts 30 seconds)
• Experiments show: a syllable of 3 letters remembered 50% of the time after 3 seconds. Totally forgotten end of 30 seconds.
• S-T memory – limited capacity = holds average of 7 items.
• More than 7 items -- jettisons some to make room.
• To hold items in STM, must rehearse -- must hear <u>sound</u> of words internally or externally.
— Long-Term memory [LTM] (lasts a lifetime or short time).
• Transfer fact or idea by:
(1) <u>Associating</u> w/information already in LTM
(2) <u>Organizing</u> information into meaningful units
(3) <u>Understanding</u> by comparing & making relationships.
(4) <u>Frameworking</u> – fit pieces in like in a jigsaw puzzle.
(5) <u>Reorganizing</u> – combing new & old into a new unit.
(6) <u>Rehearsing</u> – aloud to keep memory trace strong

Three kinds of memory systems are sensory, which retains information for about one second; short-term, which retains for a maximum of thirty seconds; and long-term, which varies from a lifetime of retention to a relatively short time.

The six ways (activities) to transfer information to the long-term memory are: associating, organizing, understanding, frameworking, reorganizing and rehearsing.

FIGURE 5.2   A Cornell Note Sheet with Jottings in the Cue Column and Summary Area

demands. The format you choose for taking your notes and the ideas you take down are almost entirely up to you. If you have a special way of jotting down your notes, you should be able to use it with the Cornell note sheet. Figure 5.2 shows notes taken on a Cornell note sheet.

In general, however, avoid taking notes in outline form because this forces you to fit the material into a highly regimented pattern. It's fine to indent and even number your notes, but don't get so caught up in numbers, letters, and Roman numerals that you overlook content.

RECORDING INFORMATION EFFICIENTLY

Strive to make your note taking both speedy and sparing. Of course, if you scribble down information too quickly, your notes may be illegible. And if you're too choosy about what you record, you may be left with costly gaps in your information. The way to circumvent these problems and record legible, useful notes at a reasonable speed is by adopting the modified printing style, using telegraphic sentences, and recording selectively.

Adopt the Modified Printing Style

Poor handwriting need not keep you from taking legible notes. You can develop legible writing by adopting the _modified printing style,_ a system that combines the rapidity of writing with the legibility of printing. Letters are formed smoothly, as with cursive writing, but are punctuated with the sort of stops and starts characteristic of printing. That means your words take on a cursive look, and at the same time the periodic breaks between letters prevent your writing from eroding into an unreadable blur.

What makes the modified printing style so effective and easy to learn is that it combines your style of printing with your style of cursive in a mixture that brings out the best elements of both. Here's how your individual letters might appear in the modified printing style:

$$a \; b \; c \; d \; e \; f \; g \; h \; i \; j \; k \; l \; m \; n \; o \; p \; q \; r \; s \; t \; u \; v \; w \; x \; y \; z$$

Figure 5.3 shows how modified printing looks in a typical paragraph.

> There are four advantages to using this modified printing style. First, it is faster than cursive writing; second, it is neater, permitting easy and direct comprehension; third, it saves time by pre-cluding rewriting or typing; and fourth, it per-mits easy and clear reforming of letters that are ill-formed due to haste.

FIGURE 5.3   Modified Printing Style

Use Telegraphic Sentences

Long before the fax machine was invented and when telephones were not so numerous as they are today, important business and personal messages were sent by telegraph. The sender paid by the word; the fewer the words, the lower the cost. A three-word message such as "Arriving three pm" was much less expensive than an eleven-word message: "I will arrive home promptly at three o'clock in the afternoon."

Of course, taking notes doesn't cost money, but it does cost time. You can save time and still extract the important information from lectures and textbook material by using telegraphic sentences in your notes. To do so, leave out unnecessary words such as articles (a, an, the), abbreviate words you use often (see Table 5.1, on pages 117–118), and streamline definitions by using a colon (":") or a dash ("—"). Two examples of this telegraphic style are shown in Figure 5.4.

Record Information Selectively

Taking thorough notes, regardless of the format you choose, should not involve writing down everything you read or hear. Your emphasis should be on the ideas, not the words. And you don't want all the ideas, either, just the key ones, along with any details or examples you need to make those ideas easier to understand.

Lecturer's words in a marketing course

In selling, you can overcome a customer's objections to almost any product if

you can come up with a good idea. Here are two examples. First, a woman who

objected to a square fly swatter bought it when the sales manager said, "These

are square, madam. They get them in the corners." Second, a woman who wanted

round clothespins bought the square ones when the clerk said, "They don't roll

out of reach under a sink." So don't sell the steak — sell the sizzle.

Student's telegraphic sentence

1. People buy ideas, not products.
   a. Ex. square fly swatter = "get in corners."
   b. Ex. square clothespins = "won't roll--sink."
   c. Don't sell steak -- sell sizzle.

Lecturer's words

The U.S. Patent Office has granted numerous patents for perpetual motion

machines based upon applications with complete detailed drawings. Some

years ago, however, the patent office began requiring working models of such a

machine before a patent would be granted. Result: no patents granted for

perpetual motion machines since that time.

Student's telegraphic sentences

1. Perpetual motion machine (drawings) = many patents.
2. Required working model = no patents since.

FIGURE 5.4   Examples of Telegraphic Sentences

TABLE 5.1   Abbreviations and Symbols

Use only the abbreviations that fit your needs and that you will remember easily. A good idea is to introduce only a few abbreviations into your note taking at a time.

1. Symbols are especially helpful in engineering and mathematics. Lists of commonly used symbols are given in most texts and reference books.

≠	does not equal
f	frequency

2. Create a family of symbols.

○	organism
⊙	individual
Ⓢ	individuals

3. Leave out the periods in standard abbreviations.

cf	compare
eg	for example
dept	department
NYC	New York City

4. Use only the first syllable of a word.

pol	politics
dem	democracy
lib	liberal
cap	capitalism

5. Use the entire first syllable and only the first letter of a second syllable.

subj	subject
cons	conservative
tot	totalitarianism
ind	individual

6. Eliminate final letters. Use just enough of the beginning of a word to form an easily recognizable abbreviation.

assoc	associate, associated
ach	achievement
biol	biological
info	information
intro	introduction
chem	chemistry
conc	concentration
max	maximum
rep	repetition

7. Omit vowels from the middle of words, and retain only enough consonants to provide a recognizable skeleton of the word.

bkgd	background
ppd	prepared
prblm	problem
estmt	estimate
gvt	government

8. Use an apostrophe in place of letters.

gov't	government
am't	amount

TABLE 5.1 *(Continued)*

cont'd	continued
educat'l	educational

9. Form the plural of a symbol or abbreviated word by adding "s."

□s	areas
chaps	chapters
coops	cooperatives
f̱s	frequencies
/s	ratios

10. Use "g" to represent *ing* endings.

decrg	decreasing
ckg	checking
estg	establishing
exptg	experimenting

11. Spell out short words such as "in," "at," "to," "but," "for," and "key." Symbols or abbreviations for short words will make the notes too dense with "shorthand."

12. Leave out unimportant verbs.

13. Leave out the words *a* and *the.*

14. If a term, phrase, or name is written out in full during the lecture, substitute initials whenever the term, phrase, or name is used again.

Initial writing:	Modern Massachusetts Party
Subsequently:	MMP

15. Use symbols for commonly recurring connective or transitional words.

&	and
w/	with
w/o	without
vs	against
∴	therefore
=	equals

SUMMARY

What is the purpose of taking notes?

The primary purpose of taking notes is to slow the process of forgetting by supplying a motivation that focuses your attention and by producing a written record to alleviate the task of trying to remember everything you've learned.

What is the value of the Cornell system?

The Cornell system enables you to take notes with ease and then master those notes once you've taken them.

What is the purpose of the cue column?

The cue column gives you room to write in cues that help you rehearse and master the information from lectures and text-book assignments.

What is the purpose of the summary area?

The summary area is where you sum up the most important ideas from each note sheet. It provides a quick synopsis for each sheet of your notes and helps you step back and take a broader look at what you learned so you don't get bogged down in specific facts.

What format should you use for taking notes?

Almost any format will work. One of the advantages of the Cornell system is that it accommodates a variety of note-taking styles.

How can you take notes more efficiently?

You can be more efficient by writing speedily and sparingly. Use modified printing and telegraphic sentences to jot down information quickly, and record only key ideas and examples.

HAVE YOU MISSED SOMETHING?

Matching. In each blank space in the left column, write the letter preceding the phrase in the right column that matches the left item best.

_d._ **1.** Margins

_e._ **2.** Flexibility

_f._ **3.** Outline

_a._ **4.** Attention

_b._ **5.** Instant feedback

_g._ **6.** Ideas

_c._ **7.** Cornell

a. Focused by the act of taking notes

b. Provided from taking notes

c. Time-honored system for taking notes

d. Distinguishing feature of the Cornell system

e. Permitted in the Cornell System's note-taking area

f. Only note-taking format expressly discouraged

g. Should take precedence over words in note-taking

Multiple choice. Choose the word or phrase that completes the following sentence most accurately, and circle the letter that precedes it.

1. The primary goal of taking notes is to
   a. keep you attentive during lectures.
   b. create advance organizers for review.
   c. provide you with a written record of lectures and assignments.
   d. encourage a head start on writing papers.

2. Ebbinghaus found that half of what you learn is forgotten
   a. immediately.
   b. within the hour.
   c. by the end of the day.
   d. by the end of the semester.

3. Your notes should consist mainly of
   a. key ideas.
   b. important examples.
   c. specific details.
   d. personal opinions.

4. The modified printing style is
   a. almost as fast as cursive.
   b. nearly as neat as printing.
   c. effective and easy to learn.
   d. all of the above.

5. In general, the notes you take should be
   a. speedy and sparing.
   b. timely and technical.
   c. drawn out and detailed.
   d. complete and concise.

True-false. Write *T* beside the *true* statements and *F* beside the *false* statements.

  F 1. When taking notes in lectures, you should strive to write down as much as you can.

  T 2. Each summary area should contain one or two general sentences.

  F 3. The amount of space in your short-term memory is virtually unlimited.

  T 4. Cornell-style note paper can be adapted from standard note paper.

_____ **5.** A carefully written set of notes can function as a handwritten textbook.

Short answer.   Supply a brief answer for each of the following items. The number in parentheses refers to the page where the item is discussed in the text.

1. In what way is a set of notes superior to a textbook chapter? (110–111)
2. What role does the cue column play in note taking? (111)
3. Name two advantages gained from filling in the summary area. (111)
4. What is the point of writing telegraphic sentences? (115)

BUILDING YOUR VOCABULARY STEP BY STEP: FINDING WORDS ON YOUR OWN FRONTIER

After much study, psychologist Johnson O'Connor concluded that learning new words is much like learning any other skill. We progress from simple words to more difficult ones in an orderly sequence. Using this idea, O'Connor developed the Frontier Vocabulary System, a method that adds words to your vocabulary in a way that follows natural learning processes.

According to the system, all words can be divided into three basic zones: the zone of known words, the zone of totally unknown words, and, between them, the frontier zone. It is in the frontier zone that most learning occurs.

There's no point in learning words from the zone of known words because by definition you already know them. These are words you've mastered. You use them in reading, writing, listening, and thinking.

Trying to learn from the zone of totally unknown words is equally pointless, but for a very different reason. These words are completely disconnected from your experience. You probably haven't heard or seen the words before, and it's unlikely that you would have much use for them if you had. Technical words from an unfamiliar subject are often unknown words, although the words don't always need to be obscure to be unknown.

Learning frontier words accomplishes three tasks simultaneously. Because the frontier words are connected with words you already know, you can make rapid progress in mastering these words. At the same time, your supply of frontier words is continuously replenished. Finally, as you learn new words and find others to replace them, your frontier zone pushes further into the zone of totally unknown words, reducing the words you don't know, while increasing the ones you have mastered.

Here's a list of words from the chapter you've just finished. (Page numbers indicate where.) Now that you have been introduced to the work of O'Connor and the theory behind the Frontier Vocabulary System, you may discover that many of these words belong in your own frontier.

adopted (111)	far-reaching (111)	punctuated (114)
bolster (109)	haphazardly (109)	rapidity (110)
circumvent (114)	illegible (114)	regimented (114)
continuity (111)	incentive (109)	sparing (114)
developed (110)	keystone (111)	stashing (111)
enables (109)	pitfall (111)	strive (114)
equipped (110)	potential (111)	surmise (110)
eroding (114)	primary (109)	unrehearsed (110)

Noting What's Important in Readings and Lectures

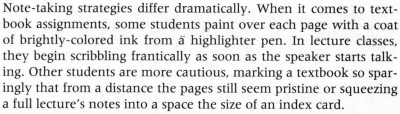

6

It shows not from afar; but seek and you shall find it.

Murasaki Shikibu
Author

Note-taking strategies differ dramatically. When it comes to textbook assignments, some students paint over each page with a coat of brightly-colored ink from a highlighter pen. In lecture classes, they begin scribbling frantically as soon as the speaker starts talking. Other students are more cautious, marking a textbook so sparingly that from a distance the pages still seem pristine or squeezing a full lecture's notes into a space the size of an index card.

Which approach is the better one? Or perhaps they're both right. Or they're both wrong. This chapter takes up this question and in doing so proposes a sensible, systematic note-taking method for readings and lectures. It's based on

- Building on what you already know
- Adopting an active approach to learning
- Paying attention to signals
- Detecting organizational patterns
- Keeping track of key ideas

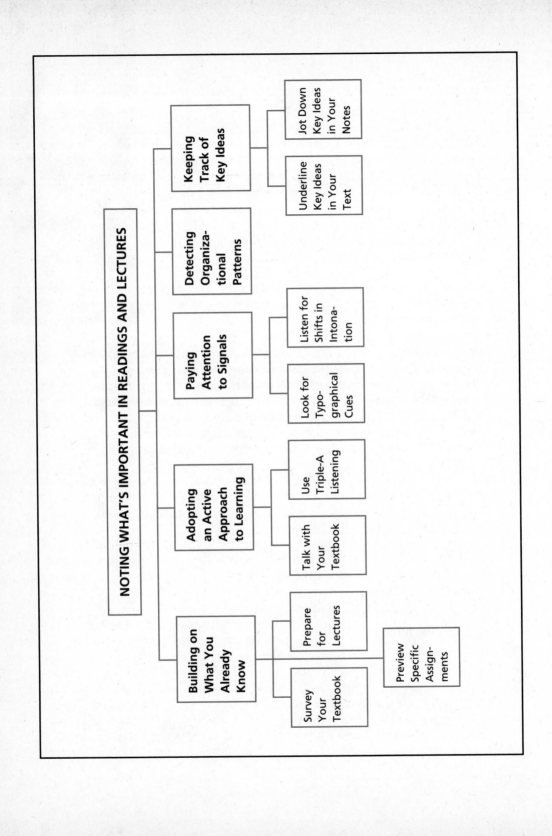

NOTING WHAT'S IMPORTANT IN READINGS AND LECTURES

Building on What You Already Know
- Survey Your Textbook
- Prepare for Lectures
- Preview Specific Assignments

Adopting an Active Approach to Learning
- Talk with Your Textbook
- Use Triple-A Listening

Paying Attention to Signals
- Look for Typographical Cues
- Listen for Shifts in Intonation

Detecting Organizational Patterns

Keeping Track of Key Ideas
- Underline Key Ideas in Your Text
- Jot Down Key Ideas in Your Notes

Most of the information you are exposed to in a college-level course comes from two sources: textbooks and lectures. Although the experiences of reading a textbook and listening to a lecture are undeniably different, they share the same basic and rather simple goal. Your purpose in reading and in listening is to get to the point of what has been written or said. It's rare that the essence of an entire chapter or lecture will be squeezed into a single sentence. Instead, you will more likely be introduced to a series of key ideas, important points, or principles that, when pieced together, will solve the puzzle of what the author or the lecturer is trying to convey.

Not surprisingly, therefore, when reading an assignment or listening to a lecture you should focus your attention on ferreting out key ideas. In general, the most successful students are those who are able to track down these all-important key ideas. Luckily, the process is far more methodical than mysterious.

First, you prepare for learning by building on what you already know. Second, you adopt an active approach to learning instead of waiting for the key ideas to simply reveal themselves to you. Third, you pay attention to specific signals that indicate what material is significant. Fourth, you set about detecting organizational patterns that provide a broader view of the direction in which a reading assignment or lecture may be heading. And finally, once you've gone to the effort to extract the key ideas, you keep track of what you've been able to discern.

BUILDING ON WHAT YOU ALREADY KNOW

Learning doesn't happen in a vacuum, and it doesn't happen all at once. For any new learning to take hold in your mind, it has to be connected to prior learning, to the knowledge you've already made your own. The process of connecting new information to old and comprehending a whole body of new information happens one step at a time.

The first place to start, whether you're approaching readings or lectures, is with the course syllabus. A typical syllabus provides an objective or a goal for the course and an overview of the course content. Use the syllabus to activate your mind about the subject of the course. At the beginning of the term, look over the syllabus for topics you already have some familiarity with, and spend a few minutes thinking about them. Notice, too, how and where they fit into the whole, how they relate to other topics you'll be studying in the course. Consult the syllabus throughout the term for specific reading assignments and lecture topics, and continue building your foundation by surveying your textbook, previewing specific assignments, and preparing for lectures.

Survey Your Textbook

Conducting a general survey of your entire textbook at the beginning of the term helps you understand the context of the book as a whole and of the chapters in particular. In this way, you get a head start on the semester, and you don't have to spend valuable time later on figuring out how all the pieces of the course fit together. Surveying includes reading the introductory material and previewing the book from front to back.

Read the Introductory Material   Most textbooks are written in a serious, scholarly tone. In the introductory material—which may be called "Preface," "To the Student," "Introduction," or something similar—the authors often take a more personal approach to their subjects and to their readers than they do in the body of the text. In the introductory material you have a chance to meet the authors as people and to get comfortable with them. Once you do, you'll find that you can converse and even argue with them as you read the text. Now and then, you'll find yourself saying, "No, I don't agree with that statement," or "What do you mean by that?"

In the introductory material you can also find valuable information on the concepts and content of the book. As a practical exercise, you might find it interesting to read the "To the Student" section of this book, if you have not already done so. Look for the following kinds of information:

The author's objective.   Learning the author's objective—the purpose or goal he or she meant to achieve—enables you to read and interpret the text appropriately. For instance, the authors of *American Government* state their objectives this way:

> As in the first edition, we have kept two major goals in mind. First and foremost, we present a concise yet comprehensive picture of American government and politics. . . . Our second goal is tied closely to the first. . . . We encourage students to think critically by confronting certain myths that they or other Americans may hold about government. Thus each chapter begins with a brief exposition of one or two preconceptions or misconceptions found in discussions of politics.[1]

---

[1]Alan R. Gitelson, Robert L. Dudley, and Melvin J. Dubnick, *American Government*, 2nd ed. (Boston: Houghton Mifflin, 1991), p. xiv.

These few sentences tell you straight off what you can expect and what particular approach the authors will be taking.

The organizational plan of the book. Having the book's organizational plan is like having a road map. You know not only what the authors are doing but also where they are going. In the following example, you're told the title and focus of each of the book's three parts and are given examples of some of the topics that will be covered in each part:

> The text is built on a three-part framework. Part One, "Foundations of Communication," introduces basic theoretical concepts, including an overview of the communication process as well as verbal and nonverbal transactions, critical thinking, ethics, and listening.

> Part Two: "Personal Communication," covers intrapersonal and interpersonal communication. Personal relationships, communication apprehension, the interview, and small-group functions—among other topics—are discussed.

> Part Three, "Public Communication," focuses on planning, developing, structuring, and presenting successful informative, and persuasive briefings and speeches.[2]

How and why the book is different. Recognizing what makes the textbook unique enables you to read with greater awareness and comprehension and to avoid the trap of thinking this book is just "more of the same old stuff." Notice how the specificity of the following example lets you know right away where to direct your attention: "What makes *All of Us* stand apart from other reading texts is its devotion to a curriculum of inclusion. . . . We tried to compile the richest and most ethnically diverse reading matter available."[3]

The author's qualifications. Writers usually try in some subtle way to let the reader know that their book is written by an expert on the subject and that therefore the information is trustworthy and credible. Note in the following example how the writers describe their relationship with the subject matter in a way that inspires confidence and belief in the value of their opinions:

> Economically and politically, the world has changed with the initiative of the European Community to reach economic integration (1992 initiative) and the liberalization of Eastern Europe, culminating with the dramatic events in the Soviet Union in August 1991. As authors, we have

---

[2]Roy M. Berko, Andrew D. Wolvin, and Darlyn R. Wolvin, *Communicating: A Social and Career Focus,* 5th ed. (Boston: Houghton Mifflin, 1992), pp. xv–xvi.
[3]Harvey S. Wiener and Charles Bazerman, *All of Us: A Multicultural Reading Skills Handbook* (Boston: Houghton Mifflin, 1992), p. xi.

benefited enormously from being close to these changes, both through our contacts as well as our extended trips and teaching assignments in Europe. In addition, we have worked extensively with companies who are about to embark on new types of global strategies.[4]

Supplementary learning aids. Most textbook authors provide learning aids to help you understand the material. The introductory material generally names these aids and tells how they'll benefit you. In addition to these in-text features, supplementary materials such as workbooks, study guides, computer programs, and videos are often available. Reading the introductory material will alert you to the presence of these features and ancillary materials, as you can see from the following example:

> To help students understand the various topics, we have included several pedagogical features in each chapter. **Preview outlines** open each chapter and point-by-point **summaries** appear at the end of each chapter. The **conclusion** of each chapter provides a retrospective glance at the myths in light of the whole chapter discussion.
>
> In the second edition, each chapter now ends with a list of **definitions** of **key terms and concepts** that have been used in that chapter. We have increased the number of key terms and concepts set off in boldface in the text in this edition. These terms and concepts are also defined in a **glossary** at the end of the book. A chapter-by-chapter listing of **suggested readings** on topics covered throughout the text appears at the end of the book. And an **appendix** contains important documents, such as the Declaration of Independence, the Constitution, *Federalist Papers* Nos. 10 and 51, and a list of presidents.[5]

Preview from Front to Back   After you've read the introductory material, survey the rest of the book. Begin by scanning the table of contents, which lists the parts, the chapters, and sometimes the major headings within each chapter. The contents shows the overall organization of the book and how the chapter topics relate to one another. It also shows whether the book contains extra material, such as appendixes, glossaries, bibliographies or references, and indexes.

Now turn to the back of the book and look at these extra sections. Appendixes contain additional information such as tables and graphs, documents, or details about a specific aspect of a subject. Glossaries are specialized dictionaries of terms common to the subject the book discusses. Bibliographies and references list the sources the authors consulted in writing the book and can point you in the direction of further readings. Indexes—alpha-

---

[4]Jean Pierre Jeannet and Hubert D. Hennessey, *Global Marketing Strategies,* 2nd ed. (Boston: Houghton Mifflin, 1992), p. xix.
[5]Gitelson, Dudley, and Dubnick, *American Government,* p. xvi.

betical listings of significant topics, ideas, and names that appear in the text along with page references—give you a sense of the scope of the book and help you locate specific material quickly.

By familiarizing yourself with your textbook, you not only bolster your background knowledge about the subject but also become aware of the features of the book you can use throughout the term. As a result, future assignments will be easier and less time consuming, and you'll have a greater chance to master the material.

Preview Specific Assignments

Previewing specific assignments allows you to overcome inertia, delve into the text, and get a sense of the larger picture into which you can fit specific ideas and fact. When previewing, you can use any or all of these techniques:

Think about the title. Take a few moments to reflect on the chapter's title. Is its meaning obvious? If not, can you guess what the chapter will discuss?

Read the introduction and the summary. Although they may not be marked as such, textbook chapters frequently include an introductory paragraph, a brief summary at the end, or both. Reading these paragraphs provides advance organizers, which create a framework on which you can build the information in the chapter.

Look over headings and subheadings. Flip through the pages and read the headings. Notice their hierarchy and sequence as you do.

Take note of any information set apart from the rest of the text. In general, information that is *boxed, boldfaced, bulleted* (preceded with dots or squares), *screened* (printed on a gray or colored background), or otherwise set apart is information that you won't want to miss. Take a moment to look it over now so you will already be familiar with it when you go back to read the chapter completely.

Glance at the visuals. Pictures and graphic materials can provide a distillation of an entire chapter's ideas in less than a page. The concept maps on the second page of each chapter in this book, for example, show the chapter at a glance. Other visuals supply vivid and easy-to-understand examples of key points.

You may want to limit the amount of time you spend surveying your book. Your primary purpose is to read and understand the chapter. If you spend too much time preparing to read, you'll run out of time and energy for the actual reading. Or as an old Chinese proverb warns, "Keep sharpening your knife and it will grow dull."

Prepare for Lectures

You can't glance through a lecture in advance in the same way you can preview a textbook assignment. But you can make your foundational knowledge stronger so you are better prepared when the lecture begins. There are three ways to do so: Use great recall, go over your notes, and arrive early to class.

Use Gibbon's "Great Recall"   The great English historian Edward Gibbon (1737–1794), author of *History of the Decline and Fall of the Roman Empire,* made constant use of *great recall.* He spent hours alone in his study or on long solitary walks recalling everything he knew about a subject. As he pondered some major idea, he was continually surprised by how many other ideas and fragments of ideas surfaced as well.

Gibbon's system was highly successful. His old ideas were brought to the forefront of his mind ready for use, where they could act as magnets for new ideas and new information. You can apply the same principle by spending some time pondering what you already know about the subject of an upcoming lecture.

Go Over Your Lecture Notes   Looking over previous notes not only provides you with a review of what you've already learned but it also puts you in a receptive frame of mind for the upcoming lecture. Remember that lectures normally follow in a logical progression. That means today's lecture will usually provide the background for the lecture that follows.

Arrive Early to Class   From a practical standpoint, coming to class with time to spare enables you to find a good seat, get out your notebook as well as your pen or pencil, and clear your desk of anything that might constitute a distraction during the lecture. At the same time as you're clearing your desk of distractions, clear your mind of intrusions, and focus your attention on the upcoming lecture. Giving yourself these few minutes to prepare means you'll be thinking along those lines long before the instructor says a word.

Read material

ADOPTING AN ACTIVE APPROACH TO LEARNING

Building a foundation for your learning is only the first step to knowledge. The way to make learning *last* is by acting as a full partner in the process.

That means talking with your textbook, instead of just receiving its information, and listening to a lecture, instead of just hearing it.

Talk with Your Textbook

Taking an active approach to reading involves making a fundamental change in your attitude toward textbooks. Instead of approaching a textbook as a passive recipient of its information, you engage in a dialogue between your thoughts and those on the page. You do this by listening to what you read, formulating questions as you read, and following other tips for active reading.

Listening to What You Read The best reading occurs when you use intonation, which is the natural rise and fall of your speaking voice. This doesn't mean reading out loud, but it does mean reading with expression. Intonation helps you combine individual words into meaningful mental "bites."

To engage in intonation, as your eyes move rapidly across the page as usual, let your mind swing along each line with an intonational rhythm that can be heard by your "inner ear." Read the line expressively. In doing so, you will be supplying the important rhythm, stress, emphasis, and pauses that were taken out when the words were turned into written form. This will put the meaning of the words more quickly within your grasp.

To illustrate intonational reading, the passage in Figure 6.1 has been divided into "thought units." These units are separated by slash marks. (Of course, different readers would group these words into different clusters, depending on individual intonational styles.) You will probably notice how

---

Athens and Sparta / were both Greek cities / and their people / spoke a common language. / In every other respect / they were different. / Athens rose high from the plain. / It was a city / exposed to the fresh breezes / from the sea, / willing to look / at the world / with the eyes / of a happy child. / Sparta, / on the other hand, / was built / at the bottom / of a deep valley, / and used the surrounding mountains / as a barrier / against foreign thought. / Athens / was a city of busy trade. / Sparta / was an armed camp. /

FIGURE 6.1 Using Intonation to Hear What You Read
Source: Reprinted from The Story of Mankind *by Henry B. van Loon and Gerard W. van Loon, by permission of Liveright Publishing Corporation. Copyright © 1972 by Henry B. van Loon and Gerard W. van Loon.*

rapidly your eyes move and how easily you comprehend the meaning when you read with intonation.

To make silent intonation a regular habit, take a few minutes to read aloud in the privacy of your room. This will establish your own speech patterns in your mind so you will "hear" them more readily when you read silently.

Formulate Questions as You Read   Reading with intonation enables you to hear the textbook's authors as you read. You can hold up your end of the conversation by constantly formulating questions as you read, by wondering out loud about issues or aspects that concern you, and by writing out questions that help you pinpoint and remember the most important information. The latter really serves as the foundation for taking notes and mastering them.

Follow Other Tips for Active Reading   Engaging your book in steady conversation is the best way to encourage active reading. But there are some other ways to ensure that you stay on your toes as you move through a textbook assignment.

Relax. Stress can hinder both learning and remembering, the two most important aspects of reading.[6] Before you begin reading, take a moment to use one of the relaxation techniques recommended in Chapter 1. Optimum learning occurs when you are in a relaxed state. Keep in mind that being relaxed is not the same as being sluggish. A sense of relaxation makes you more, not less, alert and relieves the stress and anxiety that can make learning a chore.

Vary your speed as you read.   Match the speed of your reading to what you are reading. If the chapter starts out with some introductory material, move through that section quickly. When you come to the first substantial paragraph, slow down and start looking for important names, terms, and ideas. These will often serve as keys to the rest of the chapter. Once you're clear on what the chapter is going to cover and how, you can pick up the pace of your reading. But be ready to slow down when you come across a paragraph that's filled with new ideas. There is no reason to expect that you will read at a constant rate.

Focus on the ideas, not the words.   Memory research has shown that we remember the gist of what we've read, not the actual words. So if you get

---

[6]Kenneth L. Higbee, *Your Memory: How It Works and How to Improve It,* 2nd ed. (New York: Prentice-Hall, 1988), pp. 64–65.

bogged down in a difficult sentence, read it through once while skipping any modifying phrases. Find the simple subject of the sentence, the verb, and the simple object to avoid getting lost in a maze of language. (Extend this process to an entire paragraph if necessary.) When the framework of this sentence shows through clearly, so that you can grasp the main idea, then go back and read the material with all its "trimmings" to get the full sense of what's being communicated.

✓   *Use the Corson technique.*   Dale Corson, former president of Cornell University, recognized the role that well-composed questions could play in getting to the heart of a difficult concept. He observed that engineers and other students in science and mathematics must often crack the meaning of an idea or concept one sentence at a time. If comprehension does not occur even at this snail's pace, then students should ask their instructors for help. "But before you do," says Dr. Corson, "ask yourself this question: What is it that I don't understand?"[7] When you go for help, you should be able to say, "I understand and follow the author's idea up to this point and even beyond this point, but this particular section has no meaning for me." That way, the instructor knows how to help you as well as what you have done to achieve understanding. And by analyzing and verbalizing your problem, you may even be able to solve it yourself.

Use Triple-A Listening

A lecture's value can be extracted only through listening. But listening is not the same as hearing. It isn't simply a matter of acting as a human microphone and picking up the sound of the lecturer's voice. Listening is a conscious activity based on three basic skills: *a*ttitude, *a*ttention, and *a*djustment. These skills are known collectively as *triple-A listening.*

Maintain a Constructive Attitude   A positive attitude paves the way for open-mindedness. As businessperson and author Kevin J. Murphy says in *Effective Listening,* "Minds are like parachutes; they only function when open."[8]

Don't assume from the outset that a lecture is going to be dull. And even if the lecturer makes statements you don't agree with, don't decide he or she is automatically wrong. If you hear something that rubs you the wrong way, write it down, but keep on listening. Voice your opinion by

---

[7]Personal interview with the author.
[8]Kevin J. Murphy, *Effective Listening: Hearing What People Say and Making It Work for You* (New York: Bantam Books, 1987), p. 28.

asking intelligent, clarifying questions after the lecture. In the meantime, don't let reactive interference prevent you from recalling the speaker's key points (see Chapter 4). All in all, attitude involves giving the lecturer the benefit of the doubt.

Strive to Pay Attention   You cannot attain concentration by concentrating on the act of concentration. Your attention must focus on the lecture. Deep thinking is vital. When you hear a lecture, the words enter your short-term memory, where they have to be swiftly processed into ideas. Attentive listening sets that process in motion. If you do not process the speaker's words through attentive listening that results from focus and concentration, they will be dumped from short-term memory and will be gone forever. But if you process the words into ideas, in a flash the ideas will be stored in your long-term memory.

One of the inherent problems with lectures is that thought is faster than speech. When a lecturer speaks slowly, a listener has moments of free time to dart off on mental side trips. To keep your mind from wandering, concentrate fully on what the speaker is saying. When you have time to think between ideas, mentally enumerate the ideas that have been expressed and then summarize them. Keep alternating in this way throughout the lecture.

If you truly want to pay attention but can't, you're probably being distracted. Tune out auditory and visual disturbances by riveting your eyes on the speaker when you have a chance and by focusing on note taking the rest of the time.

Cultivate a Capacity for Adjustment   Although some speakers clearly indicate what they intend to cover in their lectures, you need to be flexible enough to follow a lecture regardless of the direction it may take. Sometimes a speaker says, "This event had three important results" and then goes on to discuss four or five. Other times a question from the audience suddenly shifts the speaker's focus. In such cases, you can't simply tune out the parts of the lecture that don't fit with your expectations. You have to be able to "roll with the punches." That's why adjustment is such an important component of active listening.

If, however, you are thoroughly lost, or if the speaker's message is not coming across and you need to ask a clarifying question, do so. The speaker will be encouraged and gratified to know that the audience is interested, and you can feel good about raising a question that was probably troubling less intrepid members of the audience.

PAYING ATTENTION TO SIGNALS

Although some textbook assignments can be hard to understand and some lectures difficult to follow, it is safe to say that no author or speaker is deliberately trying to obscure his or her ideas. On the contrary, both readings and lectures are peppered with signal words designed to keep you on track and lead you directly to the key ideas. If, as a note taker, you know the importance and meaning of these signal words and phrases (see Table 6.1), you'll be able to perceive the organization and direction of the information you read and hear.

In addition to signal words, textbook passages and classroom lectures offer further clues for pinpointing important information: typography and intonation.

Look for Typographical Cues

Open any textbook and you'll quickly discover that the words aren't all printed in the same size or the same style. The format may differ from text to text, but in general each book takes advantage of a variety of type sizes and styles to convey its information. By noting these typographical differences, you can pick up on signals for organization and emphasis.

Boldface (thick, dark type) often signals a textbook heading or subheading. It may also be used to draw your attention to a specific principle, definition, or key word within the text.

Italics (type that slopes to the right) places emphasis on a word or a phrase.

Underlining often performs the same functions as either boldface or italics, depending on the format of the particular textbook.

- "Bullets" (small markers, often circular or square) set off the items in lists.

Size, color and placement of type often call attention to headings or subheadings. Take note of words printed in larger type, in color, or on lines by themselves.

You can usually crack a book's particular typographical code simply by skimming through your text before you start reading. In addition, look for an explanation of format—especially if it is unconventional—in the book's introductory material.

TABLE 6.1   Signal Words and Phrases

Categories and Examples	When you come across these words, immediately think...

Example Words
   to illustrate
   for example
   for instance
	"Here comes an example. Must be double-checking to make sure I understood the point just made."

Time Words
   before, after
   formerly
   subsequently
   prior
   meanwhile
	"Hmm! A time relationship is being established. Let's see: What came first, what came last, and what came in-between?"

Addition Words
   furthermore
   in addition
   moreover
   also
	"Seems there's always something else that needs to be added. Must be worth remembering."

Cause-and-Effect Words
   therefore
   as a result
   if...then
   accordingly
   thus, so
	"There's an effect word. Better check back when I have a chance to make sure I can find the cause now that I know what the effect is."

Contrast Words
   on the other hand
   in contrast
   conversely
   pros and cons
   although
	"Here comes the other side of the coin. Let's see how it differs from what's already been said."

Enumeration Words
   the four steps...
   first, second, third
   next
   finally
	"That's a lot of steps. I'd better be sure I'm keeping track of all of them and getting them in the right order."

Listen for Shifts in Intonation

Clearly, lecturers aren't able to use different kinds of type, but they do have analogous tools at their disposal: their voices. Most college lecturers speak about 120 words per minute, which means that in a fifty-minute lecture you hear roughly 6,000 words. Listening for signals in a lecture is an especially helpful activity because, unlike in reading, you don't have the luxury of retracing your steps if you discover you're lost. In addition to

TABLE 6.1 *(Continued)*

Categories and Examples	When you come across these words, immediately think...

Emphasis Words
   more important
   above all
   remember
	"Looks as though what's coming up is going to be important."

Repeat Words
   in other words
   it simply means
   that is
   briefly
   in essence
	"Here comes another explanation. Maybe I'll understand this one a little better."

Swivel Words
   however
   nevertheless
   yet
   but
   still
	"Looks like there's going to be a little bit of doubt or 'give back' on the point just made. Better pay attention to this qualifying remark."

Concession Words
   to be sure
   indeed
   though
   granted
   of course
	"Okay. Here comes an argument or two from the opposing point of view."

Summary Words
   in a nutshell
   to sum up
   in conclusion
	"Good. Now I'll get a simple wrap-up of the points that have been made. It's almost sure to be full of key ideas."

Test Words (lectures only)
   This is important.
   Remember this.
   You'll see this again.
   Here's a pitfall.
	"Sounds like a potential test item. Better be sure to pay close attention to it."

words, intonation—variations in the lecturer's voice—is the most significant signal in spoken language. Intonation has three components: volume, pauses, and cadence.

Volume In general, the introduction of a crucial idea is preceded by a change in volume; the speaker raises or lowers his or her voice.

Pauses By pausing before and after main ideas, a speaker sets these ideas apart from the rest of the lecture. She or he uses pauses to achieve a dramatic effect and, on a practical level, to provide note-takers with extra writing time.

Cadence The rhythm of a lecturer's speaking patterns can be particularly helpful. Often, like the bulleted lists you find in textbooks, the speaker lists a series of important ideas by using a steady speaking rhythm, sometimes even beginning each idea with the same words or phrase. Whenever you detect these oral signals, your pencil should be moving steadily, adding these important points to your notes.

DETECTING ORGANIZATIONAL PATTERNS

Signal words enable you to keep track of the individual twists and turns in the chapter you are reading or the lecture you are listening to. Of course, gaining a broader view of where things are heading is even more useful. The kind of perspective you gain from an outline, a summary, or some recognized type of organizational pattern gives you the luxury of anticipating each new idea and of following your own progress.

Many of the signal words not only assist you in finding your way through a particular sentence, but also hint at a larger pattern. For example, suppose you've come across the signal words *then* and *next* in a reading or lecture. Spotting these two words may lead you to conclude that the author or speaker is following a process pattern. You may say to yourself, "Yes, I see what she's doing. She's explaining the steps involved in adopting a bill into law." Once you've drawn this conclusion, thanks to the clues provided by the signal words, you have a better understanding of the way the information is organized.

The process pattern is just one of the many organizational patterns used in both writing and speaking. Here are brief descriptions of the most commonly used patterns. You should have no trouble recognizing them when you run into them in a reading or a lecture, especially after you've been tipped off by a signal word or two.

Time or chronological pattern.   Events are presented in the chronological order in which they occurred. This pattern can be recognized quickly from its use of dates or from the presence of signal words such as "in previous years," "the next day," and "two years later," all of which denote the passage of time.

Process pattern.   Steps or events are presented in an orderly sequence that leads to a desired situation or product. A recipe for chocolate cake and instructions for assembling a bicycle are examples of process patterns. They often include signal words such as "first," "after this," "then," "next," and "finally."

Place or spatial pattern.   Items are presented or discussed on the basis of their locations or their arrangement relative to each other. For example, an author might use this pattern to describe the geographical features of the United States from the West Coast to the East Coast. In such a case, this pattern is often called the "geographical pattern." It is also called the "topical pattern" when used to describe the organization of a corporation along the lines of purchasing, manufacturing, sales, and so forth. The progression from item to item is usually orderly and easy to follow: from left to right, high to low, north to south, and so on.

Increasing-importance pattern.   In this pattern, the most important or most dramatic item in a series is placed at the end. A crescendo effect is created as each succeeding item becomes more important than the previous one.

Decreasing-importance pattern.   In this pattern, the most important or most dramatic item in a series is placed at the beginning. Such an organization grabs the interest of the listener or reader almost immediately.

Cause-and-effect pattern.   This pattern includes variations such as the "problem-cause-solution pattern" and the "problem-effect-solution pattern." Whatever the combination, you should be able to identify the various parts of the pattern—the problem, cause, effects, and solution—and think along with the author or speaker as you move from one part of the discussion to the next.

Compare or contrast pattern.   Comparisons stress similarities whereas contrasts emphasize differences. In this pattern, individual characteristics may be compared or contrasted one at a time, or lists of characteristics may be discussed as a group. In either case, the pattern can be recognized from the various similarities or differences and from signal words such as "similarly," "likewise," "conversely," and "on the other hand."

KEEPING TRACK OF KEY IDEAS

Your purpose both in reading a textbook assignment and listening to a lecture is to track down the key ideas that facilitate understanding. Preparation helps put you in the proper frame of mind, signals point you in the right direction, and organizational patterns provide a context for these ideas.

The next step is to make a note of these key ideas. If a key idea is especially important or particularly difficult, you may also want to record supporting points and memorable examples that clarify or elaborate the idea.

Whether you are taking notes by marking directly in your text or jotting information down on Cornell-style note paper, your goal will be the same. But the procedure you use will differ slightly with the differing format.

Underline Key Ideas in Your Text

Read your textbook assignments a paragraph at a time. When you come to the end of a paragraph, look back at it and determine which sentence or sentences are most important. Then underline the key idea. In a different color, or with a different pen or pencil, mark any especially important secondary ideas you find. If you are marking your book with a highlighter pen, use another color or another writing instrument to mark the supporting ideas. You want to be able to pick out the key ideas easily without confusing them with ideas of lesser importance.

Remember that each paragraph generally has only one key idea, so be careful not to overmark your textbook or mark it hastily. A textbook assignment in which you have highlighted or underlined virtually every other sentence or where you have mistaken minor points for major ones will do you little good when you begin reviewing and mastering your material.

Jot Down Key Ideas in Your Notes

When it comes to lectures, use signals and organizational patterns to help pick out the key ideas. Record each key idea in the summary area of your Cornell-style note sheet. Also jot down important supporting material and clarifying examples. Be sure to differentiate these secondary points from the primary ones. For example, you may want to capitalize or underline the main ideas. Or perhaps you'd prefer to indent the supporting materials beneath the key ideas they refer to. Whatever system you devise, use it consistently to keep your notes clear and reliable.

SUMMARY

What's the goal in reading a textbook assignment or listening to a lecture?	The purpose in each case is the same: to track down the key ideas and discover how they connect.

How do you build on what you already know so that effective learning can take place?

Start off by scanning the course syllabus and thinking about the objectives and subject of the course. In addition, at the beginning of the semester systematically survey the textbook. Then throughout the course, preview each reading assignment, and refresh your memory of the subject matter before each lecture.

What is meant by "talking with your textbook"?

Reading a textbook should be like engaging in a conversation: You listen carefully and then you respond. Listening to a passage in your textbook means becoming aware of its intonation, the rises and falls in the words you would hear if the sentences were spoken. When you can hear what you read, it becomes easier to do what is natural in conversation—respond with questions and comments.

What are the components of triple-A listening?

The *A*'s in *triple-A* refer to attitude, attention, and adjustment, the three basic criteria of active listening. You can actively follow a lecture by adopting an open-minded attitude to what you're hearing, by truly paying attention, and by remaining flexible enough to adjust to any unexpected twists or turns the lecture may take.

What are signal words and what is their purpose?

Signal words are those words that provide you with clues as to where information in a chapter or lecture is going. Their purpose is to help you organize information, recognize key ideas, and notice shifts in focus in the text or lecture.

What is the value of detecting organizational patterns?

Searching out organizational patterns enables you to determine how the chapter or lecture has been arranged. Once you understand this, you have an easier time following and anticipating the information.

What should you do when you spot the key ideas in a reading or lecture?

When you find these ideas, mark or underline the ideas in your textbook, or jot them down in the note-taking area of a Cornell-style note sheet.

HAVE YOU MISSED SOMETHING?

Matching. In each blank space in the left column, write the letter preceding the phrase in the right column that matches the left item best.

__d__ **1.** Intonation

__f g__ **2.** Attention

__e__ **3.** Ideas

__b__ **4.** Surveying

__a__ **5.** Introduction

__c f__ **6.** Adjustment

a. Gives the author a chance to be more informal with the reader

b. Serves as a preview for what's to come in the book

c. Listening skill that enables you to follow unexpected changes in a lecture

d. Replaces the rhythm, stress, emphasis, and expression often lost in writing

e. Should serve as the primary focus of reading

f. Enables words to be processed into ideas

Multiple choice. Choose the word or phrase that completes the following sentence most accurately, and circle the letter that precedes it.

1. The introductory material in a textbook does *not* include
    a. the book's purpose.
    b. the author's credentials.
    c. the book's organization.
    d. the course's objective.

2. The value of surveying your textbook is that it
    a. allows you merely to skim your reading assignments.
    b. motivates you to do additional reading on the subject.
    c. allows you to find the answers at the back of the book.
    d. bolsters your knowledge of the subject.

3. Reading with intonation means reading with
    a. a partner.
    b. a loud voice.
    c. expression.
    d. apprehension.

4. A lecture that explains how to install a computer is following a
    _____ pattern.
    a. decreasing-importance

    b. process
    c. chronological
    d. cause-and-effect

True-false.   Write *T* beside the *true* statements and *F* beside the *false* statements.

F   **1.** Sophisticated authors and speakers deliberately try to make their ideas difficult to decipher.

F   **2.** The introductory material in a textbook is of limited value.

T   **3.** Most college lecturers speak about 120 words per minute.

T   **4.** In listening, attitude involves giving the lecturer the benefit of the doubt.

T   **5.** Textbook reading gives you a chance to hold a continuing conversation with the author.

F   **6.** You should always read at a constant rate of speed.

Short answer.   Supply a brief answer for each of the following items. The number in parentheses refers to the page where the item is discussed in the text.

1. Why is building on what you already know the first step in learning new information? (125)
2. What distinguishes active reading from your usual approach to reading? (131)
3. What are the benefits of talking with your textbook? (131–133)
4. How do signal words increase your understanding of a text or lecture? (135)

BUILDING YOUR VOCABULARY STEP BY STEP: WHERE TO FIND NEW WORDS

If you're interested in searching for words to add to your vocabulary, you need look no further than the realm of your own experience. The very best new words are words you don't really know, although you've heard them, read them, or even used them in writing or conversation. You've probably been exposed to hundreds of words that fit this description.

To find words that are logical additions to your vocabulary, first become aware of your daily speech, making a list of the unusual words you use. Next, listen attentively while others speak. Although you may know and recognize many of the words you hear, you may not be able to precisely define them all. Television and radio newscasts often provide excellent examples of words you hear again and again and yet don't really know. Finally, be on the lookout for words you recognize in your reading but do not use in speaking or writing. You may have found words of this sort in the chapter you've just finished. The following list is made up of words from the chapter (with page number references). Look them over and decide which words would be appropriate to add to your vocabulary.

components (134)	intonation (131)	pristine (123)
crescendo (139)	intrepid (134)	riveting (134)
denote (138)	luxury (136)	scholarly (126)
engaging (132)	outset (133)	standpoint (130)
enumerate (134)	passive (131)	topical (139)
hinder (132)		

Mastering Your Material

7

Order and simplification are the first steps toward the mastery of a subject—the actual enemy is the unknown.

THOMAS MANN
Author

Between the time you close your textbook or leave the classroom and the moment you begin answering a test or writing a term paper, you need to commit to memory the important ideas you've read and heard so they're ready when you need them. To get you started in mastering your material, this chapter takes a look at

- Learning the requirements of mastery
- Conducting an immediate review
- Converting key ideas into questions
- Summarizing your information
- Reflecting on your notes
- Using a study system

145

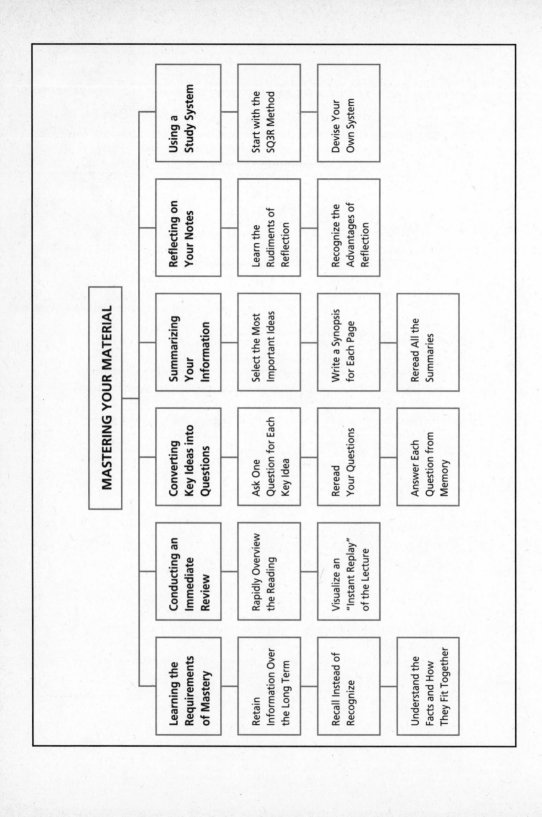

MASTERING YOUR MATERIAL

Learning the Requirements of Mastery
- Retain Information Over the Long Term
- Recall Instead of Recognize
- Understand the Facts and How They Fit Together

Conducting an Immediate Review
- Rapidly Overview the Reading
- Visualize an "Instant Replay" of the Lecture

Converting Key Ideas into Questions
- Ask One Question for Each Key Idea
- Reread Your Questions
- Answer Each Question from Memory

Summarizing Your Information
- Select the Most Important Ideas
- Write a Synopsis for Each Page
- Reread All the Summaries

Reflecting on Your Notes
- Learn the Rudiments of Reflection
- Recognize the Advantages of Reflection

Using a Study System
- Start with the SQ3R Method
- Devise Your Own System

S ometimes described as "knowing things cold" or "inside and out," mastery is your primary tactic for protecting what you've learned against forgetting. Once you know the requirements for mastery, you can master material from readings and lectures by conducting an immediate review, converting key ideas into questions, summarizing your information, reflecting on your notes, and combining these steps into a study system.

LEARNING THE REQUIREMENTS OF MASTERY

Mastery involves retaining information over the long term, learning that information to the point of recall, and understanding the facts and how they fit together.

Retain Information Over the Long Term

Newly learned ideas rest in a precarious position in short-term memory, an informational limbo where data wait until they are either retained or lost forever. In most cases, information makes the leap from short-term to long-term memory only after it has been processed repeatedly or connected with information already in long-term memory. Mastery provides opportunities for both.

Recall Instead of Recognize

One all-too-common method of studying—simply reading and rereading your assignments again and again—may eventually enable you to recognize information when you encounter it in a test but discourages you from studying to the point of recall. There is an important distinction between recognition and recall. Unlike recognition, which is triggered by a cue such as a familiar face or an option in a multiple-choice question, recall occurs when you are able to retrieve a piece of information from memory without any hints or cues.

If someone asked you to name the capital of Massachusetts and you came up with the answer *Boston*, you'd be demonstrating pure recall. If someone asked you to name the only U.S. president who was a bachelor, you might be stumped. "I know the answer," you might say, "but I just can't come up with it." But if you were given a list of presidents to choose from

Franklin D. Roosevelt

Gerald R. Ford

James Buchanan

Thomas Jefferson

you probably would have no trouble identifying James Buchanan as the bachelor president. You recognized this name. You did not recall it even though it may have been buried somewhere in your memory. You required a hint to trigger your answer.

Understand the Facts and How They Fit Together

Unlike rereading, which normally halts learning at the recognition stage, mastery brings studying to the point of recall. Rather than simply serving as a method for learning facts and ideas in isolation, mastery ensures that you learn information in context. When reinforced and integrated in this way, the knowledge you glean from your studying has a far greater chance of being retained.

If you've watched people in an art museum, you've probably noticed that those visitors who are looking at paintings appear to be doing a strange sort of dance, walking up closely to examine each work of art and then stepping back, walking up closely again and again stepping back. If you've ever done a jigsaw puzzle, you've probably followed a similar process. You alternate between picking out pieces to fit together and consulting the picture on the lid of the box to compare how your picture is progressing.

Many of us understand instinctively with pictures what we need to know with words. Mastery follows the same stepping up, stepping back process we use in examining pictures. To master something thoroughly, you need to step up by learning and reciting the individual ideas, and you need to step back by reviewing, summarizing, and reflecting on how those ideas relate to one another.

CONDUCTING AN IMMEDIATE REVIEW

You can begin mastering your notes on a reading or a lecture as soon as you have taken them. The first step is to rapidly review the material. By refreshing your memory right away, you reinforce your brain's original record of the new information and ensure that the key ideas will remain in your memory until you have time for prolonged study.

Rapidly Overview the Reading

After you've completed a reading assignment, step back and quickly overview what you've just read. Here are two ways to do so:

1. *Reread the abstract, introduction, or summary.* Any one of these three common elements provides a brief overview of what you've just read and puts the ideas you've picked up in an appropriate context.

2. *Reread the title and headings.* If the text doesn't include an obvious overview, create one yourself by rereading the title, headings, and subheadings. In combination, these elements can help you mentally organize the information you've just learned. Don't spend a great deal of time doing this rereading. The purpose is primarily to refresh your memory of the important points so that later you'll be able to focus more carefully on them. If you find you have any questions, jot these down so you can ask them in class.

Visualize an "Instant Replay" of the Lecture

As you're leaving the lecture room, mentally recall the lecture from beginning to end. Visualize the classroom and the lecturer and any blackboard work. After mentally recalling the lecture, ask yourself some questions to bring the lecture into greater focus: What was the central point of the lecture? What did I learn? How does what I learned fit in with what I already know? If you discover that you don't quite understand something, no matter how small, make a note of it, and ask the instructor to explain it before the next class.

CONVERTING KEY IDEAS INTO QUESTIONS

In your first study session after you've read an assignment or attended a lecture, expand your notes into mastery tools. Look at each key idea you've jotted down or underlined, and write a question that it answers. Then gain a new perspective on the material by reading over just your questions, and begin to solidify the material in your mind by answering each question from memory.

Ask One Question for Each Key Idea

Each key idea in your notes can be seen as the answer to a question. With that in mind, take a moment to think in reverse. You already have the answer. Now see if you can come up with the question. Your goal is to devise a specific question for which the key idea is the only appropriate answer.

If you're taking notes on Cornell-style paper, jot each question in the cue column alongside the idea to which it refers. You'll now have a column of questions and a column of answers, much like the summary questions and answers toward the end of each chapter in this book.

If you've written your notes directly in your textbook, strive for a similar setup by writing your question in the margin next to the sentence or sentences in each paragraph that you underlined or otherwise marked. Figure 7.1 provides an example. Of course, some textbook margins may provide you with very little room for writing. If that's the case, try one of these options:

Use an extra-thin mechanical pencil.   A 0.3 mm pencil lead provides a sharp, thin line that should enable you to squeeze a surprising amount of information into a very small space.

Jot your questions on bookmark-sized sheets of paper.   Write all your questions for a textbook page on a thin, separate strip of paper, and then stick that strip in at the page where it belongs. (Write the page number at the top of the strip in case it gets shuffled or falls out of your book.)

Put your questions on self-adhesive note slips.   Jot each question on a small adhesive sheet of paper, and then stick that sheet directly over the paragraph it refers to. When the time comes to review your questions, they'll be easy to see and easy to read.

Reread Your Questions

Once you've written a question for each idea from the reading assignment or lecture, go back and reread these questions. Although reading over the main ideas of your notes or your chapter should have refreshed your memory on the important points, rereading the questions you've written should do even more. It provides an opportunity to not only step back and review what you've written but also to recall the thought processes you underwent to come up with these questions. When you think about information deeply and from several different angles you improve your chances of mastering it.

To reread questions from Cornell-style notes, survey all your questions at once simply by overlapping your note pages so that only the cue column

What is
The Assignment
of Meaning?

How is meaning assigned to a message?

Once we have paid attention to the material that has been presented, the next stage in the listening process is to categorize the message so as to assign meanings to its verbal and nonverbal stimuli. Only recently have researchers begun to understand something about this assignment naming. Some researchers suggest that once we receive a stimulus, we process it mentally and put the stimulus into some predetermined category.[20] This process, the **assignment of meaning,** develops as we acquire our language system, which provides us with the mental categories for interpreting the messages we receive. For instance, our categorizing system for the word *cheese* may include such factors as food, dairy products, taste, and nourishment—all of which help us to relate the word *cheese* to the context in which it is used.

What is a schema?

What role do schemas play in assignment of meaning?

The categorical assignment of meaning that provides listeners with the interpretation of the message is affected by the human cognitive process. This categorical context creates what cognitive psychologists have identified as a **schema**—a script for processing information. The cognitive process draws on all of a person's schemas for the purpose of interpretation, and these schemas provide the mental links for understanding and creating meaning from the stimuli we receive.[21]

How has brain research affected understanding of assignment of meaning?

Today's research suggests that the two hemispheres of our brain handle information differently and have different functions. The left hemisphere deals with verbal and numerical information in a linear form, providing the analytical process, whereas the right hemisphere specializes in processing shapes and images and in treating nonverbal, intuitive matters.[22] As researchers come to understand the implications of this division in more detail, we communicators will better understand why we assign the meanings we do to the messages we receive. This understanding could also allow us to become better listeners because we may be able to learn how to better utilize whatever part of the brain deals with particular materials.

We assign meaning to the verbal and nonverbal stimuli we receive in a lecture by using schemas (mental links for understanding) and by processing information on both sides of our brain.

FIGURE 7.1 Textbook Page with Cue Questions and Summary
Source: Reprinted from Roy Berko, Andrew D. Wolvin, and Darlyn K. Wolvin, Communicating: A Social and Career Focus, *Fifth Edition (Boston: Houghton Mifflin, 1992), p. 115.*

from each page is exposed. (Use a blank piece of paper to cover the notes on the top sheet.) Then begin with the first question and continue reading each one right up to the last one you've written. Don't linger over any one question. Keep reading, placing your emphasis on how the questions fit together instead of on the ideas that make up each answer.

To reread questions written in your textbook, use a plain piece of paper as a cover sheet to obscure the print as you read each question in the margin. If your questions are written on bookmark-sized strips, take the strips out of the book and lay them side by side. If your questions are written on self-adhesive note slips, just flip through the article or chapter and read each question you've written.

Rereading the questions, regardless of the specific method you have used, should have a positive psychological effect. Because you move rapidly from one question to the next, reviewing a long lecture or a large chapter will seem more manageable than it would if you were rereading everything you had written down.

Answer Each Question from Memory

Now reverse the process you used to devise the cue column questions by using these same questions to help you recall the answers they were based on. To do so, cover the large column of your notes or the text in your book with a plain sheet of paper. Then simply ask each question on the page one at a time, and answer it from memory, either by writing out your answer on a separate sheet of paper or by speaking that answer out loud. After you provide each answer, lift the cover sheet and compare your response with the key idea you wrote in your notes or underlined in your text. If the answer you gave is incorrect or doesn't closely match the key idea, try again. With the correct answer still fresh in your mind, of course, you will have little trouble coming up with it the second time.

Continue answering each of the questions on a page in this way. When you finish a page, move on to the next page and then to the next, repeating the procedure until all the questions from the set of notes or pages of your text have been accurately answered.

SUMMARIZING YOUR INFORMATION

Writing a summary is not easy, but the rewards are great. Summarizing is a sure-fire way to gain a deep understanding of the facts and ideas in your notes, and reviewing summaries makes studying for exams a breeze. By summarizing your notes, you gain mastery because you have the whole picture instead of an assortment of facts. Summarizing is composed of three tasks: selecting the most important ideas, writing a synopsis for each page, and rereading all the summaries.

Select the Most Important Ideas

Summarizing begins with selectivity. Pick the most important idea on the page and mark it. If there are several ideas of great and equal importance, mark each of them. If you have trouble determining which of the ideas on each page of your notes is most important, try using the Silver Dollar System (explained in Chapter 4.)

Write a Synopsis for Each Page

Once you've marked the most important ideas, combine them into a sentence or two. If you've taken Cornell-style notes, write your summaries in the two-inch summary area at the bottom of each page. If you've been jotting your markings directly in your textbook, try to write your summary sentences at the bottom of each page (see Figure 7.1, on page 151). If there's not enough room, write your sentences on a separate sheet of notebook paper. The process of distilling information down to just a couple of sentences will prompt you to think deeply about the ideas on each page, weigh their relative importance, and discover how they connect.

Reread All the Summaries

After you have written summaries for each sheet in your notes or page in your textbook, reread them. The highly concentrated synopsis of your note sheets will not only permit you to review an entire chapter or lecture in a matter of minutes but should also provide you with a broader context for understanding individual facts and ideas.

REFLECTING ON YOUR NOTES

Perhaps the most powerful learning tool you can use is reflection, thinking about and applying the facts and ideas that you've learned. Reviewing your notes and reciting them out loud or on paper will enable you to retain information long enough to pass a test or write a paper. But if you want this information to become a permanent part of your knowledge, then reflection is the key. With reflection you take an extra step back, a step with consequences far larger than the mere memorization of facts. In the words of the philosopher Arthur Schopenhauer (1788–1860): "A man may have a great mass of knowledge, but if he has not worked it up by thinking it over for himself, it has much less value than a far smaller amount which he has thoroughly pondered."[1] Once you have learned its rudiments and recognized its advantages, you can use reflection to ensure a deep, long-lasting understanding of your notes.

Learn the Rudiments of Reflection

Reflection provides you with a method for thoroughly pondering the information you have learned. You reflect on the ideas in your notes by rearranging them, by comparing them to ideas that you already know, and most of all by subjecting them to questions.

Rearrange Your Information   Information can be organized in a variety of ways, with each arrangement providing a different perspective and in the process a clearer picture and a fuller understanding. Group information from your notes into categories. Then see what conclusions you can draw. Next, group your information into other categories, and note how those conclusions differ. Clustering the same information under different categories can lead to varying conclusions and greater understanding.

Make Thoughtful Comparisons   New information you learn may support or refute what you already know or may provide an alternative to facts and ideas you have previously learned. By comparing what you're learning with what you already know, you improve your understanding of both.

Ask Some Far-Reaching Questions   Questioning is the essence of reflection. Simply taking the time to wonder and ask why can dramatically enhance your learning and deepen your understanding. Unlike the straightforward questions you've written in the margin, the questions you ask for reflection must reach beyond the confines of a particular lecture or reading assignment. Ask yourself such questions as these:

---

[1]Arthur Schopenhauer, "On Thinking For One's Self," *Essays* (New York: A.L. Burt, 1893), p. 321.

What is the significance of these facts and ideas?

What principle or principles are they based on?

What else could they be applied to?

How do they fit in with what I already know?

From these facts and ideas, what else can I learn?

Recognize the Advantages of Reflection

Reflection provides benefits that you can't obtain from conventional studying. It encourages advantageous learning, it promotes creativity, and, perhaps best of all, it enables you to study virtually anywhere.

Uncover the Secret of Advantageous Learning The only type of learning that increases your innate wisdom and becomes a permanent part of you is advantageous learning—learning that is propelled by a burning desire to know something. Advantageous learning occurs when you take a voluntary extra step beyond the mere memorization of facts. That extra step is reflection.

Harness the Power of Creativity There's a difference between proficiency and creativity. You can become proficient by studying your textbooks and lecture notes, but you will never be creative until you try to see beyond the facts, until you step back and look at things from the broadest possible context. When done properly, recitation and review result in proficiency and equip you with the knowledge you'll require for academic achievement. But recitation and review, no matter how diligent and conscientious, will not yield the creativity that leads to breakthroughs in art, science, and business. As Hans Bethe, a nuclear physicist and winner of the Nobel Prize once explained, "Creativity comes only through reflection."[2]

Learn How to Study Anywhere Unlike reviewing and reciting, which require that you have your notes or textbook handy, reflection is a skill you can take with you wherever you go and use whenever you have the time. You can reflect while walking from one building to another, standing in line, waiting for a friend, or riding a bus. Great discoveries and insights have come in unlikely places and at odd times. A classic example is that of

---

[2]Personal interview with the author.

Archimedes (287?–212 B.C.), the greatest mathematician of ancient times, who discovered the natural law of buoyancy while taking a bath. He became so excited that he leapt out of the water and ran naked through the streets shouting, "Eureka!"

Or take an example from our own time. In 1941, when Swiss engineer George de Mestral came down from the mountains after a hunting trip, his woolen pants were covered with burrs. Instead of annoying him, the prickly weeds made de Mestral wonder, "How do they stick so securely?" His reflection on this question resulted in the invention of Velcro, one of the most common and versatile fasteners used today.

USING A STUDY SYSTEM

Over the years, educators have combined the elements of mastery into easy-to-remember study systems. The best known of these systems is the *SQ3R Method*, but many others are available. In addition, you can create your own study system.

Start with the SQ3R Method

The SQ3R Method was devised during World War II by Francis P. Robinson, an Ohio State University psychologist. The aim of the system was to help military personnel enrolled in special programs at the university read faster and study better. The steps of the SQ3R Method are as follows:[3]

S Survey. Glance through all the headings in the chapter, and read the final summary paragraph (if the chapter has one). This survey should not take more than a minute, and it will show you the three to six core ideas on which the discussion will be based. This orientation will help you organize the ideas as you read them later.

Q Question. Now begin to work. Turn the first heading into a question. This will arouse your curiosity and thereby increase comprehension. It will bring to mind information you already know, thus helping you understand that section more quickly. The question also will make important points

---

[3]"SQ3R Method" from *Effective Study*, 4/e, by Francis P. Robinson. Copyright © 1961, 1970 by Francis P. Robinson. Copyright 1941, 1946 by Harper & Row Publishers, Inc. Reprinted by permission of HarperCollins Publishers.

stand out from explanatory details. You can turn a heading into a question as you read the heading, but it demands conscious effort on your part.

R₁ Read.   Read so as to answer that question, but read only to the end of the first section. This should not be a passive plodding along each line, but an active search for the answer.

R₂ Recite.   Having read the first section, look away from the book and try briefly to recite the answer to your question. Use your own words, and cite an example. If you can do this, you know what is in the book; if you cannot, glance over the section again. An excellent way to do this reciting from memory is to jot down brief cue phrases in outline form on a sheet of paper.

Now repeat the second to fourth steps for each successive section: That is, turn the next heading into a question, read to answer that question, and recite the answer by jotting down cue phrases in your outline. Read in this way until the entire lesson is completed.

R₃ Review.   When you have read through in this way, look over your notes to get a bird's eye view of the points and their relationships to each other. Check your memory by reciting the major subpoints under each heading. This can be done by covering up your notes and trying to recall the main points. Then expose each major point and try to recall the subpoints listed under it.

SQ3R is the best known of dozens of mastery systems. Although widely accepted, even SQ3R has its drawbacks. For example, it applies only to textbook assignments, it offers no guidelines for mastering lectures, and it does not use the reflection step. Despite these shortcomings, SQ3R was a valuable breakthrough in learning techniques. It demonstrated clearly that the process of mastering information could be expressed in a concrete, step-by-step system.

Devise Your Own System

Now that you understand the basic elements of taking notes, noting the key ideas, and mastering your material, you can combine these elements into your own study system, one that suits your particular learning style and addresses your individual needs. A good way to start is by modifying the SQ3R Method.

Use the form on page 158 to list the steps in your custom-made study system and to summarize the process involved in each step. Then test your system. Use it to study a subject for one or two weeks, and make sure that

A Personal Study System

In a brief statement, summarize the goal of your system (for example: to master textbook assignments using Cornell-style paper). Then jot down each step and an explanation of how it should be carried out. Limit your system to no more than seven steps so it is easy to remember.

Goal: _____

_____

The Step   What It Involves

_____   _____

                              _____

                              _____

                              _____

_____   _____

                              _____

                              _____

_____   _____

                              _____

                              _____

_____   _____

                              _____

                              _____

_____   _____

                              _____

                              _____

_____   _____

                              _____

                              _____

you've clearly defined each step and put it in the right order. Based on what worked and what didn't, modify the steps or what they involve. Finally, place a copy of your system in the front of your notebook for easy access throughout the term.

As you design and test your system, remember that the most important aspect of any study system is an active approach. In fact, in the process of designing your own system, you're already becoming an active learner.

SUMMARY

What are the requirements of mastery?

Mastery requires learning information for the long term, knowing it to the point of recall, and understanding how each fact or idea fits in with others you already know.

How do you conduct an immediate review?

Overview a reading assignment by rereading the abstract, introduction, or summary or by rereading the title, headings, and subheadings. Overview a lecture by mentally recalling the lecture and then asking yourself questions about it to fix the key ideas in your mind.

How do you convert the key ideas from your notes into questions?

Whether you made your jottings on Cornell-style paper or directly in your textbook, think of each key idea you've taken down as the answer to an unasked question. Write that question in the cue column of your Cornell paper, in the textbook margin, or on a separate sheet of paper.

What's the benefit of rereading your questions all at once?

Rereading the questions enables you to step back and review what you've written and recall the logic you used in arriving at each question.

How should you answer the questions?

Cover your notes or your text with a sheet of paper so that only the questions are revealed. Then move systematically through the questions, answering each one in your own words and from memory either by reciting the answer out loud or by writing it on a separate sheet of paper. Check your answers simply by lifting the cover sheet. If your answer is wrong or inadequate, try again.

How do you summarize your notes?

Select the most important ideas from each page of your note sheets or each page of text and combine them into a one- or two-sentence synopsis. If you have difficulty choosing the most important ideas, use the Silver Dollar System. Write your synopsis at the bottom of each page.

Why should you reread your summaries?

Rereading your summaries provides you with a convenient, concise review of an entire chapter or lecture. It also helps you put what you've just read or heard into a larger context.

How do you reflect on your notes?

You reflect on your notes by clustering them into different categories to gain a different perspective, by comparing them with information you already know, and by taking the time to explore the ramifications and significance of what you've learned through asking thoughtful questions.

What are the advantages of reflection?

Reflection is a powerful tool for making newly learned information a permanent part of your knowledge. It promotes advantageous learning, the only kind of learning that really lasts. In addition, it encourages creativity and enables you to study virtually anywhere.

Why should you use a study system?

A study system puts the key elements of mastery into a convenient set of steps. You can use a well-known study system such as the SQ3R Method, or you can tailor the elements of mastery into a customized system that fits your learning style.

HAVE YOU MISSED SOMETHING?

Matching.   In each blank space in the left column, write the letter preceding the phrase in the right column that matches the left item best.

_____ **1.** Archimedes

a. Retrieving information from memory without the aid of hints or cues _d._ _b_   **2.** Questions   _b._ Provides an "instant replay" of a lecture

__c__   **3.** Reflection   _c._ Opening summary that often helps put
                                      an article in context

__g__   **4.** Velcro   _d._ The primary tool for both recitation
                                      and reflection

__C__   **5.** Abstract   _e._ May be the most powerful learning tool
                                      you can use

_b_ _e_   **6.** Visualization   _f._ Used reflection to arrive at the law of
                                      buoyancy

__a.__   **7.** Recall   _g._ Developed as a result of its inventor's
                                      reflection

Multiple choice.   Choose the word or phrase that completes the following sentence most accurately, and circle the letter that precedes it.

1. According to Bethe, "creativity comes only through

   a. textbooks."
   b. recitation."
   c. understanding."
   d. reflection."

2. Mastery is your primary weapon against

   a. rereading.
   b. boredom.
   c. overwork.
   d. forgetting.

3. The questions that accompany your notes should always be answered

   a. from memory.
   b. on paper.
   c. out loud.
   d. in complete sentences.

4. Summarizing your notes begins with

   a. consolidation.
   b. selectivity.
   c. recitation.
   d. recognition.

5. Reflection is done by

 a. rearranging.
 b. comparing.
 c. questioning.
 d. doing all of the above.

6. The most important aspect of any study system is

 a. an oversized margin.
 b. the surveying step.
 c. an active approach.
 d. a memorable name.

True-false. Write *T* beside the *true* statements and *F* beside the *false* statements.

___F___ **1.** Recognition and recall are two terms that describe the same process.

___T___ **2.** The process of mastery begins by conducting an immediate review.

___T___ **3.** If a reading assignment doesn't provide an obvious overview, you can usually create one yourself.

___T___ **4.** Each key idea in your notes can be thought of as the answer to an unasked question.

___T___ **5.** Advantageous learning ensures long-term retention and increases innate wisdom.

___F___ **6.** Most of the benefits of reflection can be obtained from conventional studying.

Short answer. Supply a brief answer for each of the following items. The number in parentheses refers to the page where the item is discussed in the text.

1. Compare recall and recognition. (147–148)
2. How can you take useful notes for textbooks that have narrow margins? (150)
3. Discuss the psychological effect of viewing all your marginal questions at once. (152)
4. Why is reflection considered such a powerful study aid? (153–154)
5. What would be the most important element of your personal study system, and why? (157–158)

BUILDING YOUR VOCABULARY STEP BY STEP: KEEPING TRACK OF YOUR WORDS

As with ideas you read in a textbook or hear in a lecture, new words must be written down and mastered if you want to make them truly your own. Each word you plan to add to your vocabulary should be written on a separate index card along with all the important information that pertains to it. Here's a method for mastering new words:

1. On the front of the card, write the word, underlined, as it appeared in a sentence you either read or heard. Because the meaning of a word can vary depending on the situation, it's always important to place that word in its proper context.
2. Once you have a small stack of cards, look up the words in an unabridged dictionary. Below the excerpted sentence, print the word with its syllable divisions and pronunciation markings.
3. Next, flip each card over and on the back write out the word's prefix and root. Jot down the definition as well. If the word has several definitions, write them all, and put an asterisk beside the one that applies to the meaning of your word in its specific content.

Carry a dozen or so of these completed cards with you so you can review them whenever you happen to have a spare moment. To review the words on the cards, follow this procedure:

1. Start with the front side of the card. Pronounce the word correctly and read the sentence completely. Then without flipping over the card, see if you can define the word from memory. You don't necessarily have to use dictionary language, but your definition should be clear and specific.
2. Turn the card over after you've done your best to define the word, and check the accuracy of your definition.
3. If the definition you gave was wrong or unsatisfactory, flip the card over and put a dot in the upper right-hand corner of the card. This will let you know the next time that the word has already given you some trouble. Three dots in the corner signal that the word requires some extra attention.
4. Once you've mastered a set of cards, put them in a file box and begin working on another set of words.
5. From time to time, review the words you have already mastered to ensure you haven't forgotten them.

As you master the precise meaning of each word on your card, you'll notice a corresponding advance in your reading, writing, speaking, and thinking.

Here's a list of words from the current chapter that you may want to add to your vocabulary. The number following each word refers to the page in the chapter where the word was used and enables you to place each in its original context.

adhesive (150)	informational (147)	precarious (147)
buoyancy (156)	innate (155)	proficiency (155)
conscientious (155)	insights (155)	refute (154)
consequences (154)	integrated (148)	retrieve (147)
diligent (155)	limbo (147)	rudiments (154)
essence (154)	manageable (152)	synopsis (153)
glean (148)	mere (154)	

Thinking Visually

A picture shows me at a glance what it takes dozens of pages of a book to expound.

Ivan Turgenev
Writer

Most of us are comfortable with reading and writing in words. But the same doesn't usually hold true for pictures. This means that the entire right half of our brains, the half that processes pictures, is largely ignored or underused during a typical school day. If you can learn to read and write in pictures as comfortably as you do in words, then you will be adding a visual dimension to your studying that could dramatically affect your learning and remembering. To aid you in thinking visually, this chapter deals with

• Using your whole brain

• Extracting meaning from pictures

• Expanding understanding with graphics

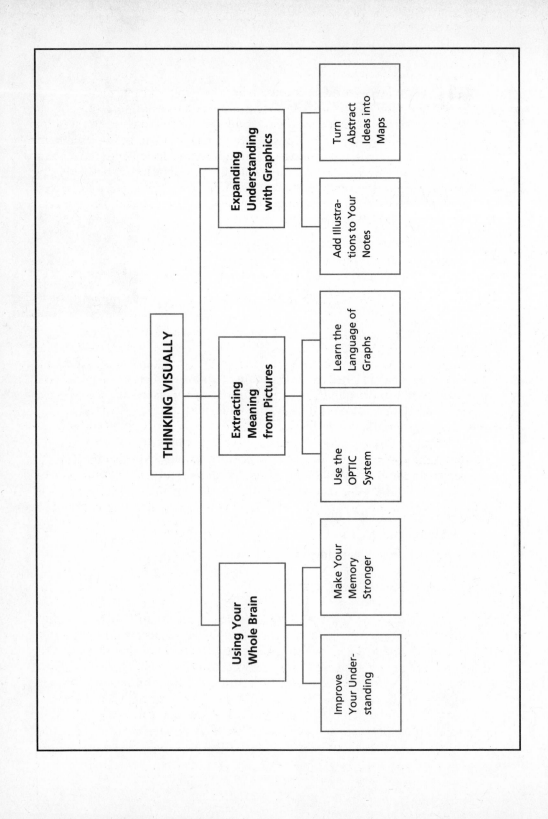

We live in a world of words, where reading and writing are crucial not only to our success but also to our survival. But words are not our only form of communication. Think of the millions of pictures that flash on your TV screen, or consider the signs that use only pictures and shapes to convey their meanings. Although there's little danger that words will become extinct, the role of visual images appears to be increasing. Learning to think visually will broaden your mind. With your whole brain engaged, you'll be able to extract messages from pictures and use visuals to expand your understanding.

USING YOUR WHOLE BRAIN

Although each of us has only one brain, that brain is divided into two distinct sides, or hemispheres, each with a separate set of functions. The chief function of the left side of the brain is to process written and spoken information. As you might expect, that side of the brain gets quite a workout. Although the right side does not get nearly as much use, its job is nevertheless important. One of the main functions of the brain's right side is to analyze and interpret visual information. Thinking in pictures puts the right side to work. Suddenly, instead of relying primarily on the left side of the brain, you're using both hemispheres. Your analysis of information is more balanced. This is why thinking in pictures can be said to broaden your mind. And with this broader mind, you are able to understand and remember information more easily than you could when you did the bulk of your thinking with only the left half of your brain.

Improve Your Understanding

There is some information that the left side of the brain may be unable to understand without help. Take, for example, an elaborate set of street directions. Written out, they become the responsibility of the left side of the brain. And yet you can read and reread all the directions and still wind up scratching your head and getting lost. But if you put this same information into a visual form—in this case, a map—you give your right brain a chance to interpret the data. With the two sides of the brain working in concert, information that would have taken time to untangle using one-sided thinking can often be grasped in an instant.

Make Your Memory Stronger

Thinking with your whole brain virtually doubles the odds of remembering what you've just learned. Memories that would normally be stored in only the left side of the brain are now filed in the right side as well. Indeed, Allan Paivio from the University of Western Ontario, using what he calls "dual coding," has concluded that pictures are easier to remember than words and that information is more readily recalled when it is learned as both pictures and words.[1] Thus, if you make a verbal and a visual effort to recall something you've learned, your memory will have two places to search for the information instead of just one.

EXTRACTING MEANING FROM PICTURES

When you read a paragraph, you're cracking a code. That code is the English language, and its message is the meaning you extract from words, sentences, and paragraphs. Although we spend a great deal of time decoding language, most of the codes around us are visual codes. We can decode a smile, for example, and know how its meaning differs from that of a frown. Visual materials in textbooks use codes as well to supply messages that are often as important as the meanings gained from sentences and paragraphs. For that reason, they must be read every bit as carefully. And as with reading a paragraph, reading a visual simply means extracting its message.

The OPTIC system enables you to extract the message from a variety of visuals. If your goal is the analysis of a graph, you will need to understand the language of that graph before you use the OPTIC system.

Use the OPTIC System

Many students mistakenly give visuals only a quick glance or even skip over them entirely. But these graphic materials should be scrutinized as carefully and as systematically as paragraphs. The OPTIC system will help you take an organized approach to this task.

---

[1]Allan Paivio, *Imagery and Verbal Processes* (New York: Holt, Rinehart, and Winston, 1971), pp. 522–523.

The five letters in the word OPTIC (which means "pertaining to the eye") provide you with a system for remembering the five steps for analyzing a visual.

O is for *overview*.

P is for *parts*.

T is for *title*.

I is for *interrelationships*.

C is for *conclusion*.

1. Begin by conducting a brief *overview* of the visual.
2. Then zero in on the *parts* of the visual. Read all labels, and note any elements or details that seem important.
3. Now read the *title* of the visual so you're clear on the subject it is covering.
4. Next use the title as your theory and the parts of the visual as your clues to detect and specify the *interrelationships* in the graphic.
5. Finally, try to reach a *conclusion* about the visual as a whole. What does it mean? Why was it included in the text? Sum up the message of the visual in just a sentence or two.

Learn the Language of Graphs

You are most likely to encounter three general types of graphs: circle graphs, bar graphs, and line graphs. The purpose of a circle graph is unique, whereas bar and line graphs share the same basic function.

Decode the Circle Graph.   The purpose of a circle graph, also known as a pie chart, is to show proportionally the relationship of parts (slices) to a whole (the pie). Although these graphs are relatively rare in highly technical books, they regularly appear in newspapers as well as in textbooks where the topic is something other than mathematics or science. The popularity of the circle graph is mainly due to its simplicity. In most cases, you can tell at a glance the proportions the graph illustrates—that is, the various-sized slices of the pie. For example, in Figure 8.1, the circle graph gives you a clear picture of the population distribution in the United States.

Decode Bar and Line Graphs.   The purpose of bar and line graphs is to illustrate the relationship of a set of dependent variables to a set of independent variables. *Variables* are numbers that can change. For example, the number we use to refer to the year is a variable. It changes every twelve

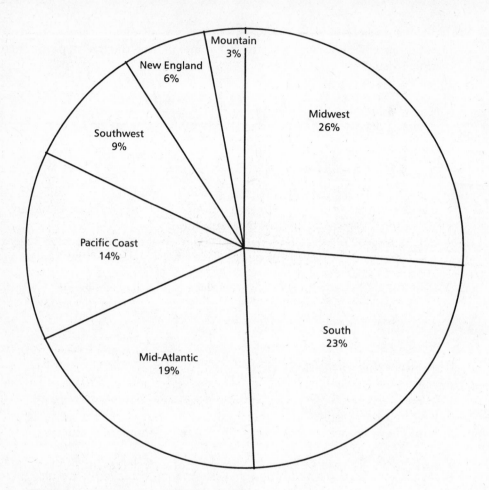

FIGURE 8.1   U.S. Population Divided by Region
Circle (Pie) graphs show the relationship of several parts to a whole.

months, when it increases by one. Population is another variable. It changes when someone is born or dies, when someone becomes a citizen, or when someone leaves the country. Years and dates in general are called *independent variables* because they change on their own. The population of the United States does not influence the fact that every 365 to 366 days we begin a new year. Quantities such as population are called *dependent variables* because their change occurs in relation to another variable, such as the year. For example, we measure the changes of U.S. population every ten years when the census is taken.

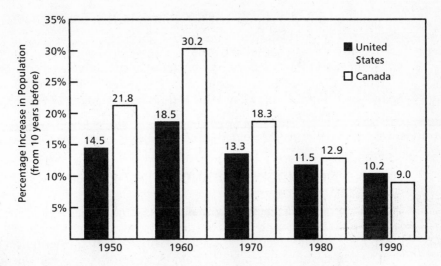

FIGURE 8.2 Population Growth in the United States and Canada, 1950–1990
Bar graphs show sizes of individual items and illustrate comparisons.

Although bar and line graphs both operate in the same basic way, (showing how a dependent variable such as population increases or decreases in relation to an independent variable such as the year), each takes a slightly different approach. Bar graphs (see Figure 8.2) focus on specific changes; line graphs (see Figure 8.3, on page 172) illustrate long-term trends. One way to visualize this distinction is to think of bar graphs as snapshots and line graphs as movies. If you were to take successive snapshots of a long jumper, you would have a series of photographs showing successive stages of the jump. If you were to film the same jump with a movie camera, you'd have a continuous record of the entire jump. Figure 8.4, on page 173, illustrates this idea.

Like snapshots and movies, each type of graph has its strengths. Bar graphs are good for comparing the individual sizes or amounts of items, and they provide clear comparisons of several sets of data at once. Line graphs are useful for showing changes in data over long periods of time. For instance, if you wanted to examine the country's population increase over a brief period of time or if you wanted to compare it with the population of another country, then you would probably use a bar graph. Figure 8.2 shows that the growth in U.S. population was relatively steady from 1950 through 1990, whereas Canada's population growth surged during the 1950s and 1960s. But if you wanted to show the percentage increase in U.S. population since the eighteenth century, a line graph would be a bet-

ter visual. Figure 8.3 shows that the growth in U.S. population has generally slowed since 1800.

Regardless of whether the graphic is a circle, bar, or line graph, once
you understand the language of the particular graph, you can methodically
extract its meaning in the same way you would with a picture or diagram—by using the OPTIC system. Figure 8.5, on pages 174–175, shows a
graph that has been analyzed using this system.

EXPANDING UNDERSTANDING WITH GRAPHICS

We now know that reading a visual means studying a diagram or a graph
and turning its message into a sentence or two. When you write in pictures, you simply reverse the process. You convert the sentences you've
read or heard into a diagram or graph. If the information you encounter is
concrete, then your task is fairly simple. For instance, you can turn a description of a computer modem into a diagram by using that description as
directions for your sketch (Figure 8.6, on page 176). If, however, the ideas

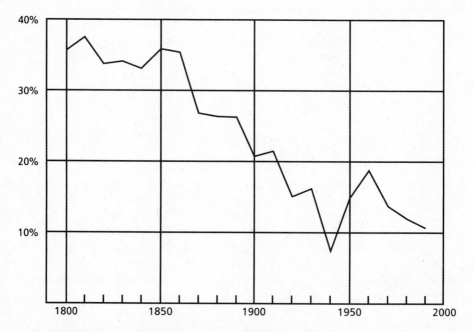

FIGURE 8.3 Percentage Increase in U.S. Population, 1800–1990
Line graphs show long-term trends in data.

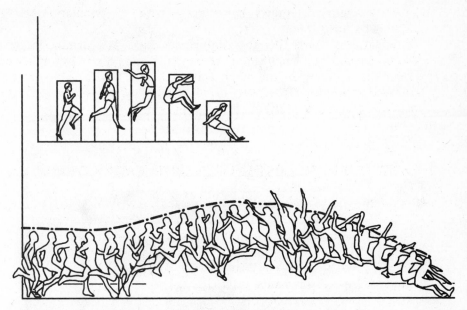

FIGURE 8.4 Snapshots versus Movies: Bar Graphs and Line Graphs
A bar graph can be compared to a set of snapshots, whereas a line graph is more like a movie.
Adapted from Track and Field Omnibook, *4th ed.*, 1985, by Ken Doherty, Tafnews Press (Track and Field News), Mountain View, CA.

you read or hear are more abstract, such as information about the characteristics of amphibians, then your approach is a bit more involved. Instead of sketching the animals, which doesn't tell you much about their characteristics, you create a concept map. Although your approach to abstract ideas is different from your approach to concrete ones, your goal is the same: to turn something you can read into something you can see (see Figure 8.7, on page 177).

When you need extra help understanding or remembering something you've read or heard, try drawing a picture of it. Concrete ideas can be expressed as illustrations in your notes. More abstract notions can be converted into schematic diagrams called concept maps.

Add Illustrations to Your Notes

As you read your textbook or go over your lecture notes, don't just jot down the key ideas in words; sketch some of them as well. In some subjects this sketching will come naturally. Science courses, for example, are

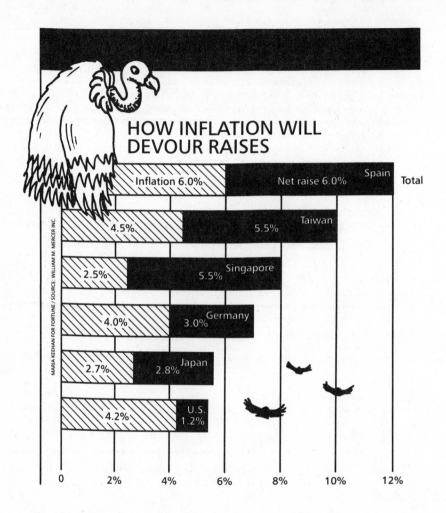

full of information that can be drawn. The parts of a one-celled organism or the connections in a computer network are much easier to understand if you put little diagrams of them in your notes. Sometimes the drawing is done for you. If the instructor puts a sketch on the board or the textbook author includes diagrams in the chapter, add these pictures to your notes in the same way that you would jot down important examples. When a drawing doesn't exist, make one of your own.

A history course may not feature easily drawn elements, but it does include plenty of concrete data that can be translated into picture form. A series of important dates, for example, can be turned into a time line, and

OVERVIEW
A bar graph with a vulture in the corner and six bars moving from longest to shortest with each bar divided into plain and hatched lined sections and marked with percentages.

PARTS
• The six bars represent six countries: Spain, Taiwan, Singapore, Germany, Japan, and the U.S.
• Percentages run horizontally at the bottom of the graph—from 0% to 12%—and represent percentage increases in salaries.
• The total length of each bar represents raises, the hatched line section stands for the rate of inflation, the plain colored part of the bar is the net raise—the raise that remains after inflation.

TITLE
"How Inflation Will Devour Raises"
The word *devour* seems to imply that inflation has a major impact on raises. The vulture is being used to make the point more dramatic and perhaps make the graph more interesting.

INTERRELATIONSHIPS
• Spain appears due for the largest raises, while the U.S. will be receiving the smallest.
• Half of the raises in Spain will be "devoured" by inflation, while roughly four-fifths of American raises will be lost to inflation.
• Of those countries listed, Spain has the highest rate of inflation (6%), while Singapore (2.5%) has the lowest rate.
• The net raises in Taiwan and Singapore are identical (5.5%), even though their rates of inflation are very different (4.5% and 2.5%).

CONCLUSION
With the exception of Singapore, inflation will devour a large portion—close to half and more—of anticipated raises. The United States is the hardest hit of all the countries represented in the graph, retaining only 1.2% of a 5.4% raise after inflation.

FIGURE 8.5   Using the OPTIC System to Analyze a Graph
Source: Fortune, *December 30, 1991, p. 10.* © *1991 Time Inc. All rights reserved.*

individual historical facts can be visualized almost as easily. Suppose you read that Abraham Lincoln was born in a log cabin in 1809. That may not seem like the sort of information you can turn into a diagram. Yet with a little imagination, you can come up with a drawing that should be easier to recall than a sentence (see page 178).

Other ideas lend themselves more easily to this picture writing. Consider this sentence, for example:

The issue of taxation has divided Republicans and Democrats.

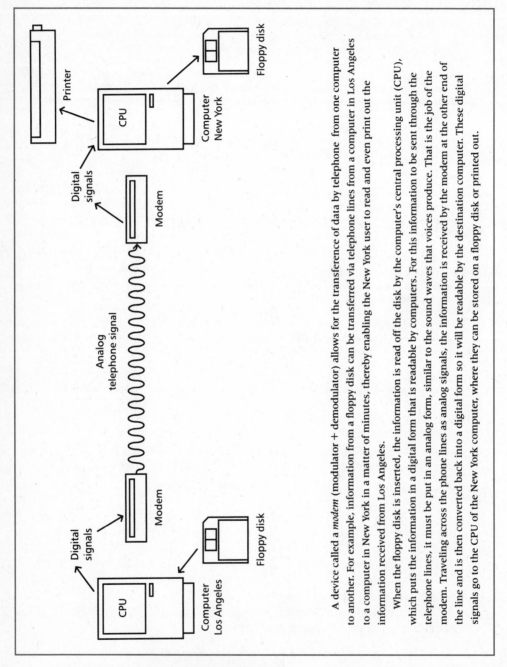

A device called a *modem* (modulator + demodulator) allows for the transference of data by telephone from one computer to another. For example, information from a floppy disk can be transferred via telephone lines from a computer in Los Angeles to a computer in New York in a matter of minutes, thereby enabling the New York user to read and even print out the information received from Los Angeles.

When the floppy disk is inserted, the information is read off the disk by the computer's central processing unit (CPU), which puts the information in a digital form that is readable by computers. For this information to be sent through the telephone lines, it must be put in an analog form, similar to the sound waves that voices produce. That is the job of the modem. Traveling across the phone lines as analog signals, the information is received by the modem at the other end of the line and is then converted back into a digital form so it will be readable by the destination computer. These digital signals go to the CPU of the New York computer, where they can be stored on a floppy disk or printed out.

FIGURE 8.6   A Diagram Based on Text Information

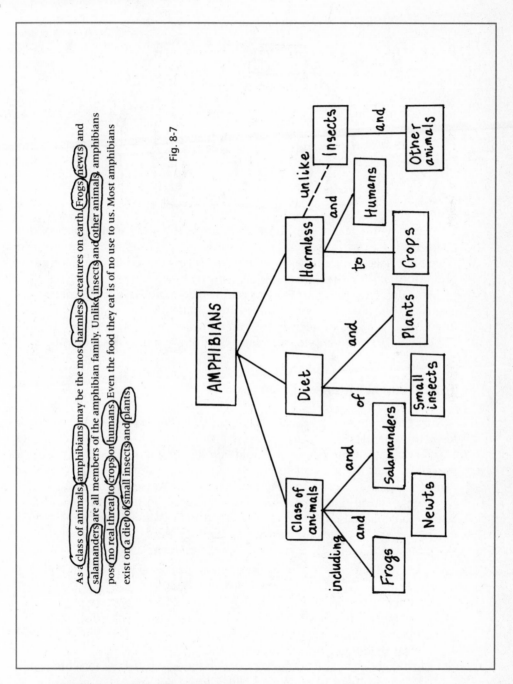

As a class of animals, amphibians may be the most harmless creatures on earth. Frogs, newts and salamanders are all members of the amphibian family. Unlike insects and other animals, amphibians pose no real threat to crops or humans. Even the food they eat is of no use to us. Most amphibians exist on a diet of small insects and plants.

Fig. 8-7

FIGURE 8.7 A Map of Text Information

These words may be no more memorable than any other ones on this page. Yet if you express them as a picture, they will suddenly stand out in your mind (see the next page). The very process of deciding how to interpret information visually strengthens your memory of it.

You don't have to be Michelangelo or Leonardo da Vinci to draw diagrams in your notes. The important point is to tap into the right side of your brain. With your full mind at work, you'll increase your brain power, regardless of whether your drawing looks like doodling or a priceless work of art.

Turn Abstract Ideas into Maps

Abstract ideas don't lend themselves quite as easily to diagrams as concrete ideas do. For example, you can draw a rough sketch of farmland, a field worker, and a tractor, but how would you diagram economic production, a procedure that involves all three? That's where a concept map comes in. Concept maps are used to diagram abstract processes and relationships. Drawing a concept map based on a set of abstract ideas is similar to drawing a road map based on a set of hard-to-follow directions. And in both cases, the map that results will make the idea easier to visualize, understand, and remember. Here are the steps for mapping a text book passage:

1. Determine the topic of the passage you are planning to map. Put the topic at the top of a sheet of paper and circle it.
2. Go back to the passage and circle or list the concepts involved.
3. Find the two to five most important concepts from your list. These are the key concepts. List them on your map in a row beneath the circled topic. Circle these key concepts as well.
4. Cluster the remaining concepts under the key concepts to which they relate. Add them to your map beneath the key concepts they support, and then circle these new concepts.

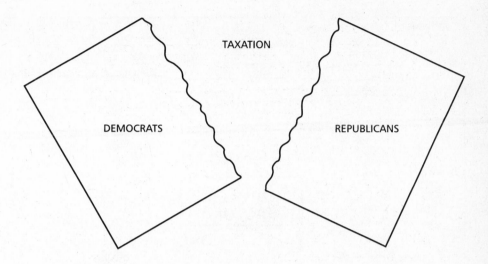

TAXATION

DEMOCRATS

REPUBLICANS

5. Draw lines connecting related concepts. Along each line, you may want to specify the relationship that connects the concepts.

Master the Map Drawing a concept map, like taking notes, does a great deal to help cement important ideas and concepts in your memory. And like your notes, your maps can be mastered. Although there are several systems for mastering your map, the simplest and most effective way is to look it over carefully and then, without peeking at the original passage, write a short summarizing paragraph explaining the key concepts and how they relate. The result is like writing your own textbook. You start out with the same concepts the textbook uses, but the words that result are your own instead of the author's. Figure 8.8 shows a map and its summarizing paragraph.

Concept maps are flexible study aids They don't lock you into just one method or approach. Here are some additional ways you can use a concept map to improve your studying.

Use the concepts for recitation Take one circled concept from your map and explain out loud and without looking at the rest of the map how it relates to the map as a whole.

Add to your map New ideas frequently connect with old information. Take a moment to think about how the concepts in your map relate to ideas you already know. Add the appropriate old ideas to your map, and connect them to what you've just learned.

Redraw your map There's no right or wrong way of drawing a concept map. The same information can be mapped in a number of ways. Look over your original map and see if you can organize the concepts a little dif-

Textbook Passage

There are three factors of production: land, labor and capital. Land includes all natural resources, labor all human inputs, and capital all human-made items used in the production process.

Concept Map

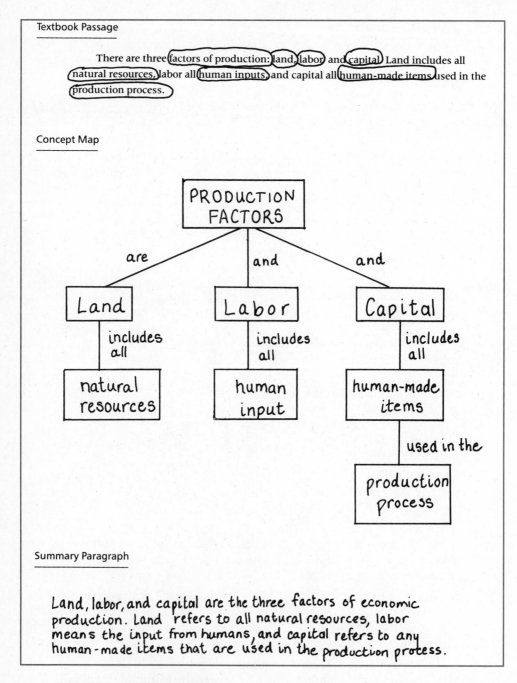

Summary Paragraph

Land, labor, and capital are the three factors of economic production. Land refers to all natural resources, labor means the input from humans, and capital refers to any human-made items that are used in the production process.

FIGURE 8.8   Mastering a Map

ferently. Looking at the information from a different angle often makes some of the concepts a little clearer. Also, creating a second map of the same information means that the concepts will be stored in your memory an additional time.

Use Maps for Summaries Although a map of every concept from a chapter would be huge and a concept map for even a small book would probably be the size of a billboard, you can use mapping to *summarize* the key concepts from chapters, articles, and books. The procedure for summarizing information with a concept map is identical to the one you just followed for mapping a single paragraph from your textbook or section from your notes except that you cover more ground. Instead of containing information from one paragraph, a summary map may draw from dozens of paragraphs. For this reason, summary maps do not contain as much detail as maps created for more specific sections. A map that covered every detail would not only be huge; it would also defeat the original purpose of mapping: to make ideas clearer and easier to understand. That's why a summary map, like a summary paragraph, covers only the most important ideas, not all the ideas. The maps that precede each chapter in this book provide good examples of summary maps. Notice how they include the most important concepts from the chapter they illustrate.

Use Maps as Planning Strategies Concept maps can be used to plan a paper (see Chapter 12) or an oral report. First write the topic you've chosen at the top of a blank sheet of paper. Then after you have done a bit of preliminary research and have come up with several main concepts, add these to your map, and connect them with lines to your topic. Finally, fill out your map with any supporting ideas you've acquired, making sure to cluster them under the main concepts to which they refer. Once again, draw connecting lines to show how each piece fits into the puzzle. Here is the step-by-step procedure for mapping a paper or an oral report:

1. Do some preliminary research on your subject.
2. Write your topic at the top of a blank sheet of paper.
3. Add two to five main ideas that you plan to cover, and link them to the topic on your map.
4. Cluster any subideas under the main ideas that they support. Link them with lines.
5. Survey your map and decide if its branches are evenly developed.
6. If your map seems lopsided, rearrange it or add information so that all its branches are balanced.
7. Use your map as a guide to do in-depth research on the concepts you plan to cover. Add to your map if necessary.

At the very least, your finished concept map can function as an outline, supplying you with all the main ideas and subideas you plan to include in your paper or oral report. In addition, the map can be used as a guide to help you do your more detailed research as systematically as possible.

Unlike a conventional outline, a map enables you to see your outline instead of just reading it. In general, a well-organized report looks fairly symmetrical when you map it. If your map has a lopsided appearance, it may mean that your report needs to be more evenly balanced. Adding some concepts or clustering your existing topics in a different arrangement should do the trick. Once you're happy with the look of your map, it can serve as a plan for further research.

SUMMARY

How can thinking visually broaden your mind?

Because the mind's interpretation of visual images occurs on the right side of your brain, thinking in pictures adds another dimension to thought and increases your chances of understanding and remembering information.

What is the OPTIC system?

The OPTIC system is a set of steps for systematically evaluating a visual. To use the system, overview the illustration, identify its constituent parts, read its title, determine the interrelationship among all these components, and arrive at a conclusion.

What is meant by the "language of graphs"?

The phrase indicates that graphs, like paragraphs, communicate key ideas. Although all graphs share some similarities, the most common graphs—circle, bar, and line graphs—speak their messages in slightly different ways.

What is the purpose of a circle graph?

The purpose of a circle graph, or pie chart, is to illustrate how a set of parts (slices) fits together to form a whole (pie). The easy readability of a circle graph makes it extremely useful for less technical articles and books.

What is the purpose of bar and line graphs?

Both graphs are primarily designed to illustrate the relationship between a set of dependent variables and a set of independent variables. In most cases, this illustration follows the form of cause and effect.

How do bar and line graphs differ?

Bar graphs usually show a few specific increases or decreases, whereas line graphs provide a broader view and are more likely to reveal an overall trend. The difference between bar graphs and line graphs is similar to that between snapshots and movies.

How can you use visuals to expand your understanding?

Drawing a picture or diagram to accompany written information often makes what you've read easier to understand. If the words are concrete, a picture usually helps. If they're more abstract, you may want to use a concept map instead.

How can you master information in a concept map?

Use each concept as a basis for recitation, explaining, or writing from memory how the concept relates to the map as a whole. You may also want to link the new ideas in your map to ones you already know or redraw your map to gain a different view of the information.

How can concept maps be used as summaries?

By selecting the most important concepts and arranging them in a map, you can create a convenient summary of an article, a chapter, or an entire book.

How do maps help you in preparing for a paper or oral report?

Arranging the important concepts you want to write or discuss in the form of a map provides you with a visual outline that makes the organization of your oral report or paper clearer. The same map can be used as a step-by-step game plan for doing your research.

HAVE YOU MISSED SOMETHING?

Matching. In each blank space in the left column, write the letter preceding the phrase in the right column that matches the left item best.

_____ **1.** Memory

a. Idea of storing information as both words and pictures

_____ **2.** Words

b. Method for systematically analyzing graphic materials

_____ **3.** Pictures

c. Strengthened when both sides of the brain are used

_____ **4.** OPTIC

d. One way to think of the function of line graphs

_____ **5.** Dual coding

e. Normally fall under the jurisdiction of the brain's right side

_____ **6.** Snapshots

f. Usually fall under the jurisdiction of the brain's left side

_____ **7.** Movies

g. One way to think of the function of bar graphs

Multiple choice. Choose the word or phrase that completes the following sentence most accurately, and circle the letter that precedes it.

1. Reading a paragraph or analyzing a visual can be considered

   a. left-brain thinking.
   b. cracking a code.
   c. identical endeavors.
   d. right-brain thinking.

2. Circle graphs are

   a. popular in newspapers.
   b. simple to understand.
   c. rare in technical books.
   d. all of the above.

3. Independent variables include

   a. years and dates.
   b. population.
   c. words.
   d. pictures.

4. The subject of a concept map is usually

   a. concrete.
   b. complex.
   c. abstract.
   d. simple.

5. Summary maps should be drawn with

    a. less detail.
    b. black marking pen.
    c. independent variables.
    d. concrete concepts.

6. When used with a paper or report, a map can function as

    a. a guide for research.
    b. a visual outline.
    c. a taking-off point.
    d. all of the above.

True-false. Write *T* beside the *true* statements and *F* beside the *false* statements.

_____ 1. In general, bar and line graphs illustrate the same relationship.

_____ 2. Line graphs can provide an effective illustration of long-term trends.

_____ 3. The OPTIC system can be used with both pictures and graphs.

_____ 4. Artistic ability isn't necessary for drawing pictures to help you study.

_____ 5. Unlike conventional notes, concept maps cannot be recited.

Short answer. Supply a brief answer for each of the following items. The number in parentheses refers to the page where the item is discussed in the text.

1. Explain the difference between the left and right sides of the brain. (167)
2. Outline the steps involved in the OPTIC system. (169)
3. What is the difference between line graphs and bar graphs?(171–172)
4. How do you master a concept map? (179–181)

BUILDING YOUR VOCABULARY STEP BY STEP: THE IMPORTANCE OF PRONUNCIATION

If you learn a new word in its proper context, memorize its definitions, familiarize yourself with its synonyms and antonyms, but fail to pronounce it properly, then you have not made the word your own.

    To become bona fide additions to your vocabulary, both the meaning and the pronunciation of new words must be learned with precision. Yet even seasoned dictionary readers sometimes overlook the pronunciation of the entries they investigate and sound misinformed or even silly when they mispronounce these words.

If you haven't already done so, get into the habit of reading the pronunciation when you look up a new word. If you are unfamiliar with the symbols and diacritical markings that indicate pronunciation, flip to the front of the dictionary for a full explanation of how each symbol is pronounced. You may be surprised to discover that many everyday words— such as "often" (only rarely is the *t* pronounced) and "asterisk" (the *s* in the last syllable is always pronounced)—are routinely mispronounced by the people around you.

Following is a list of words from the chapter you've just read (with the page numbers where they're located). As you look up their definitions, be sure to pay attention to their pronunciations as well.

analyze (167)	extinct (167)	lopsided (181)
concrete (172)	functions (167)	optic (168)
conducting (169)	hemispheres (167)	preliminary (181)
convey (167)	independent (170)	scrutinized (168)
dependent (170)	interpret (167)	symmetrical (181)
distinct (167)	interrelationships (169)	variables (169)

Succeeding at Test-Taking and Writing

Managing Test Anxiety

9

The will to win is nothing without the will to prepare.

JUMA IKANGAA
Marathoner

A walk into an exam room can be a frightening journey into the unknown. But if you're prepared before you sit down to take your test, any fear you initially feel will evaporate, and any anxiety will subside. This chapter explains how you can manage test anxiety by

- Preparing yourself academically
- Preparing yourself mentally

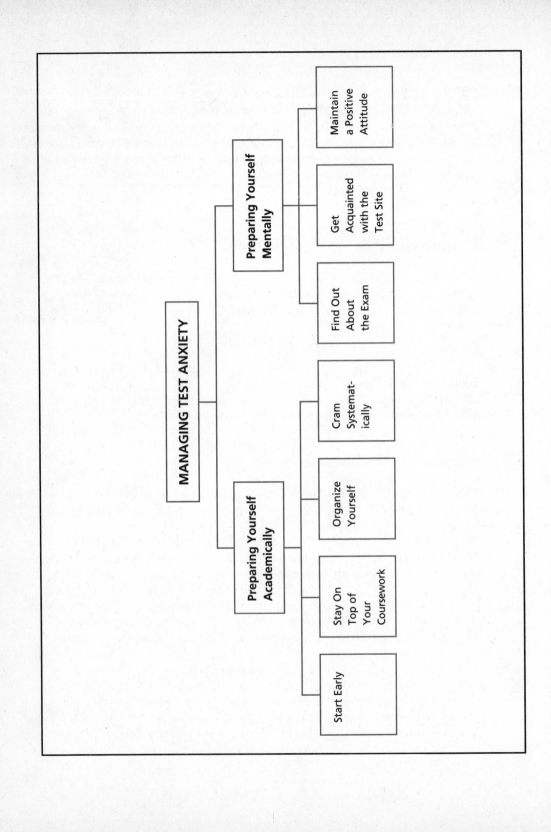

The cure for test anxiety is a simple but powerful one: preparation. Advance preparation is like a fire drill: It teaches you what to do and how to proceed, even in a high-stress situation, because you've been through the procedure so many times that you know it by heart. To manage the anxiety that often arises at test time, you can prepare yourself both academically and mentally.

PREPARING YOURSELF ACADEMICALLY

To be prepared academically, start early, stay on top of your coursework, and organize yourself and your studying plan. Even if you're forced to cram for a test, do so as sensibly and methodically as you would if you had no time constraints.

Start Early

The pressure's almost nonexistent at the start of a new term. Take advantage of this calm before the storm. Get a head start in a course by picking up your textbooks, looking over your syllabus, and familiarizing yourself with your school's tutoring services.

Pick Up Your Textbooks Early   Many students wait until the last minute, sometimes even until after the first assignment, before they pick up their textbooks. This is a common mistake. There's no reason to wait this long and every reason to buy your books as soon as you are registered for a course.

Obtaining your books in advance allows you to leisurely look through the text and get a sense of where the book and the course will be headed. Students who buy their books late in the game seldom have the opportunity to systematically go through each book, surveying the table of contents, reading both the preface and introduction, and flipping through the book as a whole. With this early start, you build a foundation of understanding.

Read Your Syllabus   One of the most frequently wasted resources in a college-level course is the *syllabus*, or course plan, usually handed out by the instructor during the first week of class. In the same way that surveying your textbook gives you a sense of the book as a whole, reading your syllabus from start to finish at the earliest opportunity provides you with a valuable overview of the course and makes preparing for tests much easier.

At times a syllabus can be an unexpected source of information. A few years ago, a student complained to the instructor that a paragraph-long essay question on the final exam was unreasonably difficult and totally unexpected. The instructor calmly pulled out a copy of the syllabus and pointed to the bottom of the page as the student's jaw dropped. The "unexpected" question had been printed on the last page of the syllabus and had been handed out at the beginning of the semester! The only problem was that the student hadn't bothered to read it.

Get Help If You Need It   As soon as you realize you're going to have trouble with one of your courses, get help. Don't struggle through a course and wait until the last minute before seeking tutoring help. By then the tutors may all have been taken.

Before the semester even begins, find out where your campus tutoring service is located and how to arrange for a tutor when you need one. New students can usually pick up this information during orientation. Keep it handy; then if you find that you are struggling with a course, you can arrange for a tutor without delay.

Stay On Top of Your Coursework

Your preparation for exams must begin on the first day of classes and continue throughout the entire semester. To be able to focus your mind and your time on an upcoming exam, the decks must be clear—that is, your coursework must be up-to-date. If you have to spend valuable time getting caught up, you can seriously endanger your performance on the exam. If you stay on top of your assignments throughout the semester—by taking notes as you read or listen and by mastering those notes at the earliest possible opportunity—they won't come back to haunt you when it's time to study for finals.

Take Notes   In most tests you are called on either to recognize or to recall a great deal of information. You can't possibly remember everything you came across in your textbook or heard in lectures during a span of several weeks. The only way to hold onto the information that will guarantee sufficient preparation for a test or exam is by taking notes.

The Cornell note-taking format, as we've seen, provides an effective framework for recording the ideas, details, and examples gleaned from both lectures and textbook assignments. The Silver Dollar System (see Chapter 4) enables you to distill that information down to its most important ideas.

If you make a regular habit of taking notes in the Cornell format for both lectures and textbook assignments and singling out the key ideas from the notes you have taken, you'll accumulate a valuable storehouse of knowledge, and you'll have an excellent start in your preparation for up-coming exams. The next step is to master the notes you have taken.

Master Your Material   The key to mastery is recitation, which is the most powerful method known to psychologists for embedding facts and ideas in your memory. If you took notes using the questions-in-the-margin system (see Chapter 7), writing the questions in the left-hand margin enabled you to recite the information you had jotted down on your note sheet. You can then take your recitation a step further by covering your notes in the wide column and using the questions to help you recall the information. This traditional method of recitation works best when you do it out loud, from memory, and in your own words. Remember: If you can't answer the questions now, you haven't learned the material, and you won't be able to recall it later during an exam.

Organize Yourself

The work you put into preparing yourself academically by starting early and by keeping up with your classes and assignments can be put to its best possible use if you make a point to organize both your time and your notes.

Organize Your Time with Schedules   Scheduling is important throughout the term. Three-part scheduling plans (explained in Chapter 2) allow you to set off times for reviewing material, so you won't get caught off-guard by a quiz or test.

As you near the end of a term or semester, scheduling your time becomes even more crucial. If you haven't been using schedules, now's a good time to start. If you have been, you probably feel on top of things already. In either case, it's a good idea to organize your time with a home-stretch schedule especially designed to help you tie any loose ends and get you through that all-important last week before exams begin. When exam week arrives, devise another schedule that specifies when each of your tests is and that enables you to schedule time for meals, sleep, and recreation, which are particularly crucial during exam week.

Make Up a "Home-Stretch" Schedule.   Use the format shown in Figure 9.1 to make up a home-stretch schedule. (This schedule uses the same grid discussed in Chapter 2.) Start by filling in the time blocks that will be taken

	M	Tu	W	Th	F	S	S
7:00							
8:00							
9:00							
10:00							
11:00							
12:00							
1:00							
2:00							
3:00							
4:00							
5:00							
6:00							
7:00							
8:00							
9:00							
10:00							

FIGURE 9.1   Format for the "Home-Stretch" Schedule

up by meals, sleep, job, and recreation. Next fill in your classes. Do not miss classes for any reason; you will want to hear the instructors' answers to students' questions about exams. Finally, fill in the time you will need to complete term papers and other assignments. Make sure you get them done before exam week. You don't want unfinished business to interfere with your studying or distract your thinking during exams.

Even after you've scheduled time for all your pre-exam obligations, you will likely find that some time is available toward the end of the week. Use it to study for your exams. Fill in the exact study times and subjects. Instead of writing "Study" in the time blocks, you are wise to write exactly what you plan to study: "Study economics, chaps 1 to 10," or "Summarize sociology notes." Make a schedule that you'll be able to follow, and then follow it.

Use an Exam Week Schedule.   Toward the end of the week before finals, make up a schedule for exam week. Fill in the times for your exams and for your meals, rest, and recreation. Remember that you must be in tiptop shape mentally, emotionally, and physically if you are to do your best on the exams. Eating the right food, getting the right amount of sleep, and exercising regularly are all important tools not only for maintaining good health but also for managing the sort of stress all too common around exam time. Therefore, don't skip meals, sleep, or recreation in an effort to squeeze in more studying time.

By finals week, the bulk of your preparation should be completed. Leave a block of time immediately before each exam to review important information. The less time you allow between this last review and the exam, the less forgetting will take place. Review calmly and thoughtfully, and carry this calm, thoughtful behavior right into the exam room.

Organize Your Notes with Summary Sheets

The best way to organize your notes before an exam is by consolidating them into a set of summary sheets (a highly concentrated version of your notes) and then reciting those sheets as you would your regular notes.

How can you reduce your notes so dramatically? You can do it by being selective. Although you may have been able to master the main ideas and subideas after each lecture or reading assignment, combining all this information and remembering it are not easy tasks. To recall all the lectures and readings without overloading your memory, you should limit your notes to only a handful of truly important ideas from each lecture and reading.

Why go through the process of making up summary sheets? First, it enables you to review and add to the notes you took throughout the semester and thereby increase the information you have retained. Second, it produces a superconcentrated set of notes that you can use as a refresher immediately before the exam. Finally, it helps you categorize your information under specific headings and thus improve your ability to retrieve it from your memory during the exam.

Make Regular Summary Sheets.   If you have used the Silver Dollar System to pick out the main ideas and subideas from your notes, reducing those notes one step further should be relatively simple. Include only those notes marked with a $ in your summary sheets. If you haven't used the Silver Dollar System, you can narrow your notes all at once by employing it now, although the process will be time consuming.

Figure 9.2 provides an example of a standard summary sheet. It is indistinguishable from a regular Cornell note sheet except that this sheet contains the most important ideas from several lectures, rather than just one, compressed into the same amount of space.

Steps in Writing

What are four elements of college writing?	**Writing must have:** basic premise, logical development of ideas, support in paragraphs, good word choice.
What are steps in prewriting?	**Prewriting** Brainstorm about a subject - generate ideas Narrow to a topic - use list or concept map Focus on a basic premise - ask a meaningful question that makes a point Plot a pattern - organize points into a framework.
What is the basic structure?	**Writing** Structure - use introduction, body paragraphs, and conclusion. - write body first
What should a body paragraph contain?	Body Paragraphs - begin each with topic sentence that supports basic premise (controlling idea) - support points with good examples and detail

What is purpose of introduction?
What does it reveal?
	Introduction - 1st paragraph-states basic premise
	  Reveals: - topic of essay
	    - opinion about topic
	    - organization pattern you'll use.

How do you conclude?	Conclusion - should leave reader with a feeling of completion
	  Either: summarize basic premise or main points
	    - state your opinion

What are the two main facets of revising?	**Revising** Strengthen support - data, examples, etc. Edit for transitions, spelling, and grammar errors.

FIGURE 9.2 A Standard Summary Sheet

Devise Advanced Summary Sheets. Although making up summary sheets of any kind gives you a chance to review your notes, devising advanced summary sheets also enables you to reflect on the information you have learned thus far. Reflection involves thinking about and applying the facts and ideas that you've learned. By rearranging your notes into categories that you've chosen yourself, you are doing just that.

Remember that "creativity comes only through reflection." That's because reflection leads to *advantageous learning*—learning propelled by a burning desire to know something. What distinguishes advantageous learning from regular learning and advanced summary sheets from ordinary summary sheets is your mental attitude. You can't help being curious about your notes when you reorganize them for your summary sheets. The knowledge you gain from doing so not only provides excellent preparation for an exam but also remains with you long after the test is over.

Figure 9.3 shows an advanced summary sheet that represents more than ten pages of notes taken during two lectures. Notice how the points are categorized by century and are placed side by side for ease of comparison. The questions in the margin are appropriately brief; they hint at, but do not supply, each comparison.

Figure 9.4 shows an advanced summary sheet derived from textbook markings. The subcategories "Advantages" and "Disadvantages" were supplied by the student who took the notes. The material in each subcategory was originally scattered throughout the chapter.

Cram Systematically

Academic preparation usually eliminates the need for cramming. But if you find yourself unprepared for an exam, then cramming is an unfortunate necessity. To cram systematically, limit the information that you attempt to commit to memory, and devote the bulk of your time to reciting what you've chosen to remember instead of trying to learn even more.

Limit What You Try to Learn   If your only chance to pass a course is to cram, then the one word to remember is *selectivity*. You must avoid falling into the trap of trying to learn too much. It will be extremely difficult to resist picking up important-looking bits of information along the way, but that is what you must do. Concentrate on essential facts, and use as much of your time as possible for remembering them.

Each textbook chapter has to be skimmed and searched, and the main ideas and pertinent supporting materials must be ferreted out and written

	Sociology 103--Dr. Lund	
	19th CENTURY	20th CENTURY
How is family governed?	1. Patriarchal, Father head of family.	1. Now, individualistic & democratic
Difference in stability?	2. Family stable	2. Family less stable
Status of extended family?	3. Many children and relatives under one roof--extended family	3. Smaller in size. Only two generations (parents & children)
Changes in mobility?	4. Non-mobile. Rarely moved "Old family homestead"	4. Mobility increased & residences changed often
Relationship between women & work?	5. Women: housework and children	5. Women: work outside & care for children after hours.
Attitude toward sex?	6. Puritanical on sex	6. Increasingly liberal
Variance in family types?	7. Family types in community alike	7. Greater variability in family type
Family's function?	8. Family had many functions: political, religious, economic	8. Now: function -- procreation and socialization

FIGURE 9.3   An Advanced Summary Sheet for Classroom Lecture Notes: Cornell System

in your own words on summary sheets ruled in the Cornell format. The same must be done with your lecture notes.

Recite Instead of Reread   Once you've extracted the most important ideas from both your textbook and lecture notes, push aside the books and notebooks. Resist the temptation to read even more in search of important information you may have missed. It's time to admit that it's too late to try learning everything. Limit yourself to only ten or so sheets of notes from your textbook and ten sheets of notes from your classroom notes. Your hope in passing the upcoming test lies, not in force-feeding yourself more and more information at the last minute, but in mastering the few facts you have in front of you.

I. Single
   Adv:
   1. freehand
   2. profits-his
Disadv:
   1. liable
   2. "venture capital"

II. Partner —
   Adv:
   1. Common pool
   2. "vertical integration"
   3. "horizontal   "   "
Disadv:
   1. death & change
   2. liable

III. Corporation
   Adv:
   1. legally formed
   2. stock-capital
   3. limited liability
   4. perpetual—
            board
Adv. to society:
   1. production - eff.
   2. continuation
   3. creates capital
   4. pays taxes

Economics 102 - Professor Maxwell

I. Single proprietorship
              ADVANTAGES
   1. Can do what desires
   2. All profit goes to owner
              DISADVANTAGES
   1. All losses hurt owner (unlimited liability)
   2. Commercial banks ordinarily will not provide
      "venture capital"

II. Partnership
              ADVANTAGES
   1. Pool wealth, profits, losses
   2. "Vertical integration" = gain control of resources,
      become own wholesaler
   3. "Horizontal integration" = buy out competitors;
      add products; improve products
              DISADVANTAGES
   1. Each time a member dies or leaves, a new
      partnership needs to be formed
   2. Unlimited liability, even if own a small share

III. Corporation
              ADVANTAGES
   1. Easy to form (legal permission needed)
   2. Issue stock to raise capital; banker underwrites
      stock issue and sells to public.
   3. Limited liability - Corp., distinct from its
      owners, can sue and be sued.
   4. "Perpetual succession", or existence. Board of
      directors.
       ADVANTAGES TO SOCIETY
   1. Technical efficiency - production of goods &
      services
   2. Pool business risks - Continuation of production
   3. Creates further capital for expansion or
      finance new
   4. It is taxed

FIGURE 9.4   An Advanced Summary Sheet from a Textbook Chapter

Now recite, recite, and recite. The notes you have selected will do you
no good unless you embed them in your mind so that you can mentally

carry them into the examination room. To make these notes your own, read each fact you've chosen, and devise a question you can jot down in the margin of your summary sheet for which that fact is the answer. Formulating these questions will act as written recitation. Then once you have a question for every idea, cover up the answers, and test yourself by reading each question and reciting the answer from memory, again and again until you know the information cold.

By judiciously selecting the very top ideas and by using your own set of questions to help you memorize them, you will have a chance of passing the examination. You may not remember much once the test is over, but for now the objective is to survive the battle so that you can come back next term and continue the war.

Next time, through organized note taking, regular recitation, and systematic review, you can avoid the pressure and anxiety of cramming. A few days spent with your summary sheets will organize vast amounts of material in your mind—far more than you could ever learn by cramming. Moreover, you will be rested, confident, and ready for exams.

PREPARING YOURSELF MENTALLY

When it comes to getting ready for an upcoming exam, there's no substitute for academic preparation. But even if you know your material inside and out, there's still an advantage to be gained from putting yourself in the proper mindset as well. Some students who experience test anxiety claim that even when they've studied hard, they freeze when the test is placed before them. Although academic preparation is essential, a little mental preparation can help take the sting out of an exam. If you take time to find out all you can about the exam, get yourself acquainted with the test site or a similar site, and work at maintaining a positive attitude, you're more likely to escape the test-taking anxiety that plagues unprepared students.

Find Out About the Exam

Fear of the unknown can be a great contributor to test anxiety. If you walk into a test without knowing what to expect, you are likely to feel anxious.

Except in those rare cases when the instructor provides you with a copy of the test in advance, you can't be expected to know exactly what the exam will contain. Does this mean that anxiety is inevitable? Not at all. By asking the instructor directly and by looking at previous exams, you should be able to "guesstimate" what might be on the exam and in the process dispel some unnecessary anxiety.

Ask the Instructor Directly   Many students overlook the most obvious method for finding out about the contents of an upcoming exam: asking the instructor directly. In many cases, instructors are not at all hesitant to discuss what the test will involve. Ask your instructor about the types of questions (objective, essay, or both) that will be asked. Find out whether your instructor will allow partial credit, how long the exam will take, and whether textbooks, notes, calculators, or other equipment will be allowed in the exam room. When you do finally sit down to take the exam, you're less apt to be knocked off balance by any surprises.

Use Past Exams   Instructors frequently take the same approach to their exams semester after semester. Therefore, a look at an old exam can often tell you something helpful about the exam you're studying for. Try to get a copy of last semester's exam to see what kinds of questions were asked and to make sure you know the meanings of the words used in the directions. Use all this information to direct your study effort and to make sure you have the background you need to take the exam.

Get Acquainted with the Test Site

Exams may be held in auditoriums, large lecture halls, or ordinary class-rooms. To be mentally prepared for an exam, get acquainted with the site where the test will take place or with a similar location. A week or two before the exam, study for a few hours each evening at the site where you will be taking the test. Your familiarity with the room and the sense of control you feel while studying will help establish a link between working in this room and actually succeeding on the exam. If you can't study at the site of the test, you can still prepare for the atmosphere of the test.

Study in quiet.   Some students who become anxious during a test are unnerved by the silence that is a normal part of an exam. If you take some time to study in silence, the quiet of the exam should be less disconcerting.

Practice at a chairdesk.   If you can't study at the actual test site, find an empty classroom that has a similar seating arrangement, and make an effort to adjust to the feel of these slightly uncomfortable accommodations.

Use a time limit.   So that you are not waiting until the last minute to discover how you perform with a deadline, spend some of your study time working under artificial time limits not only to get a sense of how quickly you work but also to grow accustomed to the inevitable pressure of time.

Maintain a Positive Attitude

One of the fundamental ways of preparing yourself mentally for any sort of challenge is by cultivating a positive attitude. Test-anxious students often sabotage their own efforts by mentally preparing themselves for failure. It's better to begin with a positive attitude: Relax, use self-talk, and engage in visualization to set a successful tone to your test taking.

Learn to Relax   Relaxation doesn't necessarily mean taking it easy or being lazy. It means being calm enough to work efficiently. If you're an accomplished runner, you know the best races start and end with a feeling of relaxation. To improve your chances of succeeding on a test, it's a good idea to prepare yourself by relaxing. Three simple but highly effective ways of relaxing are deep breathing, progressive muscle relaxation, and visualization.

Practice Deep Breathing.   When we are anxious, we take rapid, shallow breaths from the chest. But shallow breathing can actually lead to anxiety. Countless experiments have confirmed this connection. When psychologist Dr. James Loehr asked several subjects to breathe rapidly, shallowly, and irregularly for two minutes—in other words, to pant—he noticed a remarkable change in the emotional state of each subject. All found themselves feeling worried, panicked, and threatened even though nothing but their breathing patterns had changed.

Luckily, the reverse holds true as well. Deep breathing has been shown to produce a feeling of relaxation. A series of deep, slow breaths can often have a calming effect, even in the normally tense atmosphere before (or during) an exam.

If you feel tense before or during the exam, one way to cope with that feeling and to encourage relaxation is by "belly breathing"—that is, inhaling deeply beginning in the abdomen, instead of up in the chest. Here's how to do belly breathing:

1. Push out your stomach. That creates a pocket where the air can go.
2. With your stomach slightly puffed out, inhale slowly through your nose—one, two—filling up your abdomen with air.
3. Continue inhaling—three, four—this time sending air up into your lungs.
4. Exhale through your mouth, and reverse the process, counting—one, two—as you empty the air from your chest and then—three, four, five,

six, seven, eight—as the air leaves your abdomen and your stomach deflates.

5. Repeat steps 1–4 three or four times until you're feeling relaxed.

Practice Progressive Muscle Relaxation. A technique developed in the 1930s by Dr. Edmund Jacobson, progressive muscle relaxation works by diverting your attention from your mind to your body and by slowly tensing and relaxing each of your major muscle groups. This combination defuses anxiety and relaxes the muscles, which almost without exception results in a relaxed mind as well, leaving you better prepared for tackling test problems and for recalling information from your notes.

To use progressive relaxation, deliberately tense each individual muscle group, hold that tension for five seconds, and then release it. As soon as you do, reward yourself with a deep relaxing breath. Progress systematically, beginning with your toes and moving up through your body. By the time you have tensed and released the muscles in your face, you should be feeling more relaxed and at ease throughout your entire body.

Use Visualization. All of us have fond memories of places where we have felt completely relaxed. Often you can evoke a feeling of relaxation no matter where you are by imagining in detail your favorite relaxing place. If it's the seashore, for example, think not only of the sight of the slowly rolling waves but also of the sound of the surf, the smell of the salt air, the sensation of the sun on your back, and the feeling of the sand between your toes. The more vivid the image you create is, the more your body will respond as it does when you are actually there—by relaxing.

Use Self-Talk As we learned in Chapter 1, the idea of positive thinking is not just a starry-eyed slogan. You have an inner voice that is constantly chatting with you, either badgering you with negative thoughts or encouraging you with positive ones.

It helps to prepare yourself for an upcoming exam by listening carefully to what your inner voice is saying. If the message is self-destructive, now is the time to rewrite the script.

Psychologist S. C. Kobasa says that when you are facing a stressful situation, you can prevent overreaction and aggravation simply by *believing that you are in control and that you can find a solution to any problem or crisis.*[1] This means that if your inner voice is preaching doom and gloom, talk back to it, not necessarily out loud, but in your mind. Here are some examples of negative versus positive self-talk.

---

[1]S. C. Kobasa, "Stressful Life Events, Personality, and Health: An Inquiry into Hardiness," *Journal of Personality and Social Psychology* 37 (1979): 1–11.

Negative—Don't Think This:	*Positive—Think This:*
Three exams in two days is more than I can handle.	I've survived worse things than this. I'll just do the best I can.
This time there's no escape.	I'll just hang in there. There's always a way out.
I can't do these math problems.	I'll work them as far as I can and then see the TA first thing in the morning.
I don't know how to start this research paper. I never could write.	I'll make a list of ten titles or topics and then see the instructor in the morning for ideas.
I can't make heads or tails out of this chapter. I'll just forget it.	I'll go as far as I can, identify what it is I don't understand, and then see the TA or instructor immediately.

If you can change the tone of your self-talk to make it more encouraging, you can go into the test with a constructive, rather than a destructive, attitude.

Visualize Success   A number of studies have shown that visualizing an action produces many of the same responses that taking the action does. For example, if you visualize yourself eating a lemon, your body will often respond by salivating the same way it would if you were actually tasting the fruit. Similarly, if you visualize yourself taking an exam and succeeding at it, when the time comes to take the test you will have already charted a course for success. Of course, taking an exam is tougher than tasting a lemon; there's no guarantee that you will automatically succeed. But by visualizing your test-taking experience in advance, you have a much greater chance of bringing it about.

SUMMARY

How can you manage, and maybe even prevent, test anxiety?

The way to manage test anxiety is by preparing yourself both academically and mentally for any quiz or exam.

How can you prepare yourself academically for a test?

Start your test preparations early, keep up with your coursework, organize yourself, and if you have to cram, do so systematically.

What does starting early involve?

Effective test preparation begins a few days before the first class. If you buy your textbooks as soon as you're registered for a course, read your syllabus, and ask for help at the very first sign of academic trouble, you will build a strong foundation for learning thoroughly and being able to perform well.

How does keeping up with coursework prepare you for taking a test?

It's not enough to actively read your assignments and carefully listen to lectures. You must take notes and thoroughly master them to retain the information you get from lectures and readings.

What is meant by "getting yourself organized"?

Getting organized means using your primary resources—your time and your notes—as efficiently as possible. The best way of organizing your time is by using time schedules (the home-stretch schedule and the exam week schedule) geared toward the upcoming exam. The best way of organizing your notes is by compressing and categorizing them into a handful of summary sheets, both regular and advanced.

Is there such thing as systematic cramming?

Yes. You can cram systematically by limiting what you try to learn, thus avoiding memory overload, and by spending most of your time reciting the limited information you've selected.

How can you mentally prepare for an exam?

If you find out all you can in advance about the upcoming exam, get used to the test-taking site, and make a conscientious effort to maintain a positive attitude throughout, you should be able to minimize—even eliminate— test anxiety.

How do you find out what an exam will be like?

You can get a pretty good idea of what the exam will contain by asking the instructor directly about the kind of exam he or she has prepared and by looking at past exams.

What is meant by "getting acquainted with the test site"?

This phrase means if your usual study area differs sharply from the location where you'll be taking your test, it helps to spend some time studying at the actual test site or at a place that approximates it.

| How do you maintain a positive attitude about a test? | Think of a test as a challenge instead of a threat. You can boost your attitude by learning to relax, by using self-talk, and by visualizing success. |

HAVE YOU MISSED SOMETHING?

Matching. In each blank space in the left column, write the letter preceding the phrase in the right column that matches the left item best.

____ **1.** Reflection — a. Recommended cure for test anxiety

____ **2.** Cramming — b. Key to mastering your notes

____ **3.** Attitude — c. Should be done sensibly and methodically

____ **4.** Selectivity — d. Helps put a course in proper context

____ **5.** Recitation — e. Necessary to turn note sheets into summary sheets

____ **6.** Preparation — f. Bonus derived from advanced summary sheets

____ **7.** Syllabus — g. Can be improved through relaxation, self-talk, and visualization

Multiple choice. Choose the word or phrase that completes the following sentence most accurately, and circle the letter that precedes it.

1. Advance preparation for a test or exam can be compared to a(n)
    a. air raid.
    b. fire drill.
    c. road race.
    d. earthquake.

2. Deep breathing has been shown to produce feelings of
    a. anxiety.
    b. fatigue.
    c. relaxation.
    d. resentment.

3. The block of time right before an exam should be reserved for
    a. one last review session.
    b. a few moments of relaxation.

   c. a nutritious meal.

   d. rereading of a troublesome chapter.

4. Traditional reciting works best when it is done

   a. out loud.

   b. in your own words.

   c. from memory.

   d. in all of the above ways.

5. Becoming acquainted with a test site means

   a. walking through the room.

   b. spending time there practicing for the test.

   c. learning the exact time and location of the test.

   d. none of the above.

6. You can simulate the test site by

   a. working in a quiet environment.

   b. studying at a chairdesk.

   c. using a time limit.

   d. doing all of the above.

True-false. Write *T* beside the *true* statements and *F* beside the *false* statements.

_T_ **1.** The Silver Dollar System can be used to condense your notes into summary sheets.

_T_ **2.** A regular summary sheet looks just like a Cornell note sheet.

_T_ **3.** Advanced summary sheets promote advantageous learning.

_F_ **4.** You should be able to predict exactly the sort of questions a test will include.

_T_ **5.** Visualizing an activity can produce many of the same responses as occur when you peform that activity.

_F_ **6.** Awareness of an inner voice is one more distraction that is best ignored.

_T_ **7.** Relaxation provides the foundation for most mental preparation techniques.

Short answer. Supply a brief answer for each of the following items. The number in parentheses refers to the page where the item is discussed in the text.

1. What is a home-stretch schedule? (193–194)
2. How should meals, sleep, and exercise be affected by exam preparation? (193)
3. What are summary sheets? (195)
4. What is the difference between a regular and an advanced summary sheet? (195, 197)
5. What is the connection between progressive muscle relaxation and exam preparation? (203)

BUILDING YOUR VOCABULARY STEP BY STEP: CULTIVATING AN INTEREST IN WORDS

Interest can make all the difference in whether you remember something you've learned. A student who is interested in sports may be able to remember pages of baseball statistics with ease and yet struggle to recall even a single statistic from a "boring" history course. It follows, therefore, that if you can find some way of making words more interesting, then you will have an easier time remembering those words and increasing your vocabulary.

Deliberate

FIGURE 9.5 "Deliberate"

If you don't find yourself naturally drawn to new words, one way to remember the words you learn is by cultivating an interest in their origins. Most of the words you hear, read, or use didn't simply appear on the scene in their familiar form. They evolved. The trail that leads from a word's origin to its present use is often lined with fascinating history. Learning the history of a word is like discovering the story behind an invention or the motivation behind a murder. You gain a context for what you've learned, and in the process your interest is stimulated and your memory is strengthened.

Consider, for example, the word *deliberation*, which means "thoughtfulness in decision or action." Deliberation has its origins in ancient scales, the same type of scales represented in the constellation Libra. *Libra* means "a pair of scales" or "a balance." When a jury deliberates, it balances the evidence presented in the trial and weighs the possibilities of guilt and innocence. Likewise, a deliberate decision is one made after a weighing of the consequences has occurred (see Figure 9.5).

In contrast, the word *aggravation* is generally used to describe a feeling of annoyance or frustration. For example, a traffic jam can be aggravating. So can a person who shows up at a supermarket express lane with a shopping cart full of groceries. Yet the origins of this word are far more profound than simple modern inconvenience. Aggravate comes from the Latin word *gravis*, meaning "heavy," the same word that gave us *gravity*. Gravis led to another word, *aggravare*, which means "to make heavy." When it passed into English, the word took on its present spelling, *aggravate*, but it originally meant "to make heavy, weighty, serious, grievous." Somewhere along the line the meaning of the word shifted from a cause to an effect. Although we can still aggravate a situation (by rubbing salt into a wound, for example), we are more likely to encounter a situation that aggravates us.

If you want to pursue the history of a new word, a good dictionary will supply some of the story. In addition, there are dozens of books that can fill in the details in an interesting, entertaining way. Examples of some of these books follow:

Books Still in Print

Ciardi, John, *A Browser's Dictionary and Native's Guide to the Unknown American Language*. Published in 1980. Hardcover. The author discusses about 1,000 words, including "baker's dozen" and "swindle." Information and copies: Harper & Row Publisher, Keystone Industrial Park, Scranton, PA 18512.

Funk, Charles E., *A Hog on Ice, and Other Curious Expressions*. Published in 1948. Hardcover. Some illustrations or drawings. The author discusses about 750 phrases, such as "kick the bucket" and "kangaroo court." Information and copies: Harper & Row Publishers, Keystone Industrial Park, Scranton, PA 18512.

Holt, Alfred H., *Phrase and Word Origins*. Published in 1961. Paperback. The author discusses more than 1,000 words and phrases from "armed to the teeth" to "wet your whistle." Information and copies: Dover Publications, 180 Varick Street, New York, NY 10014.

Hook, J. N., *The Grand Pajundrum*. Published in 1980. The book's entries "haply" run the "gamut" from "frippery" and "furbelow" to "quaggy" and "sward." Chapter themes include people, psychology, the five senses, medicine, measurements, the landscape, and plants. The book includes an index and pronunciation guide and end-of-chapter word mastery tests. Information and copies: Macmillan Publishing Co., 866 Third Avenue, New York, NY 10022.

Maleska, Eugene T., *A Pleasure in Words*. Published in 1981. The author, a famous educator and creator of crossword puzzles, describes thousands of words through many humorous anecdotes. The book includes a section on how to construct your own crossword puzzle, in-chapter spelling, vocabulary, and etymology quizzes. Information and copies: Simon and Schuster, 1230 Avenue of the Americas, New York, NY 10020.

Mathews, Mitford M., *American Words*. Published in 1959 and again in 1976. Hardcover. The author discusses about 200 words such as "podunk" and "hickory," and many are illustrated by drawings. Information and copies: Philomel Books, 200 Madison Avenue, Suite 1405, New York, NY 10016.

Word Mysteries & Histories. Published in 1986 by the editors of the American Heritage dictionaries. As the editors note in their preface, this book "[delves] into the stories behind the *bromides* and *bluestockings*, the *Amazons* and *eunuchs*, the *ignoramuses* and *shysters*, ... the *prunes* and *pundits*, and the *wizards* and *zombies*." Information and copies: Houghton Mifflin Co., One Beacon Street, Boston, MA 02108.

Out-of-Print Books

Ernst, Margaret S., *In a Word*. Published in 1939 by Alfred A. Knopf, New York. The author discusses (and James Thurber illustrates) about 250 words, such as "abundance" and "whiskey."

Picturesque Word Origins. Published in 1933 by G & C Merriam Co., Springfield, Massachusetts. The book fully discusses 158 words and interestingly but briefly discusses 48 more under the categories of flowers, birds, animals, cloth, and gems. Forty-five of the words are graphically and meaningfully illustrated.

Here's a partial vocabulary list from the chapter you've just read. The numbers that follow refer to the page where the word was used. If the meanings of any of these words seem vague or unfamiliar, take some time to investigate the stories behind them.

accommodations (201)	extracted (198)	preaching (203)
badgering (203)	ferreted (197)	progressive (202)
deflates (203)	formulating (200)	propelled (197)
defuses (203)	inevitable (200)	reflect (197)
disconcerting (201)	judiciously (200)	salivating (204)
distill (192)	methodically (191)	unnerved (201)
embedding (193)	pertinent (197)	

Mastering Objective Tests

What is the answer?...In that case, what is the question?

GERTRUDE STEIN
Writer; reportedly her last words

The real purpose of objective tests is to test your knowledge, not try your patience. Yet when faced with the prospect of answering true-false, multiple-choice, matching, or sentence-completion questions, many students would prefer to choose "none of the above." What they may not realize is that becoming an objective test expert is one of the easiest tasks to master. To show you how, this chapter looks at

- Understanding the kinds of objective questions
- Choosing effective study methods
- Moving systematically through the test
- Learning strategies for specific question types

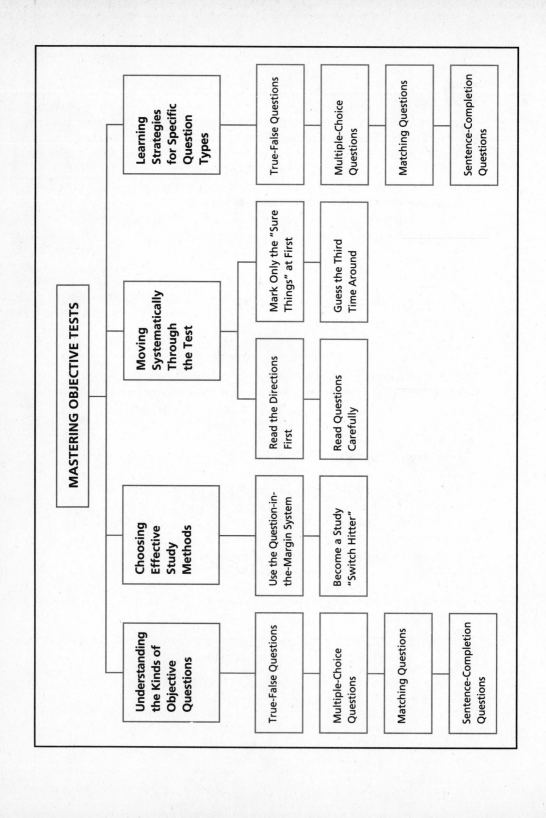

M ost of the test questions you'll be expected to answer in college fall in one of two categories: essay questions and objective questions. Essay questions take a broader view of a subject and generally place an emphasis on your ability to recall and organize what you've learned and write about it. Objective questions focus more on details and on your ability to recognize, rather than recall, them. Mastering an objective test involves understanding the kinds of questions that such a test will contain, choosing an effective study method for committing material to memory, moving systematically through the test itself, and learning strategies for specific question types.

UNDERSTANDING THE KINDS OF OBJECTIVE QUESTIONS

Although they're all basically related, true-false, multiple-choice, matching, and sentence-completion questions each have qualities and quirks of their own. Awareness of these can make you a better and more confident test taker.

True-False Questions

The basic idea behind a true-false question is simple: It consists of a single statement; your job is to decide whether it's true. What makes the choice more difficult is that to be true, this statement must be 100 percent true, not 50 percent or even 99 percent. One word is all it takes to turn a true statement into a false one. Consider, for example, the impact of a word like *always* on a true-false statement or how words like *no* or *not* radically change a statement's meaning. You have to be especially careful about reading each statement thoroughly before you answer it. Look at the following example:

> T   F   In 1787, the year the United States ratified the Constitution, Washington, D.C., became our nation's capital.

The answer to the preceding statement is false. Although it is true that the Constitution was ratified in 1787 and that the nation's capital is Washington, D.C., the United States had no federal capital until 1790, when Congress chose Philadelphia. It wasn't until ten years later, June 10, 1800, that Washington officially became the capital.

Multiple-Choice Questions

A multiple-choice question normally begins with an incomplete sentence known as a _stem_ and is followed by a series of choices, known as _options_, for completing that sentence.[1] In most cases, your job is to find the option that best completes the stem. Here is an example:

Stem ──────▶ In 1787, the year the United States ratified the Constitution,

a.   George Washington became the country's first president.

Options   b.   Washington, D.C., became the nation's capital.

c.   New Mexico was admitted to the union.

d.   the country had no official capital.

In this question, connecting option (d) to the stem results in a true statement. Linking the stem to any other option results in a false statement.

Answering multiple-choice questions entails problems you won't encounter when you're taking a true-false test:

Varying directions.   Some multiple-choice directions tell you to pick more than one correct option; others ask you to mark the one option that is incorrect. Be sure to read the directions carefully and go over all the options before you mark your selection.

Divided context.   Because each choice in a multiple-choice question is usually divided into stem and option, you have to mentally connect the two components to determine whether an option is correct. Correct answers aren't always obvious, even when you know your material.

Differing format.   Most multiple-choice questions follow the incomplete stem and option format. In some cases, however, the stem may be made up of an entire sentence. A setup of this sort can take you by surprise if you're expecting a standard multiple-choice question, but in general this variation is easier because you don't have to work with a divided context.

Matching Questions

Items in a matching test are usually divided into two columns and arranged in random order. Using a relationship that is normally explained

---

[1]Some of the ideas in this section were inspired by James F. Shepherd, _The Houghton Mifflin Study Skills Handbook_ (Boston: Houghton Mifflin, 1982), pp. 230–270.

in the directions, you systematically match the items in one column with the items in the other. Consider the following test:

Directions: Match the inventions in the right-hand column with the inventors in the left-hand column by writing the proper letter in the space provided alongside each inventor's name. Use each item in the right-hand column only once.

Inventor	**Invention**
_____ **1.** Eli Whitney	a. Automobile assembly line
_____ **2.** James Watt	b. Telephone
_____ **3.** Robert Fulton	c. Vulcanizing of rubber
_____ **4.** Cyrus McCormick	d. Six-shooter revolver
_____ **5.** Elias Howe	e. Steel plow
_____ **6.** Henry Ford	f. Steamboat
_____ **7.** James Hargreaves	g. Motion pictures
_____ **8.** Richard Arkwright	h. Cotton gin
_____ **9.** Samuel Colt	i. Dynamite
_____ **10.** Charles Goodyear	j. Steam engine
_____ **11.** Alfred Nobel	k. Telegraph
_____ **12.** Thomas Edison	l. Sewing machine
_____ **13.** Guglielmo Marconi	m. Spinning frame (textiles)
_____ **14.** John Deere	n. Radio
_____ **15.** Samuel Morse	o. Spinning jenny
_____ **16.** Alexander Bell	p. Grain-reaping machine

Answers: 1. h 2. j 3. f 4. p 5. l 6. a 7. o 8. m 9. d 10. c 11. i
12. g 13. n 14. e 15. k 16. b

Matching tests work like multiple-choice questions with an added dimension. You're faced with a *multiple* multiple choice. Instead of one stem and several options, you have several stems and several options.

This extra dimension adds extra complications as well. Matching carelessly or guessing prematurely can sometimes lead to a chain reaction of mistakes. If you make an incorrect match, you will deprive another item of its rightful match. This can aggravate your error by increasing the chances of another bad connection, which in turn can lead to another wrong match. Avoid this potential pitfall by making your matches carefully and by pairing up the items you are sure of before you begin guessing on items you're uncertain about.

Sentence-Completion Questions ⸜

A typical sentence-completion question consists of a partial sentence and one or more blanks. Your job in answering these kinds of questions is to read the sentences and determine what words belong in the blanks.

Sentence-completion questions work like multiple-choice questions without the choice. Unlike multiple-choice questions, sentence-completion questions can't actually be considered objective, but because the sentence is incomplete and because the answer is seldom vague or ambiguous, most sentence-completion questions can be answered following the same basic procedure you use for answering bona fide objective questions. For example:

Sentence-completion questions work like multiple choice without the

_____ .

CHOOSING EFFECTIVE STUDY METHODS

As we've already discovered, your success on a test is directly related to how effectively you've studied for that test. You must master your material as efficiently as possible but in a way that will prepare you for any type of test question.

Use the Question-in-the-Margin System

The safest way of preparing yourself for an objective test is the safest way of preparing yourself for any kind of test—by studying to the point of re-call. Although objective exams and quizzes generally test your ability to recognize, rather than recall, information, learning your notes to the point of recall gives you far greater control over what you've learned. You can tackle a question with confidence when you arrive at the answer independently of the cues that the rest of the question offers.

For that reason, the best way of studying for an objective test is by mastering your notes with the question-in-the-margin system. Question-in-the-margin (explained in Chapter 7) provides your notes with a built-in system for mastery. As you read each cue in the margin, you are compelled to recall the information to which it refers.

Another advantage that question-in-the-margin provides has to do with the form that the marginal cues take: They're questions! You'd be hard pressed to find a more logical way of preparing for a test filled with questions than by mastering your notes using questions as cues.

Become a Study "Switch Hitter"

Baseball players who bat from both sides of home plate are more flexible than those who can hit only right-handed or left-handed. In the same way, you can often improve your test-taking average when you master the material in your notes from both directions instead of just one. Use the question-in-the-margin system as you normally would to recall each important idea, but from time to time reverse the process by covering your questions, reading your notes, and then seeing if you can remember the questions you wrote to accompany each important idea.

If you have time and want to make absolutely certain you know your material, write down each important idea from your notes on the front of a separate 3 x 5 card, and then jot down your cue on the back. A stack of cards, instead of a few sheets of paper, enables you to constantly rearrange your notes, ensuring that you will be able to recall important information, regardless of the order in which it's presented.

MOVING SYSTEMATICALLY THROUGH THE TEST

Good students, those who understand what different objective questions require and have employed the most effective study methods, may still run into trouble unless they apply the same reasoned, organized approach they used in preparation to the process of taking the test. The only way to put what you know to good use is to move through the test systematically by reading the directions before anything else, by reading each question carefully, by initially marking only the "sure things," and by guessing only after you've made two sincere attempts to arrive at the answers logically. If you approach the test in this orderly fashion, you have an excellent chance of making the most of what you've learned.

Read the Directions First

It takes just a minute or two to read a test's directions, and yet the little time that you invest can often make a drastic difference in your score. Carelessness may do as much to torpedo a test as genuine ignorance does. If the directions for a multiple-choice test say, "Mark the two best answers," but you pass over the directions and mark only one option in each case, then most of your efforts will have been made in vain.

Read Questions Carefully

Objective questions, no matter the type, are usually filled with information. Each word in the question is likely to be far more important than a word in an ordinary sentence. For that reason, you must read each question carefully and thoroughly to pick up important details and the complete context.

Cope with Qualifiers   The English language has more than a dozen common qualifiers—including *always, most, equal, good,* and *bad*—words that we use regularly in writing and conversation and that testmakers often deliberately insert into objective test questions, especially true-false and multiple choice.

Qualifiers do precisely what their name implies: They complicate a simple statement or option by adding a qualification. The following two statements

It *often* rains in Seattle, Washington.

It *always* rains in Seattle, Washington.

are nearly identical. Yet one of them (the first one) is true, while the other (the second one) is false. In this case, the only thing that differentiates the two statements is their qualifiers: often and always. If you read through these statements too quickly, you may overlook their qualifiers.

Now look at a multiple-choice example:

The head of a kettle drum is

a. struck only with wooden mallets.
b. always made of sheepskin.
c. often made of calfskin.
d. tightened once a day.

In this example, option (d) is incorrect. Qualifiers indicate which of the three remaining options is correct. Without the qualifiers, all three options would be correct: Kettle drum heads *are* struck with wooden mallets, they *are* made of sheepskin, and they *are* made of calfskin. But because the qualifiers *only* and *always* overstate the case, options (a) and (b) are incorrect; while *often*, the qualifier in option (c), takes a more moderate stance and is therefore correct.

The qualifiers *only* and *always* in the first two options are both good examples of *100 percent words*. These qualifiers imply that the statements they appear in are true 100 percent of the time. Such qualifiers almost always make a statement false; very few things in this world are 100 percent one way or the other. Although it is wise to watch out for these words, don't automatically consider a statement wrong because it contains one of them. To keep you honest and alert, some instructors occasionally use 100 percent words in true statements:

All stars are surrounded by space.

All human beings need food to survive.

No human being can live without air.

A simple and effective strategy for coping with qualifiers is to keep careful track of them by circling each one that appears in a test question. Circling the qualifiers helps ensure that you don't ignore them. Then you can mentally substitute other words that will change the meaning of the question. This method is sometimes referred to as the *Goldilocks Technique* because you try it on several qualifiers until you find the one that's "just right." Most qualifiers are clustered in groups or "families." If you can find another family member that does a better job of completing the sentence, then the original question is probably false or, in the case of multiple choice, is probably an incorrect option. The qualifiers in the families that follow may overstate a true-false statement, understate it, or make it just right. Memorize the six families. They will help you answer true-false questions and make the right choice among multiple-choice options.

All—most—some—none (no)

Always—usually—sometimes—never

Great—much—little—no

More—equal—less

Good—bad

Is—is not

Whenever one qualifier from a set is used in a true-false statement or a multiple-choice option, substitute each of the others for it in turn. In this way, determine which of the qualifiers from the family fits best (makes the statement just right). If that is the given qualifier, the answer is true; otherwise, the answer is false.

For example, suppose you are given this question:

T   F   All birds can fly.

Substituting the other qualifiers in the "all" family gives you these four statements:

Original Statement   *Related Statements*

All birds can fly.   Most birds can fly.

Some birds can fly.

No birds can fly.

The statement that begins with *most* is just right, but that is not the statement you were originally given. Therefore, the original answer is false.

Notice Negatives   Negatives can be either words such as "no," "not," "none," and "never" or prefixes such as "il," as in illogical; "un," as in uninterested; and "im," as in impatient. Negatives are common in everyday speech and writing and almost as common in objective tests.

Negatives cause problems in objective questions because, like qualifiers, they can easily be overlooked, particularly negative prefixes that have a way of blending in with the words they modify. For example:

Because it is liquid at room temperature, mercury is indistinguishable from other metals.

If you read this sentence quickly, you may miss the two letters *i-n* and mark the statement true as a result. But if you read the statement carefully, you will realize that just the opposite is true.

Objective questions that contain two or more negatives can be even more troublesome. For example, you would probably be able to mark this statement "true" without much difficulty:

It is logical to assume that Thomas Edison's fame was due to his many practical inventions.

Yet you might have trouble with the sentence

It is illogical to assume that Thomas Edison's fame was not due to his many practical inventions.

even though it is also true.

When you find negatives in objective questions, circle them. Then disregard them for a moment, and try to gain the meaning of the question that remains. Finally, reread the sentence with the negatives included. Each negative you add reverses the meaning of the question. With two negatives, for example, the question's meaning should be the same as it was when the negatives were removed.

Use Grammatical Clues Although formats vary, all questions follow the rules of grammar. This fact can help you narrow your choices by eliminating those possible answers that don't produce grammatically correct sentences. The only way to determine if the rules of grammar are being followed or broken is by reading the entire question so you are able to get its total context. Consider this question:

The people of Iceland

a. a country located just outside the Arctic Circle.
b. are the world's most avid readers.
c. claim to be descendants of the Aztecs.
d. the capital, Reykjavik, where arms talks have been held.

If you race through this example, you might be tempted to mark either (a) or (d) as the correct response. Indeed, Iceland is a country located just outside the Arctic Circle, and Reykjavik, the capital, has been the site of important arms negotiations. But if you take the time to read the entire question, you can see that these two responses do not complete the stem grammatically. (Response [a] is missing the predicate of the sentence, and response [d] is missing any grammatical connection to "The people of Iceland.") That leaves (b) and (c) as the only legitimate options. (The correct answer is [b].)

Grammatical clues are even more helpful in sentence-completion questions, where your response must be recalled instead of chosen from a list of possible answers. For example:

Although about 75 million meteors enter our atmosphere each day, on the average only _____ of them ever reaches the ground.

Because *reaches* is a singular verb form, the only correct answer is *one*. (Otherwise the question would have read *reach*, the plural form.)

Choose the Best Response Some objective questions supply more than one *good* response, but in most cases there is only one *best* response. It's difficult to tell a good response from a best response unless you have read through the question completely. If you grow impatient and mark down the first answer that sounds right, you risk missing the best answer.

Here's a multiple-choice example:

You would expect to find an aglet

a.   on your foot.
b.   in a nest.
c.   in a small farming community.
d.   at the tip of a shoelace.

An aglet is the cap, often made of plastic, at the end of a shoelace. If you read only partway through this question, you might be tempted to pick option (a). That's a good choice, but if you read the whole way through the question, you can easily see that it's not the best choice. Only with the question's entire context can you tell which option is a good answer and which is even better. (The best option is [d].)

Mark Only the "Sure Things" at First

If a question has you stumped at first, don't feel compelled to answer it right away. And don't pick a "temporary answer" with the thought that you can come back and change it later. You may not have time, and even if you do, you may not be able to distinguish your uncertain answers from your certain ones.

On your initial pass through the test, mark only those answers you are sure of. (This is especially crucial in matching questions, where one mistake can set off a chain reaction of incorrect answers.) If an answer doesn't come to mind right away, circle any qualifiers or negatives, eliminate any choices you know are incorrect, and then move on to the next questions. These markings will provide you with a head start on your second pass.

Guess the Third Time Around

Except when there's an extra penalty for incorrect answers, guessing is always better than simply leaving a question blank. A question unanswered guarantees a zero, whereas a guess may score some points. Furthermore, if you know something about the material and have given it some genuine thought, then you should be able to make an intelligent guess. Intelligent guesses are always superior to random ones. Consider this sentence-completion item:

> You can travel by ship from New England to Florida without ever en-
> tering the usually rough open seas by using a system of rivers and
> canals called the _____ .

If you don't know the official name for the system, this sentence is long
enough and descriptive enough to help you come up with a good guess.
You might call it the "Inland Waterway." That's not the exact name, but it
is very close, and you would likely receive partial credit for it. (The answer
is Intracoastal Waterway.)

LEARNING STRATEGIES FOR SPECIFIC QUESTION TYPES

In the strictest sense, there are no tricks for taking objective tests. The requirement for taking any test is basically the same: Know your material. To
select the correct answer with any degree of certainty, you must be familiar
with the type of question, you must have studied effectively, and you are
wise to move systematically through the test. Once you've done this, there
are some other actions you can take, depending on the question type, to
improve your chances of answering correctly.

True-False Questions

Although you have a 50-50 chance of answering a single true-false statement correctly, the odds are not that high for the entire test. In fact, your
chances of guessing correctly on every statement decrease geometrically
with every question. In a ten-question test, the odds on guessing are
against you by more than a thousand to one. If you're unsure of whether
to mark "T" or "F" and you're forced to guess, adopt these two strategies to
influence your decision and improve your odds.

Mark "True" If You're Stumped   Because instructors would rather leave
true information in your mind, they tend to stack true-false tests with
more true statements than false ones. You shouldn't guess right away on a
true-false question, but if you're stumped and pressed for time, the odds
are in your favor if you choose true over false.

Be Suspicious of Longer Statements   Remember the importance of context, and remember that true-false statements must be 100 percent true.

Each word added to a true-false statement increases its chances of being false. All it takes is one incorrect word to make the statement false.

Multiple-Choice Questions

You can use several more strategies to cope with multiple-choice questions.

Pick "All of the Above" If You're in Doubt Most multiple-choice questions present just a single fact, the option that correctly completes the stem. But with "all of the above" the testmaker can include several options instead of just one. Because the purpose behind a quiz or exam is not only to test but also to teach, "all of the above" becomes an attractive choice for the testmaker.

Here's an example of a question that uses "all of the above":

Until the first half of the second millennium B.C., an army laying siege to a city had use of

a.   scaling ladders.
b.   siege towers.
c.   archery fire.
d.   all of the above.

The correct answer is (d).

One way to confirm the choice "all of the above" is to pick out two correct answers in the options. For instance, in the example just given, suppose you are sure that ladders and towers were used, but you aren't certain about archery fire. Unless the directions permit you to mark more than one option, you already have all the information you need to choose the correct answer. If option (a) is correct and option (b) is correct, then (d) is the only logical answer.

It would be a mistake to mark every "all of the above" you run into before reading the question and carefully considering the options. But if you can't seem to come up with an answer and you're running out of time, then choosing "all of the above" is usually a pretty safe bet.

Use the True-False Technique to Change Perspective If you know your material but have a mental block about the multiple-choice format, you can gain a new perspective on a difficult question by using the *true-false technique*. Almost any multiple-choice question can be thought of as a series of true-false statements. Simply rethink a troublesome multiple-choice question as a set of true-false statements.

Here's an example:

Before becoming president in 1857, James Buchanan was

    a.   married and divorced.
    b.   secretary of defense.
    c.   prime minister of Canada.
    d.   secretary of state.

This question and its options can be thought of as four true-false statements:

    T Ⓕ Before becoming president in 1857, James Buchanan was married and divorced.

    T Ⓕ Before becoming president in 1857, James Buchanan was secretary of defense.

    T Ⓕ Before becoming president in 1857, James Buchanan was prime minister of Canada.

    Ⓣ F Before becoming president in 1857, James Buchanan was secretary of state.

Viewing the question in this way can sometimes make it easier to spot the correct answer. The true statement you find in the true-false statements you create usually contains the correct multiple-choice option.

Discard Foolish Options Some multiple-choice options are distractors. Whatever the reason for their inclusion, foolish options are almost always good news for students. Exactly what the foolish option says is irrelevant. The important point is that you can eliminate it right away and pick the correct answer from the options that remain. Look at this example:

According to British tradition, the queen of England is not permitted to enter

    a.   West London.
    b.   the House of Commons.
    c.   the Soviet Union.
    d.   the Indianapolis 500.

Option (d) is so silly that you can immediately cross it out. (The correct option is [b].)

Choose the Middle Number from a Range of Numbers Questions that use numbers as choices can be easily answered if you've memorized the correct number. But if you haven't really mastered your material or if you have a tough time with numbers in general, then this kind of question can be a nightmare.

If you have no other information to go on, you can increase your chances of guessing correctly by eliminating the highest and lowest numbers. Test writers usually include at least one number lower than the correct answer and one number higher. Using this "rule," you can eliminate half the options in a four-option question. For instance:

A water polo team has _____ players.

a. three
b. ten
c. seven
d. five

Even if you know nothing about water polo, you can use the midrange rule to eliminate two options and improve your odds from one out of four to one out of two. (The correct option in this case is [c].)

Matching Questions

Answering matching questions effectively is mainly a matter of staying organized and saving time. You have a lot of items to read over, usually in a limited amount of time. A few strategies can increase your efficiency and reduce your confusion.

Mark Off Matches to Avoid Redundancy   This idea is so simple that it's often overlooked: Each time you match two items in a matching test, cross them off or mark them with a circle or an *X*. That way, when you move on to the next match, you'll have fewer items to read, and you won't be confused about which items you've chosen and which ones you haven't yet used.

Match Shorter Items to Longer Ones   In most matching tests, the items in one column are longer than the items in the other. For example, a typical matching test might contain a column of terms and a column of definitions. In cases like these, you can save yourself some time if you set out in search of matches for the longer items instead of the reverse. In other words, the column you keep reading and rereading contains the shorter items. That way you need to read each long item only once. It's a case of the dog wagging the tail instead of the other way around.

Sentence-Completion Questions

Because with a sentence-completion question the answer isn't there for you to choose, there are no real tricks to help you pick out the correct answer. But there are methods that enable you to clearly define the existing context of the question. When you do this, you zero in on the answer that will fill in the blank.

Clarify Ambiguity with a Specific Question   Sometimes a question seems to have two or more reasonable answers. In these cases, you may need to clarify the kind of answer the question is seeking. The best strategy for coping with ambiguous questions is to raise your hand and ask a well-formulated, unambiguous question of your own to clear up the confusion. Consider this item:

> In 1901, at the age of forty-two, Republican Theodore Roosevelt became the country's _____ president.

In this example, both "youngest" and "twenty-sixth" would be reasonable answers, but it's unlikely the instructor would be looking for both. If you raised your hand and said, "I don't understand this question," you would probably get a response like "Do your best." But a well-thought-out, more specific question would probably be rewarded with a more helpful response. For example, if you asked, "Are you looking for a number?" the instructor's response would enable you to decide which of your two answers is expected.

Disregard the Length of the Blank   Sometimes the length of the empty line equals the length of the answer expected. But in general there's no connection between the two. Pay attention to the words that are present, rather than to those that are missing, to come up with your answer for a sentence-completion question. Don't let the blank line distract you.

Treat Some Sentences as Two Separate Questions   Even students who aren't influenced by the size of a single blank when answering a sentence-completion question may become flustered by one that has two blanks. If the blanks are side by side, then the question may be calling for a person's name or a place name. Paying attention to the question's context should help to confirm whether this is the case. But if the blanks in a sentence-completion question are widely separated instead of side by side, then a different strategy is called for.

The best way to treat two widely separated blanks in a sentence-completion question is as though each occurred in a separate sentence.

There may or may not be a direct relationship between the missing words, so make sure that each filled-in word makes sense in its own part of the statement. Here's an example:

> Although corn is second only to _____ as the most widely grown crop in the world, no one in Europe had even heard about corn until _____ returned from the New World.

In the first portion of the sentence, the word *corn* indicates you're dealing with a grain. If you had read your textbook carefully (or if you hadn't but used your common sense), you'd know the answer is wheat. The second blank demands a person's name: Columbus.

SUMMARY

What are the distinguishing features and pitfalls of the various kinds of objective questions?

True-false, multiple-choice, matching, and sentence-completion questions are all related, but each has its peculiarities. A true-false statement must be 100 percent true before you can mark it as true; a single word can make the difference. A multiple-choice question normally asks you to complete a stem with one of four or five options. Because your choices are separated from the stem, obtaining the context can be difficult. In addition, varying directions and a differing format can complicate a multiple-choice question. A matching question operates like an expanded version of a multiple-choice question: You pair up the proper items from a column of stems and a column of options. But if you mismatch a set, you can create a chain reaction of errors. A sentence-completion question asks you to use the context of an incomplete statement to determine the word or words that are missing. The role of context is crucial because you must recall the correct answer; it isn't written out for you to choose.

What system helps you study more efficiently for objective tests?

The most efficient way of studying for an objective test is with the question-in-the-margin system. Question-in-the-margin not only helps you learn your material to the point of recall but also enables you to gear up for answering test questions by practicing with questions of your own.

How can you become a study "switch hitter"?

After you've been studying your material using the question-in-the-margin system, you can increase your flexibility by switch hitting—that is, reversing the process by covering your questions and using your notes to see if you can remember the questions.

What are the steps in moving through a test systematically?

First read the directions. Then read each question carefully and completely. Mark only the answers you're certain about at first. Then return to those questions that stumped you. If you still draw a blank, make an intelligent guess.

Why is it so important to read objective questions carefully?

Reading questions thoroughly enables you to note all of a question's details, particularly any qualifiers and negatives, which modify or reverse the meaning of a statement or option. Complete reading also allows you to use grammatical clues and contextual clues to help pinpoint your answer and pick the best response instead of just a good one.

Why should you mark only the "sure things" to start?

Marking only the answers you are certain about at first avoids the problem of not being able to distinguish later on between your certain and uncertain answers.

Should you guess on objective questions?

Except in cases where you are penalized for guessing, it usually makes sense to guess if you can't answer a question after two tries.

What strategies can you use with true-false questions?

Become aware of the types of statements that are likely to be true and those that are apt to be false. In general a true-false test contains more true statements than false ones. If you're pressed for time and have to choose, you're safer picking true than false. But view longer true-false statements with suspicion: More words in the statement mean more chances that it is false.

What strategies help you answer multiple-choice questions?

If you have to guess, pick "all of the above." If you know the material but have difficulties with the multiple-choice format, try converting the question into a series of true-false statements, which you'll probably find easier to handle. Also, eliminate foolish options right away, and choose one of the middle numbers in a range of numbers if you have to guess.

What can you do to better your chances on a matching question?

If you carefully mark each item after you've used it, you won't waste time rereading answers that you have already chosen. And if you look for matches for the column that has longer items, you'll save some time because you'll need to read each long item only once.

What strategies can you use for answering sentence-completion questions?

The best strategies are to clarify an ambiguous question by asking more specific clarifying questions of your own; to disregard the length of a question's blank, which may not indicate the length or size of the answer; and to treat a two-blank question as two questions instead of one.

HAVE YOU MISSED SOMETHING?

Matching. In each blank space in the left column, write the letter preceding the phrase in the right column that matches the left item best.

_____ **1.** Negative

a. Statement that starts off a multiple-choice question

_____ **2.** Guessing

b. One of the choices that make up a multiple-choice question _h_ **3.** Context

_a_ **4.** Stem

_e_ **5.** "Sure thing"

_c_ **6.** "Switch hitting"

_f_ **7.** True

_b_ **8.** Option

c. Mastering possible test material from both sides

d. Almost always better than leaving a question blank

e. Should be marked on first pass through the test

f. Best choice when stumped by a true-false question

g. Usually reverses meaning of a true-false statement

h. Provided when you read the entire question

Multiple choice.   Choose the word or phrase that completes the following sentence most accurately, and circle the letter that precedes it.

1. A multiple-choice question can be viewed as a series of

    a. stems.
    b. qualifiers.
    c. true-false statements.
    d. decoys or distractors.

2. One way to think of a matching question is as

    a. a multiple-choice question without the choice.
    b. a true-false question in two dimensions.
    c. a multiple multiple-choice question.
    d. none of the above.

3. Reading the entire question should help you

    a. detect grammatical clues.
    b. take advantage of context.
    c. select the best response.
    d. do all of the above.

4. If at first a question has you stumped, you should

    a. move on to another question.
    b. ask a clarifying question.
    c. pick a temporary answer.
    d. cross out any negatives or qualifiers.

5. The greatest threat of negatives is that they can be easily
   a.   replaced.
   b.   overlooked.
   c.   misunderstood.
   d.   reversed.

6. A sentence-completion question with two widely separated blanks should be treated as
   a.   a true-false question.
   b.   two questions.
   c.   a decoy or distractor.
   d.   an essay question.

True-false.   Write *T* beside the *true* statements and *F* beside the *false* statements.

___T___ **1.** For a statement to be marked true, it must be entirely true.

___F___ **2.** Some multiple-choice questions ask you to pick more than one answer.

___F___ **3.** The stem of a multiple-choice question is always an incomplete statement.

___T___ **4.** True-false tests generally contain more true statements than false ones.

___F___ **5.** Qualifiers are found only in multiple-choice questions.

___T___ **6.** Each word added to a true-false statement increases its chance of being false.

___F___ **7.** The length of the blank dictates the size of the answer in a sentence-completion question.

Short answer.   Supply a brief answer for each of the following items. The number in parentheses refers to the page where the item is discussed in the text.

1. Compare and contrast the four basic types of objective questions. (215–218)
2. What are some potential pitfalls of multiple-choice questions? (216)
3. Explain the Goldilocks Technique. (221–222)
4. What is the "chain reaction" associated with matching tests? (224)
5. What is the purpose of the true-false technique? (226–227)

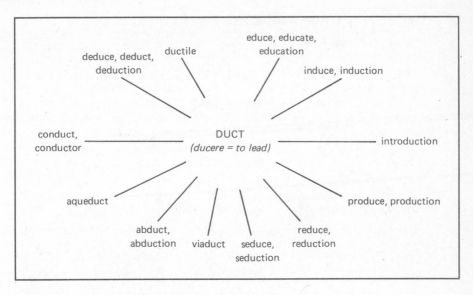

Figure 10.1   A Constellation of Words from One Root

BUILDING YOUR VOCABULARY STEP BY STEP: RECOGNIZING WORD ROOTS AND PREFIXES

The idea that a word is a single thing is a bit of a misconception. Many of the words we use routinely are actually conglomerates, combinations of prefixes and root words. Roughly 60 percent of English words in common use are partly or entirely made up of prefixes or roots derived from Latin or Greek. The value of learning prefixes and roots is that they can help you begin to "solve" words in much the same way that you solve an algebraic equation—by finding the variables, figuring out their value, and then combining them. As you do so, you also gain a better appreciation of how words evolve and how they relate. Tables 10.1 and 10.2 provide lists of common prefixes and roots. With one well-understood root as the center, you can often generate an entire "constellation" of words. Figure 10.1 shows a constellation based on the root *duct,* from the Latin *ducere* (to lead).

Once you begin to investigate prefixes, you will discover that over the centuries many prefixes have changed both in meaning and spelling. According to Lee Deighton,[2] "Of the 68 prominent and commonly used pre-

---

[2]Lee C. Deighton, *Vocabulary Development in the Classroom* (New York: Teachers College Press, 1959), p. 26.

Table 10.1   Common Word Roots

Root	Meaning	Example	Definition
agri	field	agronomy	*Field*-crop production and soil management
anthropo	human being	anthropology	The study of *human beings*
astro	star	astronaut	One who travels in interplanetary space—i.e., among the *stars*
bio	life	biology	The study of *life*
cardio	heart	cardiac	Pertaining to the *heart*
chromo	color	chromatology	The science of *colors*
demos	people	democracy	Government by the *people*
derma	skin	epidermis	The outer layer of *skin*
dyna	power	dynamic	Characterized by *power* and energy
geo	earth	geology	The study of the *earth*
helio	sun	heliotrope	Any plant that turns toward the *sun*
hydro	water	hydroponics	Growing of plants in *water* reinforced with nutrients
hypno	sleep	hypnosis	A state of *sleep* induced by suggestion
magni	great, big	magnify	To enlarge, to make *bigger*
man(u)	hand	manuscript	Written by *hand*
mono	one	monoplane	Airplane with *one* wing
ortho	straight	orthodox	Right, true, *straight* opinion
pod	foot	pseudopod	False *foot*
psycho	mind	psychology	Study of the *mind* in any of its aspects
pyro	fire	pyrotechnic	Pertaining to *fireworks*
terra	earth	terrace	A raised platform of *earth*
thermo	heat	thermometer	Instrument for measuring *heat*
zoo	animal	zoology	The study of *animals*

fixes, there are only 11 which have a single and fairly invariant meaning." The other 57 prefixes have more than one meaning each. For example, the dictionary lists four different meanings for the prefix *de-*, including two (down) and (to intensify) that are virtual opposites.

So learn as many of the common prefixes and roots as you can, but balance this knowledge with a healthy reliance on the dictionary. Use the list that follows of words from the chapter you've just read (with page

Table 10.2   Common Prefixes

Prefix	Meaning	Example	Definition
ante-	before	antebellum	*Before* the war; especially in the U.S., before the Civil War
anti-	against	antifreeze	Liquid used to guard *against* freezing
auto-	self	automatic	*Self*-acting or self-regulating
bene-	good	beneficial	Promoting a *good* result
circum-	around	circumscribe	To draw a line *around*, to encircle
contra-	against	contradict	To speak *against*
de-	reverse, remove	defoliate	*Remove* the leaves from a tree
ecto-	outside	ectoparasite	Parasite living on the *outside* of animals
endo-	within	endogamy	Marriage *within* the tribe
hyper-	over	hypercritical	*Overly* critical
hypo-	under	hypodermic	*Under* the skin
inter-	between	intervene	Come *between*
intra-	within	intramural	*Within* bounds of a school
intro-	in, into	introspect	To look with*in*, as one's own mind
macro-	large	macroscopic	*Large* enough to be observed by the naked eye
mal-	bad	maladjusted	*Badly* adjusted
micro-	small	microscopic	So *small* that one needs a microscope to observe
multi-	many	multimillionaire	One having *many* millions of dollars
neo-	new	neolithic	*New* stone age
non-	not	nonconformist	One who does *not* conform
pan-	all	pantheon	A temple dedicated to *all* gods
poly-	many	polygonal	Having *many* sides
post-	after	postgraduate	*After* graduating
pre-	before	precede	To go *before*
proto-	first	prototype	*First* or original model
pseudo-	false	pseudonym	*False* name; esp., an author's pen-name
retro-	backward	retrospect	A looking *backward*
semi-	half	semicircle	*Half* a circle
sub-	under	submerge	To put *under* water
super-	over	superimpose	To place *over* something
tele-	far	telescope	Seeing or viewing a*far*
trans-	across	transalpine	*Across* the Alps

number references) to break words down into their prefixes and roots and determine their meanings based on these word parts.

accompany (219)	efficiency (228)	irrelevant (227)
aglet (224)	employed (219)	objective (213)
ambiguity (229)	ensure (221)	perspective (226)
bona fide (218)	flustered (229)	ratified (215)
compelled (219)	formulated (229)	reasonable (229)
confirm (226)	genuine (220)	redundancy (228)
context (216)	geometrically (225)	seldom (218)
cope (220)	ignorance (220)	stumped (224)
disregard (223)	inclusion (227)	torpedo (220)

Tackling Essay Tests

Omit needless words. Vigorous writing is concise.

WILLIAM STRUNK, JR.
Professor of English; co-author of The Elements of Style

For many students, the thought of taking an essay test, of actually writing words "from scratch" instead of marking T or F or circling an option, is a terrifying prospect. Yet what these students don't realize is that writing an essay puts them in control; they are not compelled to choose from among answers someone else has devised. With a solid strategy, any student can take the dread out of the essay test and put his or her knowledge into it. To help take the sting out of essay tests, this chapter provides advice on

- Moving through the test systematically
- Learning the basics of writing an essay exam
- Writing effectively under time constraints
- Supporting your points

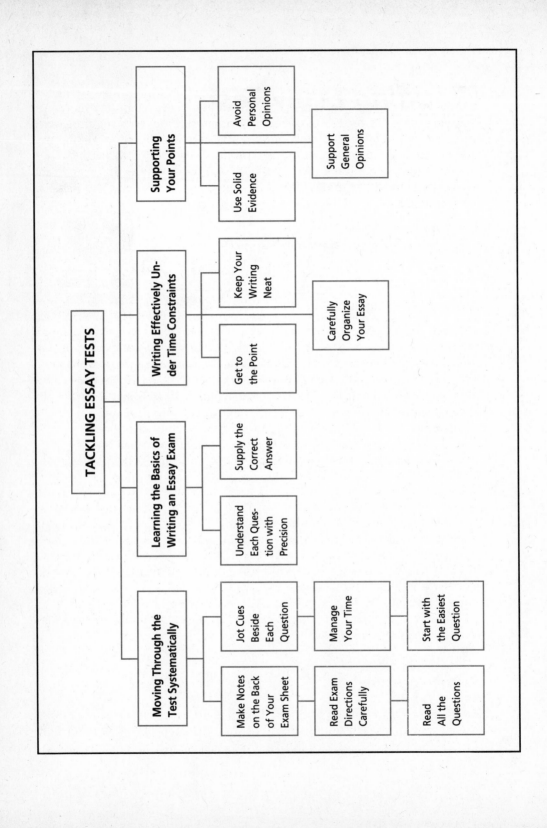

TACKLING ESSAY TESTS

Moving Through the Test Systematically

- Make Notes on the Back of Your Exam Sheet
- Jot Cues Beside Each Question
- Read Exam Directions Carefully
- Manage Your Time
- Read All the Questions
- Start with the Easiest Question

Learning the Basics of Writing an Essay Exam

- Understand Each Question with Precision
- Supply the Correct Answer

Writing Effectively Under Time Constraints

- Get to the Point
- Keep Your Writing Neat
- Carefully Organize Your Essay

Supporting Your Points

- Use Solid Evidence
- Avoid Personal Opinions
- Support General Opinions

Taking an essay test involves writing anywhere from a few paragraphs to several pages on each question. Unlike objective questions, which ask you simply to recognize correct information, essay tests require you to recall ideas and facts accurately and then to organize them into thoughtful, forceful responses to the questions. You do so by moving through the test calmly and systematically, by learning the basics of writing an essay exam, by writing effectively under time constraints, and by adequately supporting your points.

MOVING THROUGH THE TEST SYSTEMATICALLY

When an essay test is handed out, some students have difficulty resisting the temptation to jump right in and start writing. Confident students are often anxious to "get down to business" and show what they know; apprehensive test takers want to get the whole thing over with as quickly as possible. At first glance, these behaviors seem reasonable because time is limited. But if you take a few moments to plan a systematic response to the test, you'll be a lot more efficient as a result. A little preparation saves you a lot more time than it uses.

Make Notes on the Back of Your Exam Sheet

As you walk into the exam room, your brain may be buzzing with information you want to include in your essays. Before you begin reading the test, unburden your mind by quickly jotting down on the back of the exam sheet the ideas, facts, and details you think you may forget. Almost like a summary of your summary sheets, these jottings act as cues for the Silver Dollar ideas you gleaned from your lectures and readings (see Chapter 4). Furthermore, the action of writing down these notes involves you in the exam immediately. But remember: You are graded for what you write on the *front* of the exam, so don't spend more than a minute or so jotting down reminders on the *back*.

Read Exam Directions Carefully

Exam directions often contain specific instructions for answering the questions. They may establish the length of your answers (one paragraph, three hundred words, five pages), the approach you should take (explain, compare, contrast), the number of questions you should answer (say, four of the six presented), or time requirements (say, spend no more than fifteen minutes per question). If you miss such instructions, you will not only do a lot of needless writing and waste a great deal of time, but you may also invite criticism for carelessness.

Read All the Questions

Before you write anything, read all the questions. If you have a choice among questions, select those for which you are best prepared. If you have to answer every question, you'll know in advance which ones will require the most attention.

Jot Cues Beside Each Question

As you read through each question, underline or circle important words that provide clues for answering that question. Also, keep track of any key words or phrases that come to mind by jotting them in the margin. Later, when you begin writing, use these jottings and those on the back of the exam sheet to help organize your answer.

Manage Your Time

Figure out roughly how much time you can spend on each essay to complete the test. Stick as close to your time plan as you can, but don't become overly anxious or rigid about doing so.

> *If time is running out,* outline the key points you were trying to make in any unfinished essays. Instructors sometimes award partial credit when you can demonstrate that you know the material.

> *If you finish early,* use the surplus time to your advantage by going over your exam, double-checking your spelling and grammar, and, if necessary, inserting words, phrases, and examples that may make your essays clearer.

Start with the Easiest Question

Nothing inspires confidence and clear thinking more than getting off to a flying start with one question well answered. If the first question has you stumped, don't throw off your morale and your time plan. Just pick an easier question, number your answer correctly, and begin writing.

LEARNING THE BASICS OF WRITING AN ESSAY EXAM

To write an effective essay, you need to be able to understand each question with precision and to answer that question correctly.

Understand Each Question with Precision

A precise question requires a precise answer. Read each question carefully so you understand exactly what the question is asking. A good essay question is never vague or ambiguous. As you can see from Figure 11.1, words such as "analyze," "interpret," and "describe" have specific definitions. Therefore, if you have even the slightest uncertainty about what's being asked, don't hesitate to check with the instructor for clarification.

Supply the Correct Answer

Although they may require some specialized skills, essays are basically no different from any other type of question. To answer any exam question, you must have mastered your material. That means attending all lectures, reading all assignments, taking thoughtful notes, and then reviewing and reciting what you've written down until you know your information cold. Students who think they can "snow" their instructors with a long but fundamentally flawed essay are sadly mistaken. If your essay is missing the correct answer, this will be obvious to even the most inexperienced teacher.

A correct answer is often a correctly phrased answer. The tone you use or the approach you take in answering the essay can have a strong influence on the grade you receive. Most instructors have favorite approaches and ways of looking at questions and are naturally, if not unconsciously, disposed to favor essays that correspond to their ways of thinking. Theoretically you shouldn't have to worry about this—the accuracy and thoroughness of your answer should be sufficient—but practically, an essay that incorporates some of the instructor's "pet ideas" is more likely to be viewed in a better light. According to respected educator Hugo Hartig, author of *The Idea of Composition,*

Key Word	Explanation
Apply a principle	Show how a principle works, through an example.
Comment	Discuss briefly.
Compare	Emphasize similarities, but also present differences.
Contrast	Give differences only.
Criticize	Give your judgment of good points and limitations, with evidence.
Define	Give meanings but no details.
Demonstrate	Show or prove an opinion, evaluation, or judgment.
Describe	State the particulars in detail.
Diagram	Show a drawing with labels.
Differentiate	Show how two things are different.
Discuss	Give reasons pro and con, with details.
Distinguish	Show main differences between two things.
Enumerate	List the points.
Evaluate	Discuss advantages and disadvantages with your opinion.
Explain	Give reasons for happenings or situations.
Give cause and effect	Describe the steps that lead to an event or a situation.
Give an example	Give a concrete example from the textbook or from your experience.
Identify	List and describe.
Illustrate	Give an example.
Interpret	State the meaning in simpler terms, using your judgment.
Justify	Prove or give reasons.
List	List without details.
Outline	Make a short summary with headings and subheadings.
Prove	Give evidence and reasons.
Relate	Show how things interconnect.
Review	Show main points or events in summary form.
Show	List your evidence in order of time, importance, logic.
Solve	Come up with a solution based on given facts or your knowledge.
State	List main points briefly without details.
Summarize	Organize and bring together the main points only.
Support	Back up a statement with facts and proof.
Trace	Give main points from beginning to end of an event.

FIGURE 11.1 Key Words in Essay Questions
This alphabetical list contains key words encountered in the directions for essay questions, along with brief explanations of what each word means.

An alert student can easily identify these "pet ideas" and work them out carefully in his [or her] own words. The student who does this is prepared not only to see through the instructor's questions quite readily, but he [or she] also knows exactly how to answer them, using the teacher's own methods of problem solving! Perhaps this is the very essence of grade-getting in any course that depends heavily on essay exams.[1]

WRITING EFFECTIVELY UNDER TIME CONSTRAINTS

As in all tests, time plays a key role in essay exams. Well-supported essays will earn you superior scores. But at the very least, use the available time to make certain your essay gets to the point, is carefully organized, and is neat.

Get to the Point

When you are writing an essay, there's no time for obscuring facts in paragraphs filled with lavish adjectives or rambling discussions. Essay exams are written in a hurry and are often read in a hurry. You have to be concise!

Leave Off the Introduction   A good way to guarantee that your essay will get to the point is to skip writing an introduction. Don't even start off with a high-sounding sentence such as "This is indeed a crucial question that demands a swift solution; therefore...." Such a general approach scatters your ideas, thereby damaging the unity of your answer. An unfocused essay may contain all the right ideas, but if those ideas are scattered, your instructor may conclude that you don't know what you are talking about.

Put Your Answer at the Beginning   Begin with a strong opening sentence that both repeats the question and provides the answer. The example in Figure 11.2 shows how this principle works. The opening part of the first sentence restates but rearranges the question, while the second part supplies the answer. Such an approach keeps you honest and discourages partial or unfocused answers.

In Figure 11.3, the student has answered the question directly in the first sentence by naming three theories of forgetting. The rest of the essay follows a logical, predictable pattern in which she explains each theory in brief and then draws a conclusion about all of them.

---

[1]Hugo Hartig, *The Idea of Composition* (Oshkosh, Wis: Academia, 1974), p. 32.

Question: What does distributed practice involve?

Answer: Distributed practice involves dividing an assignment into several study sessions instead of one continuous session.

FIGURE 11.2   A Direct Answer

Although the essay in Figure 11.4 is longer than the ones in Figures 11.2 and 11.3, its basic format is no different from that of the previous examples. In the opening sentence the student answers the question directly by comparing reciting and rereading and then by contrasting the two methods. The next sentence states three reasons reciting is superior to rereading, and the paragraphs that follow develop those points.

In longer essays you don't have to include your answer in the first sentence. But you should make sure it is contained in the opening paragraph. Once your answer has been stated at the beginning, you can devote the rest of your essay to expanding on that answer. The ideas, facts, and details that follow all support your opening sentence or paragraph. As a result, your answer is both pertinent and unified.

Question: Identify three of the theories psychologists have suggested to explain forgetting.

Answer: Three of the theories that psychologists have suggested to explain how forgetting occurs include fading theory, retrieval theory, and reactive interference theory. Fading theory defines memories as paths or traces in the brain. According to the theory, if these paths aren't used (recalled) regularly, they fade until they eventually disappear (are forgotten). Retrieval theory claims that memories never really disappear; they simply get lost or misfiled, like important information buried under piles of paper on a messy desk. Reactive interference theory says that your attitude or emotions can interfere with your memory. If you are bored with or bothered by information, there's a greater chance that you will forget it. In certain cases, evidence seems to support all these theories of forgetting. But they remain only theories. None of them can be proved conclusively.

FIGURE 11.3   A Paragraph-Length Essay

Question: Compare and contrast reciting and rereading as methods of study.

Answer: Although reciting and rereading are both common methods of study, reciting is superior to rereading as a way of mastering your material. Unlike rereading, reciting (1) gets you involved, (2) supplies motivation, and (3) provides you with feedback on your progress.

1. Reciting gets you involved by compelling you to extract the meaning out of each paragraph you read. In contrast, it's possible to reread an assignment without understanding it.

2. Reciting supplies motivation because it encourages you to understand what you've read. If you had trouble grasping the meaning of one paragraph, you may be determined to have an easier time with the next one. If you understood a paragraph, you'll be motivated to continue your progress. But if you simply reread your assignment, you'll have no such incentive to succeed.

3. Because you know right away whether you've understood each paragraph, reciting provides you with immediate feedback on your progress. Potential trouble spots in your reading are brought to your attention right away. With rereading, the first real feedback you get is delayed until the test or quiz.

FIGURE 11.4　A Longer Essay Answer

Don't worry that by stating your answer so early in the essay that you are "jumping the gun." There's no advantage to keeping a grader in suspense, not even for a few sentences. If your answer is not included in the first few lines, your point may never become clear. Even worse, if time runs out before you have finished your answer, that key concept you were carefully saving could go unused.

Avoid Wordy, Rambling Writing Essays that are overstuffed with big words, unnecessary adjectives, and rambling philosophical discussions will leave the reader both confused and suspicious. Complex ideas don't have to be expressed in a complicated way. According to Hartig, "Quite difficult and subtle ideas can be expressed in straightforward and simple language."[2] You don't have to use large words and flowery language to prove that you are knowledgeable. In fact, as Hartig points out, a flashy essay

---

[2]Ibid.

may even put your knowledge in question, instead of confirming it: "Any teacher who has read hundreds or thousands of papers becomes very sensitive to phoniness in student writing, because he [or she] sees so much of it."[3] Don't write answers that are deliberately difficult or disingenuous. You won't fool anybody. Strive for clarity, sincerity, and simplicity.

Carefully Organize Your Essay

Organization comes easier when you leave off an introduction, put your answer at the beginning, and aim for simplicity and sincerity in your sentences. These elements provide a solid foundation for your essay's structure. Even so, you may want to take some extra steps to guarantee that the logic of your essay is easy to follow.

Use a Recognizable Pattern   Instructors don't have time to treat each essay as a puzzle in need of a solution. Take the guesswork out of your essay. Make your answer clear and obvious by following a familiar organizational pattern.

The most straightforward way of organizing your essay is by using the decreasing-importance pattern (discussed in Chapter 7). Sometimes known as the inverted pyramid, this pattern starts off with the broadest and most important information and then gradually gets narrower in scope. The advantage of this pattern is that it states the most important information at the outset so the reader can pick it up right away. It also eliminates the risk that time will run out before you've had a chance to fit in your answer.

Of course, not all essay questions are tailor-made for the decreasing-importance pattern. Key terms in the question can give you a clue as to what sort of pattern is needed. If, for example, you are asked to summarize a particular event, you'll probably want to follow the chronological pattern, progressing steadily in your description from past to present. Start off in one direction and keep moving that way until you reach the end of the essay. The same advice applies to essays that call for the spatial or the process pattern. In a descriptive essay, move systematically from one end of what you're describing to the other. Follow a process in an unbroken path from its start to its finish. And if the question asks you to compare or contrast, make sure you shift back predictably between the things you're comparing or contrasting. Whether you use the decreasing-importance pattern or some other structure, it's crucial that you move through your essay systematically and predictably.

---

[3]Ibid.

The experienced essay uses "trail markers," transitional words that provide directional clues for the reader and show the relationship between sentences in a paragraph. For example, the word *furthermore* says, "Wait! I have still more to say on the subject." So the reader holds the previously read sentences in mind while reading the next few sentences. The following list suggests other words and expressions that you might find valuable.

Transitional Words and Expressions	Intention or Relationship
For example, in other words, that is	Amplification
Accordingly, because, consequently, for this reason, hence, thus, therefore, if...then	Cause and effect
Accepting the data, granted that, of course	Concession
In another sense, but, conversely, despite, however, nevertheless, on the contrary, on the other hand, though, yet	Contrast or change
Similarly, moreover, also, too, in addition, likewise, next in importance	No change
Add to this, besides, in addition to this, even more, to repeat, above all, indeed, more important	Emphasis
At the same time, likewise, similarly	Equal value
Also, besides, furthermore, in addition, moreover, too	Increasing quantity
First, finally, last, next, second, then	Order
For these reasons, in brief, in conclusion, to sum up	Summary
Then, since then, after this, thereafter, at last, at length, from now on, afterwards, before, formerly, later, meanwhile, now, presently, previously, subsequently, ultimately, since	Time

FIGURE 11.5 Transitional Words and Expressions

Use Transitions The transitions that help make textbooks and lectures easier to follow can play a similar role in your essays, letting the reader know just where you're headed. When transitions lead from one idea to the next, the reader finds the essay clear, logical, and refreshing. A number of transitional words are listed in Figure 11.5.

End with a Summary Summarize your essay in a final sentence or two. Finishing off your essay with a summarizing conclusion ties your points to-

---

Behind the Scenes at an Essay Exam

What happens after you finish your last essay, heave a sigh of relief, and hand in your exam? Although grading procedures may vary from school to school, here is how more than two hundred examination booklets in a popular introductory history course are graded at one college.

The day of the exam, each grader in the history department has time to scan, but not to grade, the answer booklets. Then at a meeting the next day, each grader reads aloud what he or she thinks is the one best answer for each question. A model answer for each question is then agreed on by the staff. The essential points in the model answers are noted by all the graders for use as common criteria in grading the responses.

Unfortunately, simply listing all the essential points in your essay won't automatically earn you a superior score. During the reading of the answers, one grader remarks, "Yes, this student mentioned points five and six . . . but I think he didn't realize what he was doing. He just happened to use the right words as he was explaining point four."

These comments reinforce the importance of crystal-clear organization in your essay. You may also want to underline the main point of the essay so it's obvious and mark off your subpoints with dark numbers. Don't forget to include transitional words to show how you got from one idea to the next. Make sure that no one thinks you just stumbled onto the correct answer.

FIGURE 11.6   The Essay Grading Process

gether and reminds the grader of the original answer that you've devoted the rest of your essay to supporting.

These suggestions for organizing your essay become even more compelling when you learn how essays are actually graded. Figure 11.6 takes a brief look behind the scenes at an essay exam grading session.

Keep Your Writing Neat

In a carefully controlled experiment, a group of teachers was asked to grade a stack of examination papers solely on the basis of content. Unbeknownst to these instructors, several of the papers they were asked to grade were actually word-for-word duplicates, with one paper written in a good handwriting and the other in a poor one. In spite of instructions, on the average the teachers gave the neater papers the higher grades—by a full letter grade. Most instructors are unwilling to spend extra time interpreting sloppy papers. If your paper is messy, your meaning may be lost, and your grade could suffer. Take these few precautions to ensure that your paper is neat.

Use Ink   Most instructors ask specifically that you write your essays in pen, not pencil, so that they are bold and clear, not faint and smeary.

Write Legibly   If your penmanship is less than it should be, then you should probably start using the modified printing style, explained in Chapter 5. The modified printing style is easy to learn and should enable you to write your essays quickly but neatly. Both qualities are crucial in an essay exam.

Write on Only One Side of Each Sheet   When you write on both sides of the paper, the writing usually shows through, resulting in an essay that looks messy and that in some cases may even be unreadable. Besides, if your essays are written in an exam booklet, writing on only one side of each page can provide you with some last-minute room. Should you need to change or add something, you can write it on the blank page and draw a neat arrow to the spot where you want it inserted on the facing page.

Leave Plenty of Space   A little extra space in the margins (especially the left-hand margin) and between your essays provides room for the grader to make comments and for you to add any important idea or fact that occurs to you later. These "late entries" can be blended into your original answer by using an appropriate transitional phrase, such as "An additional idea that pertains to this question is...."

Guard Against Careless Errors   Neatness goes beyond the readability of your handwriting and the appearance of your essay on the page. It includes an essay that is free of careless spelling and grammatical errors. As Hartig observes:

> If you misspell common words, and make clumsy errors in sentence structure, or even if you write paragraphs that lack unity and coherence, many of your instructors are going to take it as a sure sign that you are sadly lacking in basic academic ability. Once a teacher thinks this about you, you will not get much credit for your ideas, even if they are brilliant.[4]

---

[4]Ibid.

SUPPORTING YOUR POINTS

A well-supported essay goes a long way in convincing graders that they are reading the work of a superior student. You can ensure that your essay is well supported by backing your answer with solid evidence, by supporting general opinions, and by avoiding personal opinions.

Use Solid Evidence

Obviously, whether you correctly answer an essay question is important. But because a well-written essay usually contains the answer in the first sentence (or, in longer essays, the first paragraph), the bulk of your essay should be devoted to the evidence that supports your answer.

If you've mastered your material and included your answer at the start of your essay, then providing support should be relatively easy. Every sentence that follows the first one should provide supporting ideas, facts, and details. Notice how natural this approach is. Your first sentence addresses the question directly, and the sentence that follows outlines the major points that support your answer. Then subsequent sentences—or paragraphs, if your essay is longer—will provide examples, details, and further evidence for your initial answer and its major points. When everything you write pertains to the first sentence, you cannot help but achieve unity; all your sentences will be both pertinent and cohesive.

Support General Opinions

The evidence you supply should be factual, not opinionated. Even generally accepted opinions should be backed up with facts. According to Hartig:

> An opinion that is not supported by some kind of logical or factual evidence is not worth anything at all, even if it is absolutely correct. For example, if you make the statement: "*Huckleberry Finn* is a masterpiece of American literature," and do not give any good reason to show that the statement is true, you get a zero for the statement.[5]

In the same way, you could expect to be marked off for writing, "John F. Kennedy has been the most popular president since the end of World War II." If, however, you wrote, "Based on an average of Gallup polls conducted during his presidency, John F. Kennedy had an approval rating of

---

[5]Ibid., p. 31.

70 percent, higher than any other president since the end of World War II," you'd be adequately supporting that opinion.

Avoid Personal Opinions

The opinions of "experts" have a place in an essay exam, but the same can't be said for your own opinions. All of us have personal opinions, but unless a question specifically asks for yours, leave it out of your essay. The purpose of essay exams, after all, is to see what you've learned and how you can apply it.

SUMMARY

What's the best way of tackling an essay test?

If you move systematically through the test, understand what writing an essay exam requires, work effectively within the time given, and substantiate your answer, you are more likely to tackle an essay test successfully.

How do you move systematically through an essay test?

Before you begin writing, jot down any key ideas, facts, and details you think you might forget. Then study the directions carefully, look over all the questions, and develop a rough time schedule for each question. Answer an easy question first to build your confidence and momentum.

What are the basic skills needed to answer an essay question effectively?

Most instructors expect your essay to demonstrate that you have understood the wording of the question and, of course, that you can arrive at the correct answer. Also, from a practical standpoint, an essay that incorporates some of the instructor's favorite ideas or approaches is more likely to be viewed in a better light.

How do you demonstrate that you can write well under time pressure?

If your essay makes its point quickly and is well organized and neat, you will convince most instructors that you can write well in a limited amount of time. To get to the point, omit any introduction, answer the question at the very start, and don't use any more words than are necessary to make your case. Structure your essay around a recognizable pattern, make sure that pattern is well marked with transitions, and restate your answer at the end. Finally, don't underestimate the importance of neatness. The appearance of your essays can affect your grade.

How can you ensure that your answer is well supported?

By answering the question at the beginning, you can devote the rest of your essay to supporting that answer. Back up every point you make with solid evidence. Support general opinions as well. Do not include personal opinions; the purpose of an essay is to show what you've learned, not what you believe.

HAVE YOU MISSED SOMETHING?

Matching. In each blank space in the left column, write the letter preceding the phrase in the right column that matches the left item best.

___d___ **1.** Suspense

___a___ **2.** Directions

___b___ **3.** Simplicity

___f___ **4.** Space

___c___ **5.** Scope

___e___ **6.** Transitions

a. Often provide specifics on how each question should be answered

b. The best approach to writing essay answers

c. Narrows gradually in an essay written in the decreasing-importance pattern

d. Unnecessary and undesirable in essay answers

e. Can be employed to make your logic more transparent

f. Allows room for late additions as well as for instructor's comments

Multiple choice. Choose the word or phrase that completes the following sentence most accurately, and circle the letter that precedes it.

1. Jotting down notes on the back of the test sheet

    a. gets you involved right away.

    b. is usually not permitted in an essay exam.

    c. takes time that could be better spent.

    d. will often gain you partial credit.

2. In an essay test, it helps to start off with the _____ question.

    a. most difficult

    b. first

    c. last

    d. easiest

3. Key words in an essay question should be

    a. paraphrased.

    b. circled.

    c. discussed.

    d. replaced.

4. You'll help prove that you write well under time constraints if your essay is

    a. concise.

    b. well organized.

    c. neat.

    d. all of the above.

5. A good way to ensure that your essay gets right to the point is by

    a. leaving off the introduction.

    b. writing telegraphic sentences.

    c. avoiding complicated words.

    d. scattering your ideas.

6. In a sharply focused essay, a strong opening sentence

    a. restates the question.

    b. provides the answer.

    c. helps unify the answer.

    d. does all of the above.

7. Poor handwriting can be improved through the use of

    a. the modified printing style.

    b. every other line of your exam booklet.

    c. a pencil instead of a pen.

    d. all of the above.

8. Key points in an unfinished essay should be

    a.   outlined.

    b.   combined.

    c.   included.

    d.   deleted.

True-false.   Write *T* beside the *true* statements and *F* beside the *false* statements.

    1. You should develop a time plan for taking your test and then follow it strictly.

    2. It's a good idea to read all the questions before you begin writing.

    3. Leftover time should be used for double-checking your answers.

    4. The appearance of your essay will have no influence on the grade you receive.

    5. Instructors prefer that you write in ink because it makes your answers easier to read.

Short answer.   Supply a brief answer for each of the following items. The number in parentheses refers to the page where the item is discussed in the text.

1. Why are some students particularly nervous about taking essay exams? (239)

2. What should you do if you are unable to finish an essay answer before time runs out? (242)

3. Explain the role of precision in taking an essay exam. (243)

4. What constitutes a "neat" essay? (250–251)

5. How should opinions be treated in an essay answer? (252–253)

BUILDING YOUR VOCABULARY STEP BY STEP: LEARNING TECHNICAL TERMS

Although precision is important in the learning of any new word, it's crucial when that word is a technical term. Unlike words in common usage, which may have synonyms that are acceptable replacements, the general rule for technical terms is this: Accept no substitutes. Physics, for instance, gives common words such as "work," "force," and "energy" highly specific meanings. You wouldn't replace "work" with "labor" in a sentence in a physics textbook, even though in everyday speech the two terms are almost interchangeable. Similarly, when we speak of a winning team's "momentum," we're talking about its successful trend, not about the product of its mass and velocity.

The chapter you've just finished provides some excellent examples of common words, such as *describe, list,* and *evaluate,* that have precise meanings in the context of an essay exam. You can use "compare" and "contrast" interchangeably in conversation, for example, but in an essay exam you would be penalized for writing a comparison when a contrast was specified.

Learning technical terms needn't be drudgery. Although this task requires meticulous study, it can also provide inspiration and encouragement.

Here's a list of words from the chapter you've just finished. (Page numbers in parentheses indicate where the words appear.) Try to learn them with the attention to precision you give to technical terms and the enthusiasm you give to words that interest you.

ambiguous (243)	guarantee (245)	rambling (245)
apprehensive (241)	inspires (242)	scattered (245)
chronological (248)	làvish (245)	scope (248)
cohesive (252)	logic (248)	substantiate (253)
concise (245)	morale (243)	unbeknownst (250)
crucial (245)	pertains (251)	unburden (241)
flashy (247)	philosophical (247)	unity (245)
flowery (247)	progressing (248)	vague (243)
fundamentally (243)		

Writing a Research Paper

If your writing falls apart, it probably has no primary idea to hold it together.

SHERIDAN BAKER
Professor; author of The Practical Stylist

From the time it is assigned until the day it is due, a research paper can occupy your mind like no other type of assignment. Although writing a research paper can be time consuming, it doesn't have to be overwhelming if you take the process one step at a time. To give you a head start in the art of the research paper, this chapter provides a calm and well-organized system for

- Deciding what to investigate
- Gathering information
- Devising a framework
- Writing the paper

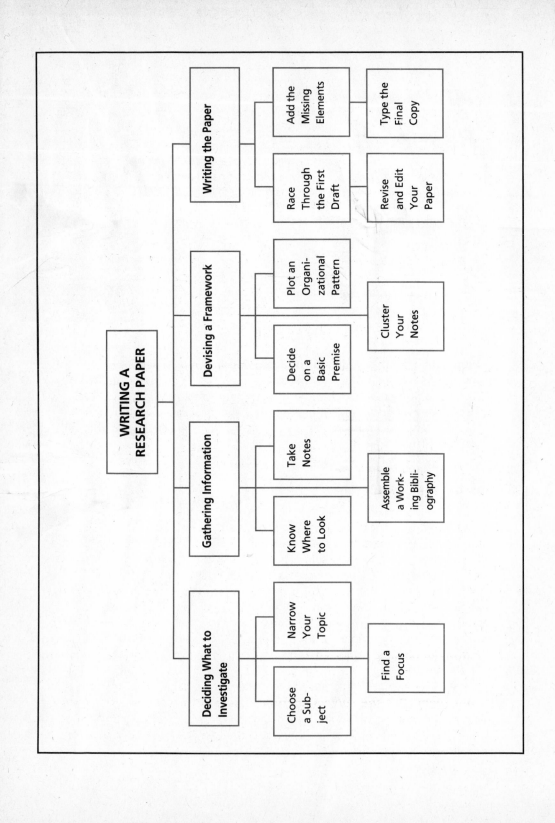

Writing even a modest research paper can take a lot of effort. Yet even though the task is long, the skills it requires aren't difficult, and most of them aren't new. In fact, writing a paper isn't much more difficult than reading about a subject in detail, taking notes on your reading, organizing your notes, and reciting, all the activities you undertake to prepare for a test or quiz. The difference is that instead of reciting out loud, you put your recitation on paper in a form that makes what you've learned readable for others. If you realize that writing a paper is not much different from studying your notes, and if you systematically decide what to write about, gather information, devise a framework, and then do the actual writing, you may even find that writing papers can be a most absorbing way to learn about a subject.

DECIDING WHAT TO INVESTIGATE

Finding a suitable topic is often the biggest stumbling block in research. It's essential that you know how to choose a topic easily and efficiently. There are three steps in the process of selecting a topic: Begin with a general subject that interests you, narrow it down, and then sharpen it even further by finding a focus. If you follow these steps, you'll wind up with a topic that is both interesting and specific.

Choose a Subject

In most cases, you'll be selecting a topic from a broad subject area. Because you'll be spending a great deal of time on the subject, your best bet is to choose one you are interested in or can develop an interest in. And if it isn't a subject that others are researching, then so much the better.

If you aren't sure what subject to select, do some preliminary research at the library. Scanning the bookshelves in your area of interest, consulting the *Reader's Guide to Periodical Literature* or a computerized periodical listing, and asking for assistance from a reference librarian will introduce you to an array of possible topics. In addition, the trip to the library will warm you up for the full-fledged research that lies ahead.

Suppose you are fascinated by natural disasters and want to learn more about them. But the subject "natural disasters" includes scores of topics: droughts, floods, tornadoes, hurricanes, volcanoes, and earthquakes, to name just a few. How can you do justice to them all? Obviously, you can't. You must narrow your topic.

Narrow Your Topic

Selecting a topic that interests you is just the beginning. The most common criticism of a research paper is that its topic is too broad. A Cornell professor of English suggests this method for narrowing your topic: Put your subject through three or four significant narrowings, moving from a given category to a class within that category each time. This method is similar to the Silver Dollar System (see Chapter 4), which enables you to select the main ideas from your notes.

For example, if you select natural disasters as the topic for a ten- to fifteen-page research paper, then you have to narrow the scope of your topic before you can cover it in adequate depth. Three narrowings will probably reduce the subject down to a manageable size, although four may be necessary.

General Topic: Natural Disasters

First narrowing: earthquakes

Second narrowing: earthquake prediction

Third narrowing: scientific developments in earthquake prediction

Fourth narrowing: computer simulations in earthquake prediction

Concept maps, which are explained in Chapter 8 and are similar to those in this book, can be used to "visually" narrow a topic. Write your general subject on a blank sheet of paper and circle it. Next write down subtopics of your general subject, circle each, and connect them with lines to the general subject. Then write and circle subtopics of your subtopics. At this point, you may have a suitably narrow subject. If not, keep adding levels of subtopics until you arrive at one. (See Figure 12.1.) The advantage of narrowing your topic with a concept map is that you provide yourself with a number of alternate topics should your original topic choice prove unworkable.

Find a Focus

Once you've narrowed your topic, give your research direction and purpose by developing a compelling question about your topic. The information you gather from your research can then be used to develop an answer. For the topic "The use of computer simulations in earthquake prediction," you might ask, "How helpful are computer simulations in earthquake prediction?"

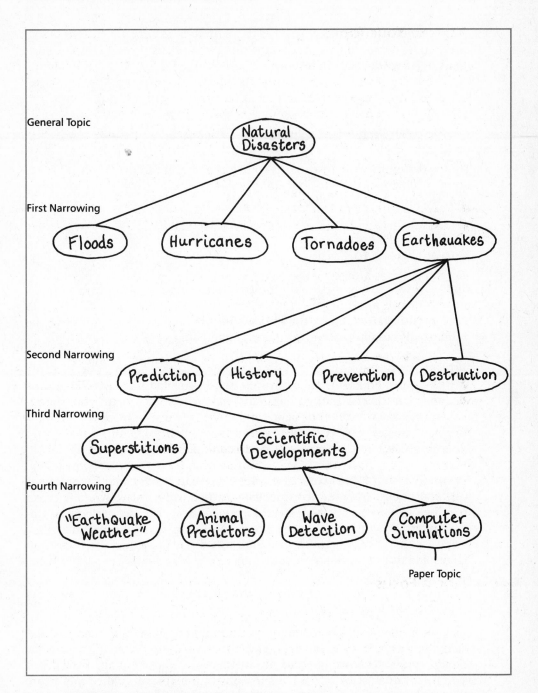

FIGURE 12.1 Using a Concept Map to Narrow a Topic

Whether you actually arrive at a definitive answer to your research question isn't crucial. The important thing is to focus your research efforts on answering the broad question.

GATHERING INFORMATION

The next step in your research is to begin gathering information. That requires knowing where to look (and what you're looking for), building a working bibliography, and then taking detailed notes.

Know Where to Look

Unless you're using firsthand information—from interviews or experiments—nearly all your material will come from the library. During this stage of your investigation, the library's most valuable resources will be the reference librarian, indexes, periodicals, and books.

Get Help from the Reference Librarian   Before you begin your research as well as any time during the process when you hit a snag, seek out the reference librarian. Although librarians may not be experts on your particular subject, they *are* experts at using the library's research tools. Librarians can often suggest indexes you may not have heard of, sources you didn't think to consult, and searching strategies you didn't try.

Consult Periodical Indexes   Most of your research will come from periodicals and books. It's wise to consult the articles that relate to your paper topic before you begin to delve into books. Not only do periodicals frequently provide the most recent information on a subject; sometimes they supply the only information. In addition, articles often include important names and titles that relate to your subject and occasionally provide a valuable overview of your topic.

There are a number of general and specific indexes, both bound and computerized, for periodicals.

Use Bound Indexes.   The most prevalent bound index is the *Reader's Guide to Periodical Literature*. Each green-colored volume lists by author and subject all the articles that appeared in several dozen magazines during a given year. To locate articles on your topic, consult the years in which you think those articles may have been published. Each entry in the *Reader's Guide* gives you the information you need to locate the appropriate journal or magazine.

Your paper topic may pertain to a subject that has its own index. For example, if you are doing research in psychology, you can refer to several indexes that deal specifically with psychology and that include journals and magazines that aren't listed in the *Reader's Guide*. A number of other subjects, such as business and education, have their own indexes. In addition, large newspapers such as the *New York Times* publish indexes of their articles.

Use Computerized Indexes. Many libraries now use computerized magazine indexes such as Info-trac that enable you to type in the name of a subject, author, or title and receive a list of relevant articles. You may also be able to customize your search with key words and/or Boolean searching.

Key word search. Key words can provide the most direct route to the articles you are seeking, especially when searching by subject isn't convenient or fruitful. For example, if you want information on Gregg Toland, the cinematographer who worked with Orson Welles on the movie *Citizen Kane*, you may come up empty if you use the subjects "Toland" or "Citizen Kane" in your search. The database simply may not have enough articles on these topics to justify a separate subject heading. If, however, you search for articles under a broader subject, such as "Motion pictures—American," you may have to scan through hundreds of citations before you find appropriate ones. With a key word search, by contrast, you can type in a word (or name) such as "Toland," and the computer will reply with every article in its database that contains the key word you have typed.

Boolean search. A Boolean search enables you to narrow your search by combining two key words. Suppose you need information on the Detroit Lions football team. If you search under the subject "Detroit," "Football," or "Lions," you would have to scan thousands of citations that have nothing to do with your particular topic. But by searching for titles that contain both key words—"Football" and "Lions,"—you are likelier to pinpoint articles that deal directly with your topic.

These computerized indexes have some advantages over bound indexes and some disadvantages as well.

Advantages

Speed. If you know what you're looking for, you can usually come up with a list of periodical entries in less than a minute.

Consolidation. Unlike many bound indexes, which have a separate volume for each year, a computerized index normally includes a wide range of years. A single computerized search can cover more ground.

A written record. Most computerized indexes are connected to a printer. Once you find the sources you are looking for, you can print out the citations immediately.

Abstracts. Some computerized citations include an abstract that summarizes the points of the articles and that helps you determine whether it would be worth your while to read.

Disadvantages

Limited listings. Most computer indexes list only relatively recent entries. If you're searching for an article that is more than fifteen years old, for example, you will probably have to look for the citation in a bound index.

Outdated information. The information in a computerized index is stored on a compact disc, which must be replaced whenever the listings need to be updated. Some libraries update their discs frequently; others do not.

Limited availability. If the wait at the computer index looks long, you may be wise to do your research with the bound indexes instead. The time-saving advantage of the computer index will be lost if you have to wait too long to use it.

Consult Book Indexes   Books usually have their own indexes—on individual cards or in a computer.

Use a Card Catalog.   The card catalog generally consists of several large cabinets and a series of long, small drawers divided by author, title, and subject and arranged alphabetically. To use the card catalog effectively, you may need to use the author, the title, and the subject sections. If you know the names of experts in the area you are researching or if you're already aware of titles of books on the subject, you'll want to consult both the author and title catalogs. If while scanning articles in magazines or journals you've uncovered the names of authors or books that relate to your subject, you'll want to find out whether your library has any of these books. Finally, you'll want to check in the subject catalog for other books pertaining to your topic.

Use a Computerized Catalog.   Many libraries have replaced the traditional card catalog with a set of computer terminals that enable you to quickly find the same information without flipping through dozens of index cards. Instead of scanning a large list of books, as you did with the card catalog, you simply type in the information you are seeking and the computer responds. Like the traditional card catalog, most computer catalogs allow you to search for a book based on its subject, title, or author. In addition, many computer catalogs include advanced commands similar to those used with the periodical index.

Assemble a Working Bibliography

As you discover magazines and books that relate to your research, add them to a *working bibliography*—a list of promising sources that you plan to consult. Be generous in compiling your list. It's better to check out several references that do not help than to miss a good one because its title isn't appealing.

Instead of listing all these references on a large sheet of paper, you can use a separate 3 x 5 card for each reference. Then later on, if you decide that a particular reference doesn't help you, you can simply throw away its card.

Figure 12.2 provides an efficient format for putting your bibliography on 3 x 5 cards. On the front of the card, record the following information:

The name of the library where the periodical or book is located

A short title of your subject. A title will make it easier to locate a particular card and will aid in clustering your information.

The library call number

The reference information—that is, the author, title, publishing data, and page references—in exactly the form that you plan to use it in the bibliographical portion of your paper. This ensures that you will include all the essential parts of the reference and that typing your paper will be much easier.

Olin Library	Theories of Memory
Q 360 .C33	Campbell, Jeremy *Grammatical Man*. New York: Simon & Schuster, Inc., 1982.

Bottom-up and top-down theories of memory described in Chapter 18.

Refers back to previous chapters and is difficult to read in spots. Provides solid summary of the two theories.
Uses simple, vivid examples to explain difficult points.

3 x 5 Card with Data   Reverse of 3 x 5 Card with Comments

FIGURE 12.2   Working Bibliography: 3 x 5 Card Method

On the back of the card, jot down your assessment of the reference. If the source doesn't seem useful, then briefly explain why. If the source appears helpful, jot down how. Then when you have a chance to take another look at the article or book, you'll know why you thought it would or would not be useful. And if you shift the focus of your paper, you'll be able to determine whether sources you had eliminated should now be consulted and whether previously promising sources will no longer be of help.

Take Notes

Using your bibliography as a springboard, you can investigate your sources and begin taking notes. There's no getting around it—taking notes is time consuming. But if your notes are easy to use, neat, brief, and accurate, then the bulk of your paper will be written by the time you have completed the note-taking step.

Making Sure Your Notes Are Easy to Use   To make your notes easy to use, jot each note on a separate piece of paper rather than writing them one after the other on regular-sized sheets. Three-by-five-inch index cards are commonly used for notes, although you can use slips of paper instead. Whether you use cards or slips, you will be able to rearrange them easily and often because each note is separate.

Another way to make your notes easier to use is by conscientiously identifying each card or slip. In the top left corner, write the author's name or the title of the source you consulted. Then at the bottom right, jot down the specific page on which you found the information. With these two markings on every note card, you can easily verify or add to any information you've gathered for your paper. In addition, you'll have all the information you may need for your citations (see Figure 12.3).

Keep Your Note Cards Neat   Detailed notes are useless if you can't read them. Write your notes neatly the first time, even if it takes a little longer to do so. Use the modified printing system (see Chapter 5) to write quickly but legibly, and write in pen, instead of pencil, to avoid smears and fading.

Keep Your Note Cards Brief   Brevity is the secret behind a useful note card. Get to the heart of the matter with each note you take. Make your notes concise, yet sufficiently detailed to provide accurate meaning.

One simple way to limit the length of each note card is by abbreviating common words. For example, use "w/" instead of "with," "co." instead of

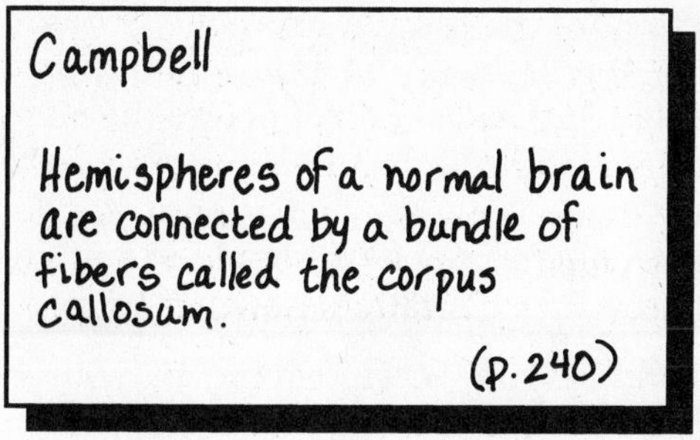

> Campbell
>
> Hemispheres of a normal brain are connected by a bundle of fibers called the corpus callosum.
>
> (p. 240)

FIGURE 12.3   Detailed Note Written on One Side of a 3 x 5 Card

"company," and "govt" in place of "government." Develop your own abbreviations for words you commonly use. For example, if you're doing research on earthquakes, you may want to use "RS" to stand for "Richter scale" and "tct plates" to abbreviate "tectonic plates." Be careful not to go overboard with abbreviations, however. Abbreviating words may save you time to begin with, but you don't want to waste that time later trying to decipher your unfamiliar shorthand.

Strive for Accuracy   Because you're dealing in facts, you must make certain that the information you jot down is accurate. It's relatively easy to remember as you're taking notes who said what and which of the thoughts you are writing down are your own and which are the thoughts of the author. But between the time you fill your last note card and the moment you write the first line of your paper, you're liable to forget these crucial details. To counteract forgetting and to ensure the information in your paper is accurate, distinguish clearly on your note cards between quoted ideas and paraphrased ideas and between the writer's thoughts and your own.

Copy Quotations Carefully.   When you quote from a book or an article, make sure that you do so carefully. Place quotation marks on your card around the exact words you copied from the reference. Compare your version with the original quotation to make sure you copied it correctly. Don't change the wording or the spelling of the author's quotation. If you find a misspelling or a grammatical error in the quotation, you may use the bracketed notation [sic] to make it clear to your reader that you're aware of the mistake.

If you leave out a section or even one word from a quote, use three ellipsis points (...) to indicate the omission. If the words you left out came at the end of a sentence, add a period before the ellipses.

The purpose of an ellipsis is to leave out information that doesn't relate to the point you are using the quotation to support. An ellipsis should not be used to rearrange a quotation simply to suit your needs. Ellipses are intended to abbreviate a quotation, not alter its meaning.

Mark Thoughts of Your Own.   Some of your best ideas may occur as you're taking notes. Put these thoughts on paper right away, but do so on a separate note card marked "my idea" or something similar. That way you'll be sure not to confuse your original ideas with the ones you've encountered in your reading.

Paraphrase What You Read.   Although it is important to distinguish your original ideas from the ones you have read, there's nothing wrong with paraphrasing—expressing someone else's ideas in your own words—as long as you give proper credit to the source. If you paraphrase as you take notes, you'll often be able to transfer what you've written on your note cards to your draft without changing a word.

DEVISING A FRAMEWORK

You can devise a solid framework for your paper out of a pile of disconnected note cards by deciding on a basic premise, clustering your notes under a handful of main ideas, and plotting out a clear, logical organizational pattern.

Decide on a Basic Premise

In the same way that choosing a focus helped provide direction for your research, deciding on a basic *premise* from the notes you now have lays the foundation for your paper's organization. Potential arguments, apparent similarities, and possible theories all have a way of rising to the surface in the process of taking notes. Any of these can be used to form a basic premise, which is the fundamental approach that underlies your paper. If a premise doesn't become obvious to you as you're taking notes, go back over the information and ask yourself some hard questions. For example:

Where is this paper heading?

What are the ramifications of the information I've assembled?

What point is most important?

What am I saying?

What do I want to say?

If there's a choice of viewpoint—for or against a question, for example—which view has the most evidence to support it? If you've done a good job of research, you should be able to decide now what you want to say in your paper, and you should have the evidence to support that view right on your 3 x 5 cards.

Cluster Your Notes

The paper's basic premise should act as a magnet for clustering your notes, which enables you to draw out the most important ideas from the dozens and perhaps hundreds of notes you have written. In most cases, a research paper should incorporate fewer than seven main ideas. These ideas will form the framework for your paper. The cards that remain won't be wasted but will be used as support for the more important ideas. Of course, if a note isn't important enough to be considered a main idea and doesn't provide support for the main ideas, that note should be left out of your paper.

Choosing the main ideas and clustering your research notes require selectivity, the same skill you used not only in narrowing your original paper topic but in studying conventional notes as well (see Chapter 4). In fact, if you find it difficult to pick out a handful of main ideas from a pile of notes, apply the following three-step system to help pinpoint the pillars that will form your paper's supports.

1. Read through your note cards and pick out those cards that seem more important than the others.
2. Now that you have two piles of notes instead of one, pick up the smaller pile and repeat the process, pulling out the most important notes and using them to make up a third pile.
3. Finally, pick up the third pile, which by now should contain only a dozen or so note cards, and find four or five ideas that seem to be the most important ones. These ideas will be the basis of your premise and of the pattern for your paper.

Plot an Organizational Pattern

Your basic premise and personal choice largely determine the pattern your paper will follow. You could use any of the organizational patterns listed in Chapter 6 as the framework for your paper. The time pattern or the process pattern is appropriate for most college papers. For some papers, however, you may be required to develop an argument. A good pattern for such papers is to begin with a statement of your premise and then support it with logical examples that build to a conclusion. This kind of organization affords more flexibility than the others.

You may need to experiment with several patterns before you arrive at a framework that adequately accommodates the information you want to include in your paper. Don't be discouraged by the inevitable period of trial and error.

There's no one "correct" way of plotting your paper. You may feel most comfortable using a traditional outline. Or you may find the process of *mapping* easier and more enjoyable.

To map out your research paper, use the index cards that contain your paper's main ideas and subideas (or jot these ideas down on small slips of paper). On a clear surface such as a desk or a tabletop, shift the cards around like checkers on a checkerboard, clustering them in various ways, according to the premise of your paper.

If you're planning to structure your paper using the time or process pattern, arrange your ideas so they follow logically from the earliest to the latest or from the start of the process to the end. If you're structuring your paper as an argument, decide which of the major points should be made first; then arrange the remaining points in an order that will make your argument smooth, logical, and easy to follow.

The chapter maps in this book provide examples of the process and argument patterns. The map in this chapter, for example, uses the process pattern, spelling out, in order, the steps for writing a research paper. The map for Chapter 9, in contrast, develops an argument; it asserts a premise—managing test anxiety requires preparation—and supports the premise by detailing the ways to prepare.

When you arrive at an arrangement that incorporates your information and makes logical sense, you have found a suitable pattern for your paper. Once you have arranged the cards that contain your major points in an effective order, repeat the procedure by arranging the cards that contain your minor points. Think of each major point as a premise in itself. Then arrange the minor points that support a major point in a clear and effective way.

If, as you arrange your cards, you find gaps in your organization, you may need to create new categories or perhaps even return to the library to take more notes.

Finally, with all points arranged to your satisfaction, go back and number your cards according to the order in which they'll appear in your paper.

WRITING THE PAPER

You already have most of your paper worked out—information, sources, organization. Now all you have to do is put your data into sentences and paragraphs and work up a first draft of your paper. Once that is accomplished, allow yourself plenty of time to go back and revise and edit what you've written, add the missing elements, and type the final copy.

Race Through the First Draft

The best way to start writing is simply to write. Pausing with your pen poised over an empty page or with your fingers resting idly on a keyboard waiting for inspiration to strike is a useless endeavor. Inspiration, like concentration, seldom comes when you call it. Once your hands are engaged in the physical motions of writing, your brain will follow.

Write your first draft as rapidly and spontaneously as possible. To ensure continuity, record your thoughts on paper as they go through your mind. Don't stop to ponder alternatives. Although you will probably write too much, don't be concerned; it's easier to cut out than to add.

In your first draft your goal is simply to transfer information from your notes to your paper. Take each card in order and write. Start with major point one. State what it is, and then use supporting evidence to show why it is so. As you use a reference from the card, note the card number on your paper. You can put the footnotes in later, taking the exact information from the card. Continue to write, following your organized and numbered cards.

Only after you've completed your first draft should you step back and take a look at what you've written. If you typed your draft into a computer, print out a hard copy so you can jot down your comments. Regardless of whether your draft was handwritten, typewritten, or printed on a computer, go over what you've written and pencil in changes, adding words or phrases and circling lines or paragraphs you want to move or re-

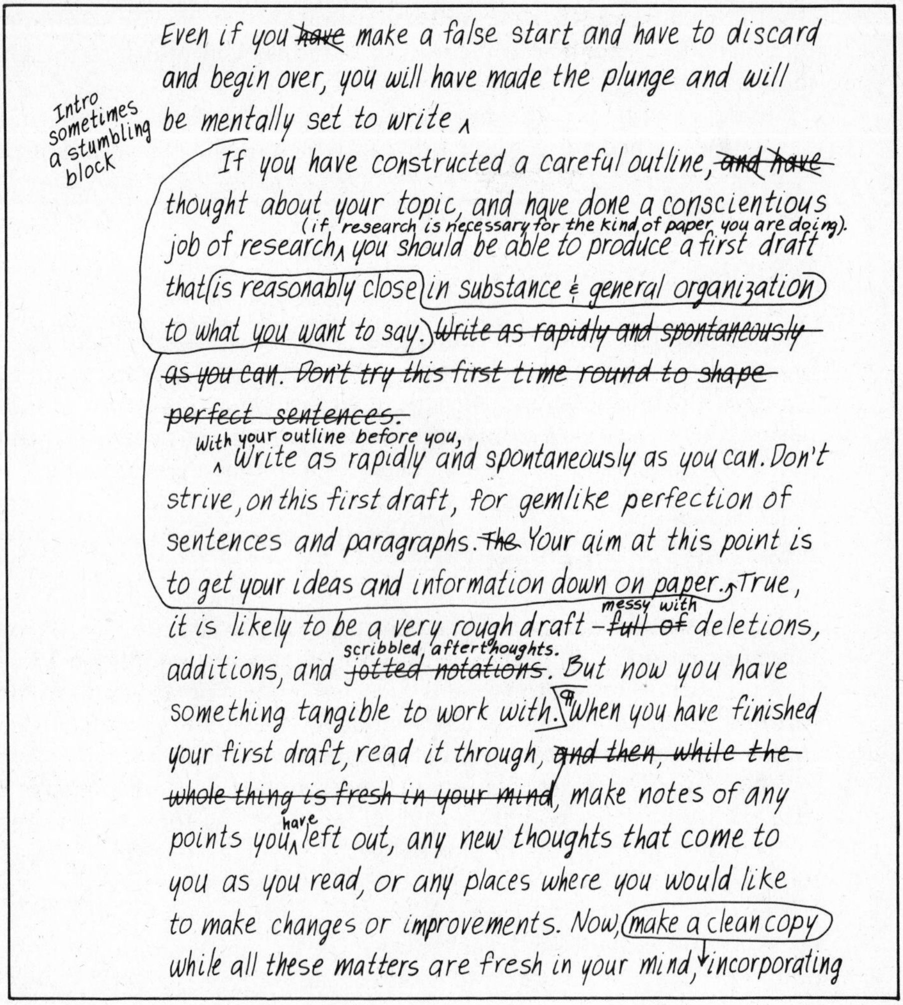

Even if you ~~have~~ make a false start and have to discard and begin over, you will have made the plunge and will

Intro sometimes a stumbling block be mentally set to write ∧

If you have constructed a careful outline, ~~and have~~ thought about your topic, and have done a conscientious job of research∧ *(if research is necessary for the kind of paper you are doing).* you should be able to produce a first draft that ⟨is reasonably close⟩ in substance & general organization to what you want to say. ~~Write as rapidly and spontaneously as you can. Don't try this first time round to shape perfect sentences.~~

With your outline before you, ∧ Write as rapidly and spontaneously as you can. Don't strive, on this first draft, for gemlike perfection of sentences and paragraphs. ~~The~~ Your aim at this point is to get your ideas and information down on paper. ∧True, it is likely to be a very rough draft — *messy with* ~~full of~~ deletions, additions, and ~~jotted notations~~. *scribbled afterthoughts.* But now you have something tangible to work with. When you have finished your first draft, read it through, ~~and then, while the whole thing is fresh in your mind~~, make notes of any points you ∧left out, *have* any new thoughts that come to you as you read, or any places where you would like to make changes or improvements. Now, ⟨make a clean copy⟩ while all these matters are fresh in your mind, ∨incorporating

FIGURE 12.4   Page from a First Draft

move. Figure 12.4 shows a page from a first draft, complete with annotations, insertions, and other marginal markings.

While your markings are still fresh in your mind, write or type a clear copy that incorporates all your changes. Don't wait before adding in these corrections. If you delay even a day, you may lose a lot of time trying to recall exactly what you meant by some of your notes. And if you type or rewrite the material while it's still fresh, you may find that you do some spontaneous revision.

Once you have made these changes, put your draft aside for a while. To gain objectivity on what is in the paper and what is still missing, you need a cooling off period of at least a day. When you return to your paper, you'll then easily spot errors and weaknesses in your writing.

Revise and Edit Your Paper

The hardest part of writing a research paper is completing the first draft. From that point on, you'll be refining what you've already written. In the next drafts—and you may write two, three, or even four drafts before you are satisfied with your paper—you'll focus on strengthening supporting evidence and fine-tuning technical details such as transitions, grammar, and spelling.

Strengthen Supporting Evidence   Students often state a main point and then go on to something else without supporting it. The kinds of evidence you need to support a major point are statistics, quotations from other published works, facts, examples, comparisons and contrasts in views, expert opinion, and description. If you make statements and follow them up with generalities, you will not convince your reader that your main point is true. Use what you have collected on your cards to support your points. Here, with examples, are the steps you can take to develop a major point:

1. State your point clearly.

   The two sides of the human brain perform distinct functions.

2. Develop the point beyond a brief statement.

   According to the theory of brain laterality, the left hemisphere of the brain handles analytical thinking, while the right hemisphere is the home of abstract thought.

3. Support with data from authorities and with statistics

   Drs. Michael Gazzaniga and Roger Sperry found that the cerebral hemispheres process information differently. Subsequent research determined that the brain's left and right sides contrast information that is symbolic and conceptual versus information that is nonsymbolic and directly perceived.

4. Illustrate with examples.

   For example, if you were to add up a column of numbers, you would probably be using the left side of your brain. But if you were sketching a picture, you would be engaging the right side.

Be sure that all the main points are supported about equally with this kind of evidence. If you can't find enough evidence to support one point, perhaps it's not a major one. You may need to reorganize the structure to include that point under one of the other major points.

Avoid padding. You may be tempted to add words or to rephrase a point to make the paper longer. Such padding is obvious to the reader, who's looking for logical arguments and good sense, and will not improve your grade. If you haven't enough evidence to support a statement, leave it out or get more information.

Fine-Tune Technical Details   Although awkward transitions, clumsy grammar, and poor spelling may not affect the basic meaning of your paper, they do affect the reader's perception of how you have thought about your topic and what you have written.

Provide Transitions.   In writing your paper, consider how to help your readers move easily from one main point to the next. If they feel that there's no connection, they will find it hard to follow the logical sequence that you have established in your own mind. You must therefore use transitional words and phrases to make your paper easy to follow. (See Table 11.5 for a list of these words.) Check carefully for transitions, and insert them where they are needed.

Correct Grammar.   Students who use the English language correctly get their ideas across to other people more clearly and forcibly than do those who stumble over every sentence. Moreover, students who apply the rules of grammar in their papers earn better grades. If you are unsure about these rules or careless with them, your meaning may get lost. If you feel that you could use a review of grammar, there are good texts that give you the elements of English grammar by a programmed method. Some of them are even fun to read.

Here's a brief list of some popular handbooks of English grammar:

Corder, Jim W. *Handbook of Current English*, 7th ed. Glenview, Ill.: Scott, Foresman, 1985.

Diamond, Harriet, and Phyllis Dutwin. *Grammar in Plain English*. New York: Barron's Educational Series, 1989.

Feigenbaum, Irwin. *The Grammar Handbook*. New York: Oxford University Press, 1985.

Hodges, John C. et al. *Harbrace College Handbook,* 11th ed. San Diego, Calif.: Harcourt Brace Jovanovich, 1990.

Shertzer, Margaret D. *The Elements of Grammar*. New York: Collier Books, 1986.

Check Spelling. If your spelling problems are not severe, you will find a dictionary helpful. If your spelling is poor, look for one of the paperback books that list the most commonly misspelled words. If you cannot recognize that you are spelling words incorrectly, have someone who is good at spelling read your paper and mark, not correct, the words that are wrong. Then look up and insert the correct spellings. If you do this conscientiously over a period of time, you will improve your spelling.

Of course, if you are writing your paper on a computer, you can use a spell-checking program to pinpoint your spelling mistakes. The spell-checker compares each word you have typed with the words stored in its dictionary and calls your attention to words that don't appear there. Although the computer can catch many of your spelling errors, it isn't infallible. The size of the dictionary is limited, and the spell-checker is unable to recognize words that are spelled correctly but used incorrectly (such as "there" instead of "their").

Add the Missing Elements

Having revised and edited your writing, you can now add the missing elements that will make your paper complete. Because your paper is a research paper, you must give credit for your information by including citations and a bibliography. In addition, the paper will need a title, an introduction, and a conclusion.

Give Credit Where It's Needed To avoid any appearance of plagiarism and to demonstrate the depth of your research, attribute quoted or paraphrased material and include a bibliography.

Avoid Plagiarism. Plagiarism is stealing other people's words and ideas and making them appear to be your own. It need not be as blatant as copying whole passages without giving credit. If you paraphrase something from already published material and do not cite your source, you're guilty of plagiarism even though you may have no intention of stealing. Simply rearranging sentences or rephrasing a little without crediting is still plagiarism.

Those who grade papers are quick to notice a change in writing style from one of your papers to another or from one part of your paper to another. Your writing is like your fingerprints—individual. If you try to use another's work, his or her style will not match the rest of your paper, and the difference will be obvious. Instructors may give you the benefit of the doubt if they cannot prove where you got plagiarized material. But if they can—and doing so is usually not difficult—plagiarism is grounds for expulsion from college. In a world where the written word is a major product, stealing it from someone else is a serious offense.

Include Citations.   Avoid plagiarism by crediting material you've quoted or paraphrased to its source. You may include a credit right after the quoted material, within the body of the paper, in a format like this: (Jones 1965, p. 264). This citation refers to page 264 of the work by Jones that was published in 1965 and is listed in your bibliography. Or you can use a superscript [1] and cite the full source at the bottom of the page or in a complete listing at the end of the paper. Credits that appear at the bottom of the page are called *footnotes*. Figure 12.5 shows a format for footnotes and for credits at the end of the paper. References are numbered in the order in which they appear in your paper. Other forms are given in handbooks on English usage.

Supply a Bibliography.   The bibliography lists the sources you cited in your credits and may include other books or published material that you read as background for the paper but did not quote. A bibliography is not "notes," "endnotes," or "sources." It is a listing of the books that you used in preparing the paper, and you should use the correct title for this listing. When you compile the bibliography, use the 3 x 5 cards you prepared earlier. Each entry should include enough information so that a reader can identify the work and find it in a library.

Entries are listed alphabetically by author. Different bibliographic forms are used in different fields. Either select a standard form from a handbook on English usage, or follow the form used in one of the journals on your subject.

Here's a list of style manuals that will provide you with a form for your citations and bibliography.

Achtert, Walter S., and Joseph Gibaldi. *The MLA Style Manual.* New York: The Modern Language Association of America, 1985.

American Institute of Physics Publication Board. *Style Manual for Guidance in the Preparation of Papers,* 3rd ed. New York: American Institute of Physics, 1978.

---

1. Hunter Shirley, <u>Your Mind May Be Programmed Against You!</u> (Lafayette, La.: 21st Century Books, 1982), pp. 112–115.

2. Frank H. Winter, <u>Prelude to the Space Age</u> (Washington, D.C.: Smithsonian Institution Press, 1983), p. 18.

FIGURE 12.5   Format for Footnotes and End-of-Paper Credits

American Chemical Society. *American Chemical Society Style Guide and Handbook.* Washington, D.C.: American Chemical Society, 1985.

American Mathematical Society. *A Manual for Authors of Mathematical Papers,* 7th ed. Providence, R.I.: American Mathematical Society, 1980.

American Psychological Association. *Publication Manual of the American Psychological Association,* 3rd ed. Washington, D.C.: American Psychological Association, 1983.

The Chicago Manual of Style, 13th ed. Chicago: University of Chicago Press, 1982.

Council of Biology Editors, Style Manual Committee. *CBE Style Manual: A Guide for Authors, Editors, and Publishers in the Biological Sciences,* 5th ed. Bethesda, Md.: Council of Biology Editors, 1983.

Harvard Law Review. *A Uniform System of Citation,* 13th ed. Cambridge, Mass.: Harvard Law Review Association, 1981.

Webster's Standard American Style Manual. Springfield, Mass.: Merriam-Webster, 1985.

No matter what form you use, follow it consistently for every entry in your bibliography. Figure 12.6 shows a common bibliographic form.

Bibliography

Boyer, Ernest. L., and Fred M. Hechinger, Higher Learning in the National Interest. Washington, D.C.: Carnegie Foundation, 1981.

Chaplin, James P., and T. S. Krawiec, Systems and Theories of Psychology. 4th ed. New York: Holt, Rinehart, and Winston, 1979.

Kleppner, Paul. Who Voted? New York: Praeger, 1982.

Shirley, Hunter. Your Mind May Be Programmed Against You! Lafayette, La.: 21st Century Books, 1982.

Uhler, Harry B. "Semicentennial: Baltimore-to-Venus Attempt," Science News 114 (July 1978): 78–79.

Winter, Frank H. Prelude to the Space Age. Washington, D.C.: Smithsonian Institution Press, 1983.

FIGURE 12.6 Format for a Bibliography

Choose a Suitable Title   It is often a good idea to wait until you have written the paper before you decide on a title. Although the title should reflect the content of the paper, you can give it an interesting twist or perhaps make use of part of a quotation that seems particularly appropriate. Of course, there's nothing wrong with a straightforward title. In many cases, a no-nonsense title that gets straight to the point is your best choice.

Write an Introduction   The paper's premise serves as the basis of the introduction. In revising your paper, you can expand on this premise and come up with the introduction in its final form. In addition to stating your premise, the introduction explains how you plan to support it and can include an apt example, anecdote, or quotation. Choose any of these devices carefully; they must be right on target. If you're not sure they will contribute to the paper, then write a straightforward statement.

State a Conclusion   Don't end the paper without a concluding passage. If you do, your readers will be left dangling, wondering what happened to you and the rest of the paper. Let them know they have come to the end.

By now, all your major points should have been made and adequately supported. The primary purpose of your conclusion is to restate or summarize your basic premise. In addition, you may want to use your premise to draw a related conclusion. For example, if your premise states that alcohol is one of the country's leading causes of death and your paper has supported that contention with data and examples, you may want to conclude with some suggestions for dealing with the problem of alcohol abuse:

> Taxes on alcoholic beverages should be increased.
>
> Beer, wine, and liquor companies should be made to subsidize alcohol treatment programs.
>
> Americans must overcome their tendency toward self-destructive addictive behavior.
>
> Alcohol education should begin at the elementary school level.

Although the rest of your paper should be backed up with information you discovered through research, the conclusion affords you the opportunity to state your own opinion and draw a personal conclusion.

In general, of course, the kind of conclusion you write depends on the paper and the subject. In most cases, the conclusion need not be long and involved. But be certain you include one.

Type the Final Copy

All the time and energy you have spent on your research paper should be reflected in the appearance of the final copy. Make it neat, clean, and attractive.

1. Use only one side of white paper. Although instructors seldom specify, most assume that your paper will be written on 8-1/2 by 11 sheets.
2. Type your paper or have it typed. Of course, if you've written your paper on a computer, you can have it printed. Handwritten papers are difficult to read and may not even be accepted in some courses.
3. Leave a generous margin at the top and bottom of each page and a margin of 1-1/2 inches on both sides to provide room for the instructor's comments.
4. Type your paper without any strikeovers. Erase errors thoroughly and neatly.
5. Set up long, direct quotations (of five or more lines) in block style—that is, single space and indent the lines from both sides about a half inch or five typewriter spaces. Omit the quotation marks when you block a quotation in this way—the block setup shows that you are quoting.
6. Proofread your final copy. Go over it carefully to catch spelling errors, typing errors, and other minor flaws. This is a very important step that is often neglected.

SUMMARY

How do you arrive at research topic?

Start by selecting a general subject that interests you. Then narrow it down to a topic that's specific enough to cover in depth but large enough to allow you to find a sufficient amount of information. Finally, focus your topic by asking a question that gives your paper direction and purpose.

What sort of information should you look for, and where can you find it?

Look for books and magazine articles that deal with your specific topic. You can find them in the library by searching the card catalog (or computerized card catalog) for books and by consulting an index such as the *Reader's Guide* or Info-trac for magazine articles. If you get stuck in your search, ask a reference librarian for help.

How do you assemble a working bibliography?

Write the bibliographical information for each reference you plan to consult on the front of a 3 x 5 card. Use the back to summarize your opinion of each article or book.

How can you ensure that your notes are easy to use?

Jot each note on a separate 3 x 5 card. On each card, write the author and the page number of the source so you'll be able to verify the accuracy of your notes with ease and have all the information you need for citations. Use the modified printing style to write both quickly and neatly, and write in pen to prevent your notes from fading or smearing. Take concise but detailed notes. Use abbreviations for common words.

How can you ensure that your notes are accurate?

To ensure that the information in your notes is accurate, make a clear distinction among your own ideas, paraphrased information and quoted material. Copy quotations exactly as they appear in the source. If you shorten a quotation, insert an ellipsis in place of the words you've removed.

How do you decide on your paper's basic premise?

The premise for your paper can grow out of potential arguments, apparent similarities, or possible theories that you've developed from going over your notes.

How do you cluster your notes?

Select the note cards with the most important ideas you have jotted down, and then group the other notes beneath the idea they support. If a note doesn't support any of the main ideas, do not include it in your paper.

How do you plot out a pattern for your paper?

Use your premise as a starting point to organize your clusters of information into a logical pattern. Most college research papers follow one of three basic forms: the time pattern, the process pattern, or the development of an argument.

How should you write the first draft?

Speed, not style, is the key to completing your first draft. For now your goal is simply to get everything written down. Move systematically through your note cards, turning notes into sentences and combining sentences into paragraphs.

How can you strengthen your paper's supporting material?

You can do so by double-checking your paragraphs to make sure that each idea is sufficiently developed. If an idea lacks support, bolster it with further explanation, data from authorities, statistics, or examples.

How do you fine-tune technical details?

Use transitional words and phrases to guide your reader through your paper. Make sure your grammar and spelling are correct; consult an English handbook or a dictionary when in doubt.

What missing elements do you need to add?

You should include a citation for every reference you make, a bibliography of the sources you used, a title, an introduction, and a conclusion. These make your paper complete.

What are the requirements for the final copy?

Your final copy should be neat, clean, and attractive. Type it carefully with generous margins, using only one side of each sheet of white paper, and double-check each page to make sure it is free of errors.

HAVE YOU MISSED SOMETHING?

Matching. In each blank space in the left column, write the letter preceding the phrase in the right column that matches the left item best.

_____ **1.** Compelling question

a. Can help you find a suitable topic

_____ **2.** *Reader's Guide*

b. Synopsis found at the beginning of some journal articles

_____ **3.** Abstract

c. Can be used to "visually" plan your paper

_____ **4.** Index

d. Helps provide a focus for your paper

_____ **5.** Ellipsis

e. Primary source for most of your paper's information

_____ **6.** Concept map

f. Good starting point in the search for books or magazines

_____ **7.** Preliminary research

g. Best-known index of periodicals

_____ **8.** Library

h. Indicates that part of a quotation has been omitted

Multiple choice.   Choose the word or phrase that completes the following sentence most accurately, and circle the letter that precedes it.

1. The basic skills for writing a research paper are similar to those for

   a. writing a novel or short story.
   b. preparing for a test or quiz.
   c. taking notes during a lecture.
   d. doing none of the above.

2. The most common criticism of research papers is that they are

   a. too broad.
   b. too long.
   c. poorly written.
   d. carelessly researched.

3. The *Reader's Guide* is a common example of a

   a. Boolean search.
   b. style manual.
   c. periodical index.
   d. card catalog.

4. A research librarian is an expert on

   a. most research paper topics.
   b. the proper form for footnotes.
   c. use of the library.
   d. all of the above.

5. Your notes will be easier to use if you

   a. recopy them so they are easy to read.
   b. copy all your information verbatim.
   c. jot down each note on a separate index card.
   d. fit them on as few pages as possible.

6. In writing your first draft, you should emphasize

   a. speed.
   b. accuracy.

    c.   style.
    d.   neatness.

7. You can avoid the appearance of plagiarism by including
    a.   quotation marks.
    b.   citations.
    c.   a bibliography.
    d.   all of the above.

True-false.   Write *T* beside the *true* statements and *F* beside the *false* statements.

_____ **1.** Three or four narrowings should reduce your general topic to a suitable size.

_____ **2.** A working bibliography consists of only those references you cited in your paper.

_____ **3.** Info-trac is an example of a computerized magazine index.

_____ **4.** Like a card catalog, a computerized catalog enables you to search by subject, author, or title.

_____ **5.** A "cooling off" period is helpful between the writing of your first draft and your second draft.

_____ **6.** Paraphrasing is permitted in a research paper.

_____ **7.** A conclusion isn't always necessary in a research paper.

Short answer.   Supply a brief answer for each of the following items. The number in parentheses refers to the page where the item is discussed in the text.

1. List some of the advantages and disadvantages of a computerized magazine index. (265–266)
2. How can Boolean searching be used to pinpoint references? (265)
3. How can concept maps be used in organizing a research paper? (262, 272)

BUILDING YOUR VOCABULARY STEP BY STEP: MEETING WORDS FROM THE EXTENDED FAMILY

With few exceptions, every new word you add to your vocabulary comes with its own extended family. Of course, if you have chosen your words carefully, they will relate to the ideas and concepts that are already part of your background. A new term in geology, for example, will relate to the other geological terms you already know. But there is also a set of words that relate specifically to the word you've just learned, that congregate around your new word like family members at a wedding. These are the words that make up your new word's family. They include synonyms, antonyms, and homonyms. Although you might be tempted to overlook these words or to view them as excess baggage, they provide you with an excellent opportunity to increase your vocabulary even further, enabling you to add several words to your background instead of just one. As a result, your vocabulary expands at a much faster rate, your understanding of the original word deepens, and your general flexibility with language increases.

For example, if you were to learn the word *martial* (relating to war), you would also have an opportunity to learn its sound-alike, *marshal* (an officer or sheriff); its look-alike, *marital* (relating to marriage); and its antonym, *pacifistic* (opposing war or the military). In addition, martial has many synonyms, ranging from *militant* to *belligerent*. All these words, because they are related to a word you've just learned, become easier to acquire as well. And if you follow along any or all of the branches that grow out of your new word's family, you can find a number of relatives worth meeting. For example, the words *nuptial, matrimonial,* and *connubial* are all synonyms of *marital*. Because the four words aren't identical in their meaning, when you learn each of them, you add precision to your vocabulary.

Of course, not all words come from big families. But for nearly every word you learn, you should be able to find at least two or three other words that relate to it. For example, many of the words that come from the chapter you've just read have relatives worth getting to know. *Cite* brings to mind some obvious sound-alikes—namely, *sight* and the less common *site*. *Ellipsis* has both a sound- and look-alike in the word *ellipse*.

In the list of chapter words that follows (with page numbers for reference), trace the family trees of these words. Every one of these words has at least one synonym, and many have antonyms, all of which are worth learning, particularly when you are able to relate them so readily to a word you already know.

apt (280)	cite (277)	ellipsis (270)
assessment (268)	counteract (269)	entries (278)
bibliographical (267)	decipher (269)	expulsion (277–278)
blatant (277)	delve (264)	forcibly (276)
bracketed (269)	devices (280)	fruitful (265)
brevity (268)	distinguish (269)	generalities (275)

infallible (277)   refining (275)   subsequent (275)
laterality (275)   relatively (266)   superscript (278)
paraphrasing (270)   scanning (261)   terminals (266)
periodical (261)

Appendix: Answers _____

Chapter 1   Managing Stress

Have You Missed Something?

Matching: 1. b   2. f   3. e   4. c   5. a   6. d

Multiple choice: 1. c   2. d   3. b   4. d   5. b   6. c   7. b

True-false: 1. T   2. T   3. T   4. F   5. F   6. T

Building Your Vocabulary Step by Step

1. b   2. e   3. a   4. d   5. b   6. b   7. c   8. b   9. a

10. c   11. b   12. a   13. b   14. d   15. a   16. d   17. c

18. c

Chapter 2   Finding Time

Have You Missed Something?

Matching: 1. g   2. f   3. d   4. b   5. h   6. c   7. a   8. e

Multiple choice: 1. b   2. a   3. c   4. b   5. c   6. b   7. d

8. c

True-false: 1. F   2. T   3. T   4. F   5. T   6. T

Chapter 3   Learning to Concentrate

Have You Missed Something?

Matching: 1. g   2. h   3. a   4. f   5. b   6. d   7. e   8. c

Multiple choice: 1. a   2. d   3. c   4. a   5. b   6. c

True-false: 1. T   2. F   3. T   4. F   5. F   6. F   7. T

Chapter 4   Combating Forgetting

Have You Missed Something?

Matching: 1. c   2. h   3. g   4. e   5. a   6. b   7. d   8. f

Multiple choice: 1. b   2. a   3. c   4. b   5. a

True-false: 1. T   2. T   3. T   4. F   5. F

Chapter 5   Creating a Note-Taking Framework

Have You Missed Something?

Matching: 1. d   2. e   3. f   4. a   5. b   6. g   7. c

Multiple choice: 1. c   2. b   3. a   4. d   5. a

True-false: 1. F   2. T   3. F   4. T   5. T

Chapter 6   Noting What's Important in Readings and Lectures

Have You Missed Something?

Matching: 1. d   2. f   3. e   4. b   5. a   6. c

Multiple choice: 1. d   2. d   3. c   4. b

True-false: 1. F   2. F   3. T   4. T   5. T   6. F

Chapter 7   Mastering Your Material

Have You Missed Something?

Matching: 1. f   2. d   3. e   4. g   5. c   6. b   7. a

Multiple choice: 1. d   2. d   3. a   4. b   5. d   6. c

True-false: 1. F   2. T   3. T   4. T   5. T   6. F

Chapter 8   Thinking Visually

Have You Missed Something?

Matching: 1. c   2. f   3. e   4. b   5. a   6. g   7. d

Multiple choice: 1. b   2. d   3. a   4. c   5. a   6. d

True-false: 1. T   2. T   3. T   4. T   5. F

Chapter 9   Managing Test Anxiety

Have You Missed Something?

Matching: 1. f   2. c   3. g   4. e   5. b   6. a   7. d

Multiple choice: 1. b   2. c   3. a   4. d   5. b   6. d

True-false: 1. T   2. T   3. T   4. F   5. T   6. F   7. T

Chapter 10   Mastering Objective Tests

Have You Missed Something?

Matching: 1. g   2. d   3. h   4. a   5. e   6. c   7. f
8. b

Multiple choice: 1. c   2. c   3. d   4. a   5. b   6. b

True-false: 1. T   2. T   3. F   4. T   5. F   6. T   7. F

Chapter 11   Tackling Essay Tests

Have You Missed Something?

Matching: 1. d   2. a   3. b   4. f   5. c   6. e

Multiple choice: 1. a   2. d   3. b   4. d   5. a   6. d   7. a
8. a

True-false: 1. F   2. T   3. T   4. F   5. T

Chapter 12   Writing a Research Paper

Have You Missed Something?

Matching: 1. d   2. g   3. b   4. f   5. h   6. c   7. a   8. e

Multiple choice: 1. b   2. a   3. c   4. c   5. c   6. a   7. d

True-false: 1. T   2. F   3. T   4. T   5. T   6. T   7. F

Index _____